THE
CONFESSIONS
OF LADY NIJŌ

In about 1307 a remarkable woman in Japan sat down to complete the story of her life. The result was an autobiographical narrative, a tale of thirty-six years (1271-1306) in the life of Lady Nijō, starting when she became the concubine of a retired emperor in Kyoto at the age of fourteen and ending, several love affairs later, with an account of her new life as a wandering Buddhist nun. In my judgment it is one of the finest works in classical Japanese literature.

Karen Brazell, in Introduction

THE CONFESSIONS OF LADY NIJŌ

Translated from the Japanese
by Karen Brazell

THE CONFESSIONS OF LADY NIJŌ
ISBN 0 600 20813 3

First published in Great Britain 1975
by Peter Owen Ltd
Zenith books (Hamlyn Paperbacks) edition 1983
Translation © 1973 by Karen Brazell

UNESCO COLLECTION OF
REPRESENTATIVE WORKS
JAPANESE SERIES

This book has been accepted in the Japanese
Literature Translation Series of the United
Nations Educational, Scientific and Cultural
Organization (UNESCO)

Hamlyn Paperbacks are published by
The Hamlyn Publishing Group Ltd.,
Astronaut House,
Feltham, Middlesex, England.

Reproduced, printed and bound in Great Britain by
Hazell Watson & Viney Ltd., Aylesbury, Bucks

Contents

To Jim

Introduction

In about 1307 a remarkable woman in Japan sat down to complete the story of her life. The result was an autobiographical narrative, a tale of thirty-six years (1271–1306) in the life of Lady Nijō, starting when she became the concubine of a retired emperor in Kyoto at the age of fourteen and ending, several love affairs later, with an account of her new life as a wandering Buddhist nun. In my judgment it is one of the finest works in classical Japanese literature.

Lady Nijō would have been delighted to hear this, for she wrote her memoirs in order to restore her family's waning literary prestige. Through the vagaries of history, however, her glory has taken 6½ centuries to arrive. *The Confessions of Lady Nijō*, or *Towazugatari* in Japanese, was not widely circulated after it was written, perhaps because of the dynastic quarrel that soon split the imperial family, or perhaps because of Lady Nijō's intimate portrait of a very human emperor. Whatever the cause, the book was neglected, then forgotten completely, and only a single manuscript survived. This was finally discovered in 1940 by a scholar named Yamagishi Tokuhei, who was carefully sifting through the holdings of the Imperial Household Library in Tokyo.

When he came across the title *Towazugatari* in the geography section, he decided to take the manuscript home for a closer look, and of course he soon found that it was not a treatise on geography at all, but a major new text in Japanese literature. The war delayed publication of the text until 1950, but it was not until 1966 that complete, annotated—and therefore readable—editions were published. So it is only recently that this new classic has been available to Japanese readers.

Who was Lady Nijō? Were it not for her own account, this lively personality would have died its natural death, for not even her personal name has come down through history. The common practice was to designate court ladies by street names, and our lady was called Nijō, or Second Avenue, a high-ranking designation. Her autobiography tells us, several times, of her family's high aristocratic standing, and this claim is substantiated by historical records. She is fond of reciting her pedigree and pointing out that she was sent to Retired Emperor GoFukakusa as the adopted daughter of a prime minister (who was also her paternal grandfather) and that she had been treated as a foster daughter by Lady Kitayama, the grand old lady of the period, who counted five emperors among three generations of descendants. Such affiliations were a means of social climbing in aristocratic circles, where indicators of status were minutely observed.

Lady Nijō's ties with GoFukakusa were complex. Her father, Masatada, was in the service of his father, Emperor GoSaga, and her mother, Sukedai, had served GoFukakusa before her marriage. In fact, Lady Nijō's mother was probably the woman who initiated the young GoFukakusa into the arts of love, a practical usage that had received the sanction of custom at the imperial court. Because her mother died while she was still an infant, GoFukakusa took Lady Nijō at age four into his palace to be raised. In 1271, when she was fourteen, he received her father's consent and took her as a lover.

As a court lady, Nijō was expected to participate in the elaborate ceremonial and social life of the imperial family, adding to its splendor by her skills in music, painting, and poetry, as well as by her personal charms. Lady Nijō excelled in these things, and during her years in GoFukakusa's service she was a high-ranking and favored court lady, yet she never received the rank of official consort. Given her own abilities, her family's position, and GoFukakusa's fondness for her, she might well have become an empress had it not been for her father's death when she was fifteen. Without an influential person to push her cause, there was little chance of improving her own official position. Compounding her misfortune was the early death of the only child she bore GoFukakusa. Yet despite these handicaps Lady Nijō enjoyed remarkable success in the highly competitive court circles, where she flaunted her independent nature by taking several lovers. The complications that arose in keeping these lovers happy and her children by them out of sight constitute the major action of the first three books of her memoirs. Eventually, however, she ran afoul of GoFukakusa's empress, Higashi-Nijō, and this, along with her numerous affairs and evident lack of interest in GoFukakusa, cooled his ardor enough that she was finally forced to leave his palace when she was only twenty-six. The last straw may well have been her involvement with Kameyama, GoFukakusa's brother and political rival.

After being expelled from the palace in 1283, Lady Nijō describes her attendance at one other major court function, a birthday celebration for Lady Kitayama in 1285. Her long and detailed description of this event is written in a perfunctory style quite unlike the smooth narrative she employs in the rest of her work. Her change of style here effectively reveals the drastic change that has occurred in her life. No longer is she an active member of the inner circle; now she is simply a spectator at an elaborate celebration that has little meaning for her. The ceremonies that used to be a vital part of her life are only sterile reminders of what once had been. With this event, her narrative of life at court breaks off.

When Book Four opens it is 1289, and she is a Buddhist nun setting out on a series of pilgrimages that take her to famous temples, shrines, and places of literary renown. On her journeys she exchanged poems with priests and warriors; met leaders of the military government, provincial warlords, traveling commoners, and prostitutes; and copied large sections of Buddhist sutras, which she dedicated at Shinto shrines. Throughout her travels she maintained some contact with life in Kyoto, meeting GoFukakusa twice after he too had taken religious vows, visiting him on his deathbed, looking in from the outside at his funeral, and in 1306, the year her tale ends, attending services to mark the third anniversary of his death. Nothing is known of Lady Nijō after this.

In telling the story of her life, Lady Nijō reveals

a great deal about the age in which she lived. The period was one of transition from an aristocratic tradition to a culture dominated by the warrior class. The preceding Heian period began in 794 with the building of a capital in Kyoto (then known as Heian-kyō), and lasted until the end of the twelfth century, when the Minamoto clan fought its way to national supremacy and established a military government in Kamakura, some 280 miles northeast of Kyoto. The shogun who headed this new government did not usurp the position of emperor, but instead claimed to be ruling at imperial command. Consequently during the Kamakura period, which lasted until 1333, there were two important centers in Japan: the imperial court in Kyoto, still the cultural heart of the land, and the military headquarters in Kamakura, where the actual governance of the country was carried out. By the time Lady Nijō was born in 1258, both centers had large official bureaucracies. In Kyoto all the titles and positions of an earlier day were maintained, although they were largely ceremonial, and in Kamakura the position of shogun was held by an imperial prince who was simply a figurehead controlled from behind the scenes.

Cumbersome though this government appears, it ruled Japan with notable success. In Lady Nijō's lifetime, however, there were two developments that eventually contributed to the downfall of Kamakura. One was the division of the imperial family into two feuding factions, which resulted in the only prolonged dynastic break in Japanese history. The actual split occurred in 1334 and lasted until 1392, but the roots of the dispute date from about the

time of Lady Nijō's birth and involve two of the
principal figures in her narrative.

GoFukakusa was put on the throne by his father
GoSaga in 1246; but because GoFukakusa was only
four years old, GoSaga continued to direct the affairs of the imperial court from offstage. In 1249
Empress Ōmiya bore another son, Kameyama, whom
both parents came to favor to such an extent that in
1259 GoFukakusa was forced to yield the throne to
his younger brother. After GoSaga's death in 1272,
a dispute arose between GoFukakusa and Kameyama
over whose son should become the next emperor.
Finally, after the intervention of the Kamakura
government, a compromise was reached, with
GoFukakusa's son scheduled to succeed Kameyama's. Thus began the uneasy and irregular alter-
nation between the descendants of these two
brothers that continued until 1333. The tensions
this rivalry caused are mentioned in our narrative,
where Lady Nijō herself is seen contributing directly
to the antagonism between the two brothers by becoming involved with Kameyama while still in
GoFukakusa's service.

The Mongol invasions of Japan in 1274 and 1281
were the second crucial events of the period. Of
these Lady Nijō says nothing. It is true that they occurred in the southern island of Kyushu, but
temples and shrines in Kyoto offered fervent prayers
that the invaders be repulsed, and when the fleets
were destroyed both times by typhoons—the original
kamikaze—these religious establishments were well
rewarded. Thus Lady Nijō's omission was probably
due not to her lack of knowledge, but to the con-

temporary attitude that political and military events were not a proper topic in works by women.

Because Lady Nijō accepts this literary stance, she gives us few hints of the power and prestige of her friends. The lover she calls Akebono, for example, was Saionji Sanekane, one of the most influential men in Kyoto. He served as liaison officer between the military government and the imperial court, and had an important voice in the continuing succession dispute. In Kamakura, one of Lady Nijō's close friends—and she swore to GoFukakusa that he was nothing more—was Iinuma, son of the powerful Taira no Yoritsuna. Lady Nijō describes how their friendship developed out of a common interest in poetry, but she gives us few details of his political stature and no hint of his ignoble end: He and his father were executed for treason in 1293.

What Lady Nijō does describe relates to her personal life, which at first revolved around love affairs, parties, and ceremonies in Kyoto and its environs. It is important to know that in the late thirteenth and early fourteenth centuries the imperial court did not have a proper palace. The great palace enclosure built at the beginning of the Heian period was no longer in existence, and the palace that had been used to replace it burned down in 1259. Since there was no complex worthy of the designation "imperial palace" until 1318, emperors made out as best they could, usually taking over mansions belonging to wealthy families. The Tomi Street Palace, which Lady Nijō considered home, was actually a mansion in the northeast part of Kyoto that had belonged to the Saionji family. Two other palaces frequently appear in Lady Nijō's narrative: the Saga Palace west

of Kyoto on the banks of the Ōi River opposite
Mount Arashi, which was used by Kameyama and
his mother Empress Ōmiya; and the Fushimi Palace
to the southeast of the city, which was inherited by
GoFukakusa and used by his empress, Higashi-Nijō,
and their daughter Yūgi.

Lady Nijō's account of life at the capital reveals
how the aristocracy in the Kamakura period strove
to copy the minutest features of Heian culture. *The
Tale of Genji,* which had been written 2½ centuries
before, was an important document for Lady Nijō
and her contemporaries, who were always seeking
precedents for their actions and models for their
behavior. The elaborate musical entertainment at
which Lady Nijō and her grandfather Takachika
quarreled, for example, was a deliberately contrived
replica of a concert in *Genji.* Small wonder then that
the term *imamekashi* (up-to-date), which had been
so important in Heian society, had gone out of
fashion in the Kamakura period. It gave way to a
wistful longing for the past.

The fourfold social ideal of the Heian court—
wine (*sake*), love, music, and poetry—was still very
much honored. *Sake* does not figure importantly in
the idealized world of Prince Genji, but in Lady
Nijō's narrative, where life is much more down to
earth, *sake* is frequently mentioned. Lady Nijō does
not hesitate to describe GoFukakusa well along in
his cups or falling into a drunken slumber. Parties
required entertainment, and this was generally provided by the participants themselves, who would
compose poems, sing, or play musical instruments.
Afterward, if one were sober enough, a love tryst
was the ideal way to end the night.

All court events, no matter how informal, followed complicated rules of decorum and taste that demanded accomplished participants. An educated aristocrat—and this applied to both men and women —was expected to be familiar with certain literary classics, to be able to compose poems and write them in a graceful hand, to play at least one musical instrument, paint acceptably, and be clever in the art of combining appropriate colors and textures in costumes.

In this rarefied scene, poetry was a staple form of communication. Official occasions and social gatherings were not complete without a poem or two, or perhaps a series of linked verses, such as Lady Nijō, Kameyama, GoFukakusa, and others composed after Lady Kitayama's birthday celebration. It was unthinkable to write a letter without a poem, and it was a gross breach of etiquette for a lover to neglect to send a morning-after poem as soon as he returned to his own quarters.

Given the important social function of poetry, no court literature was written entirely in prose. This means that there is an abundance of court poetry, not all of it good; and of the second- and third-rate examples that have come down to us, more than a few are in Lady Nijō's narrative. Perhaps this is as it should be. Convention demanded poems, and it is only natural that Lady Nijō wrote and received some that were uninspired. Yet even the mediocre examples fit into the thirty-one-syllable pattern of classical verse, often with a play on words or a standard allusion. These elements do not fare well in translation, however. But her work also contains poems of real beauty. In moments of heightened awareness or deep emotion, she followed the convention of expressing herself in poetry rather than prose, as when she describes her feelings at the sight of a departing lover in the snow at dawn, or expresses her delight upon seeing some commoners resting under a mountain cherry tree in full bloom.

Other aspects of court life were also elevated to an art with that zeal for refinement that characterizes Japanese aesthetics. Consider the use of incense, for example. People went to great lengths to find the proper ingredients to produce a special blend, which was then burned in skillfully concealed containers or used to scent their clothing. The arrangement of the many layers of a court lady's costume was another complex art. The textures, colors, and patterns of these gowns, made of fine silks and brocades, were artfully combined to produce a harmonious whole that reflected the wearer's status as well as the occasion. One reason for the elaborate care taken with women's costumes was that it was the only part of their person revealed to outsiders, for highly placed women normally spent their lives in dimly lit rooms behind shutters, bamboo screens, and silk curtains. When they went out, they rode in carriages, covered their heads with a gown or a veiled hat, or hid their faces behind a fan or their sleeves. To attract a decorous amount of attention they let the hems of their skirts or the bottoms of their sleeves gracefully hang out beneath the screens. Thus it is not surprising that Lady Nijō gives us very little description of her contemporaries' physical features; yet she often describes their costumes in elaborate detail, sometimes with caustic comments.

Conducting a love affair was another art that took

time, patience, and skill, especially if one tried to maintain as many relationships as Lady Nijō did. In this connection it may be helpful to know that in aristocratic circles marriage was a flexible arrangement, with several possible patterns. Rarely did a husband, wife, and children live together in a single house; more often the partners lived in separate residences with various types of visiting patterns. Well-born mothers had little direct involvement with the raising of their children, and adoption for reasons of expedience was a common practice. Monogamy was certainly not recommended for men, and even married women often managed at least an extramarital flirtation. Of course one did not need to marry at all, and Lady Nijō never did.

Lady Nijō's relationship with GoFukakusa was socially acceptable, as we can see from the fact that he formally recognized the child she bore him by presenting it with a sword. What is puzzling is his toleration of her other amours. GoFukakusa seems to have known that Nijō and Sanekane were having an affair, although they went to great lengths to keep the birth of their child a secret; he also encouraged her to sleep with the regent Kanehira, almost pushing her out of his bed on one occasion; and he even connived to bring her and the high priest Ariake together, knowing full well that this was a breach of Ariake's vow of celibacy. In fact, his interest in her romantic liaisons bordered on the morbid. Not until he suspected Nijō of having relations with his brother Kameyama did he really balk, and his objections in this case were probably occasioned by the bitter rivalry between the two. GoFukakusa himself, of course, had his share of women: In addition to the two official consorts, Higashi-Nijō and Genki, there were the court ladies within his palace and various outside possibilities. Nijō was sometimes the go-between for his affairs, and took the job as a matter of course—although she did not hesitate to offer candid remarks about the other women. Both the former high priestess and the fanmaker's daughter disappointed her because they gave in too quickly. This was surely no way to please a man. And then there were flaws in their dress and manners as well. Love affairs were fine if they were conducted adroitly and with the proper regard for decorum.

Lady Nijō was not to end her life at court, however, and when the break came that barred her from its splendors, she took her father's deathbed advice and became a Buddhist nun. Without saying when she took her vows, she simply presents herself in Book Four as a traveling nun. This unexpected leap in her narrative has caused some scholars to speculate that a book is missing from *Towazugatari*. It seems more likely that she modeled her story after *The Tale of Genji,* where the "Niou" chapter opens with the startling statement that Prince Genji is dead, without explaining the circumstances of his death. Perhaps she regarded the change in her life as drastic enough to warrant such treatment.

The act of renouncing the world and entering Buddhist orders was certainly not unusual, and for someone whose expectations had ended as abruptly as Lady Nijō's, it was a course often taken. The extent of Lady Nijō's pilgrimages, however, was very unusual indeed. High-ranking aristocrats who took religious vows generally settled down near the capital

to a quiet life of sutra copying, prayer, and even a
bit of socializing. For a woman of Nijō's high rank
to travel extensively was unprecedented and not entirely approved of. She defends her journeys on the
grounds that they helped her to forget the disap-
pointments she had suffered and claims that she was
following the example of her idol, the twelfth-
century poet-priest Saigyō.

Life within and without the capital, Lady Nijō
discovered, were quite different things. The court
society she left was an island of nostalgia for past
greatness, an enclave where old ideas and ideals were
desperately clung to. Outside, the country was in a
rapid state of transition, yet the martial society that
prevailed still looked to Kyoto for guidance in the
absence of any fully developed artistic ideals of its
own. Lady Nijō learned that no matter where she
went, the arrival of a lady from the capital caused a
stir. In Kamakura she was asked to give high officials
advice on arranging the layers of a formal gown and
on decorating the new shogun's living quarters.
Her ability at poetry helped her gain entry into
local society in Kamakura, Zenkōji, and Ise; and on
occasion the verses she wrote persuaded reluctant
hosts to extend their hospitality. But her talents
also had their drawbacks. She barely escaped being
detained as a servant by a local warlord who was
impressed by a painting she did for him.

In her journeys as a nun outside of Kyoto and
beyond the confines of aristocratic society, Lady
Nijō crossed paths with a great variety of people
and discovered a common bond of humanity with
them. Those local people resting under a cherry
tree, she realized, probably appreciated its beauty as

much as she did. She was touched to find that a woman entertainer who played the *biwa* for her at a country inn was a kindred spirit, and she admired the pluck of the ex-prostitutes who had become nuns on Taika Island. Not everything she saw pleased her. The disrespectful treatment of the shogun, who was also an imperial prince, affronted her deep-seated feelings of decorum, and the cruelty of the provincial lord at Wachi toward his servants upset her deeply.

These experiences helped change the sophisticated, high-spirited, and sometimes vain court lady that Nijō had been into a mature and patient woman capable of compassion. Compassion was probably the religious ideal that Lady Nijō admired most, and it was the keynote of the Amidist sects of Buddhism that were gaining strength in the countryside at this time. The sects of Buddhism that prevailed in the imperial court were Tendai and Shingon, whose esoteric rites and priestly hierarchy were closely linked with the class-conscious aristocracy. The Tendai and Shingon sects had been most powerful in the Heian period, but they still retained enough influence in Kyoto to hamper the growth of the newer sects there. Outside the capital, however, Amidism, Nichiren, and Zen, sects that emphasized simple piety and spiritual exercises, were predominant. Lady Nijō was most attracted to the Amidist ideal of a compassionate god extending salvation to all living creatures, and in her narrative she includes exemplary legends about the compassion of Amida and his companion Kannon. These stories, she claims, helped to strengthen her own faith.

Although she became a Buddhist nun, Lady Nijō's

many contacts with Shinto indicate how these two
religions were commingled in thirteenth-century
Japan. She made a vow to copy out five long Buddhist sutras, but after finishing each major section
she would dedicate it at a Shinto shrine. When
she discusses the Kōfuku Temple and the Kasuga
Shrine in Nara, it is difficult from her words to tell
which is Buddhist and which is Shinto. The ancestral deity of the Minamoto clan to which Lady
Nijō belonged was the Shinto god Hachiman, but
like many other Shinto gods he was also considered
a bodhisattva; and in the oaths that were commonly
sworn, both Buddhist and Shinto deities appear.
The amalgamation of the two religions was not complete, of course. Lady Nijō points out that because
of her Buddhist costume she had to be circumspect
in her activities at the Ise Shrine, the most
sacrosanct of Shinto shrines. Even there, however,
her garb certainly did not prevent her from becoming fast friends with the Shinto priests.

Features of religious belief that were neither dis-
tinctly Buddhist nor Shinto were also pervasive in
Japanese culture at this time, playing an important
role in the lives of courtiers and commoners alike.
Lady Nijō mentions directional taboos, human spirits
leaving the body, tree spirits, and other omens and
portents. Dreams were especially significant as portents. To Lady Nijō dream was a meaningful con-
cept with complex religious and literary associations,
and dreams were omens to be taken seriously. She
and her friends frequently consulted them to deter-
mine a course of conduct or to discover what the
future held in store. The night she became pregnant
by Akebono, Lady Nijō dreamed he presented her

with a silver hair-oil jar. When she conceived Ariake's second child, he dreamed that he turned into a mandarin duck and penetrated her body. Go-Fukakusa, having dreamed that Nijō received a religious implement from Ariake, abstained from visiting her for a month and found his suspicions verified. The point here is that Lady Nijō and her contemporaries assumed a close connection between their dream life, with its intimations from the past and the future, and their present existence. When her father, after his death, appeared to her in a dream and warned her not to let their family's literary reputation decline, Lady Nijō was prompted to write her autobiography.

As an autobiographical work, *The Confessions of Lady Nijō* belongs to a major category of Japanese literature. By Lady Nijō's time numerous diaries, autobiographical stories, and personal miscellanies had been written and circulated, and at least two women had attempted to write narrative memoirs. The author of *Kagerō Nikki* portrayed twenty years of her life (954–74) in terms of her difficult and disturbing relationship with her husband, and Lady Sarashina presented her life (1020–59) through a veil of romantic and religious fantasies. Both of these women give frank and human portraits of themselves. Lady Nijō's narrative is in the same genre but of a much broader scope, for Lady Nijō's life was more varied, and she made far better use of the narrative techniques Lady Murasaki employed in *The Tale of Genji*. In common with the two earlier autobiographical narratives and with much other court literature, however, *The Confessions of Lady Nijō* sometimes strikes a tone of melancholy that grates on the modern reader, who may see in it an indulgent self-pity. Sleeves damp from weeping soon become soppy. In mitigation it can be said that melancholy was an acceptable tone in Lady Nijō's day, when it was treasured as a sensitive response to the transience of life.

Fortunately, Lady Nijō's feelings of melancholy do not overcome her sense of humor. She is able to laugh at herself even in moments of distress, as she does when she is trying to ward off the persistent Ariake and suddenly realizes that the humorous poem "Love Pursues from All Sides" fits her situation exactly. She is also good at rendering the comic element in situations, as in the scene of Akebono's visit to Lady Nijō at her old nurse's house. Like the hero of an old tale, Akebono has sneaked through a break in the wall to pay a secret visit to Lady Nijō, but the lovers are constantly harassed by the unwelcome attentions of the old nurse, who bangs on their door and asks embarrassing questions in a loud voice. Then there is GoFukakusa's affair with the fanmaker's daughter, which shows the incongruity of Lady Nijō, a highly sophisticated court lady, leading the beautiful but awkward girl to GoFukakusa, conveys Lady Nijō's tone of condescension and fine malice, and finally describes her real sympathy with the girl's sad but somehow amusing plight. One of the last views we have of Lady Nijō herself is a scene of comic pathos: She is a lone nun running barefoot after the funeral procession of an emperor because she has taken off her shoes to enter a building and forgotten where she left them.

Like any writer in an established literary tradition, Lady Nijō took it for granted that her readers would catch most of her allusions and echoes. Her technique of allusion was often subtle, as an example will show. The first night that GoFukakusa visits Lady Nijō as her lover, he tells her he has raised her from childhood eagerly awaiting the day when he could make her his own. Though it is not explicitly referred to, no one who knew *The Tale of Genji* would miss the similarity to the Genji-Murasaki relationship. Later, when we learn that GoFukakusa had loved Nijō's mother, the parallel is underscored. Having set up the parallel, Lady Nijō depicts a relationship far more complex than its prototype. Another example of this technique of allusive variation occurs when Akebono is caring for Lady Nijō during the birth of their daughter. The situation and some of the words echo the scene in *Genji* where the hero is caring for Lady Aoi after the birth of their son. This allusion adds tension to Lady Nijō's story because the parallel scene in *Genji* had an ominous end: Lady Aoi was killed by the jealous spirit of one of Genji's mistresses. Lady Nijō did not die, of course, but this foreshadows the role jealousy will play in her expulsion from the palace. Throughout her memoirs Lady Nijō uses allusions, sometimes to achieve other effects: to suggest or intensify an emotion, for example, or to help describe a character, to add a touch of irony, or to dignify an event. She draws a great many allusions from both *Genji* and a tenth-century work entitled *Tales of Ise*, but she also refers to other prose works and to poems from many of the anthologies compiled at imperial command. Unfortunately, allusions that must be pointed out and explained lose their

force for modern readers not steeped in the classics
of Japanese literature known to every court lady.

Classical Japanese literature is so completely different from modern literature in English that a few
words are in order to explain what the translator is
up against. Consider the fact that the subject of a
verb does not need to be stated. For the writer who
wants to tell good anecdotes without being indis-
creet about names, it opens up all sorts of possibilities. Lady Nijō took advantage of them all. In
describing an affair that lasted three nights, the most
specific reference she makes to her companion is a
single use of the word "person."

When her love affairs become so involved that she
has to refer to her two most important lovers by
name or risk hopeless confusion, she comes up with
poetic nicknames. She calls one lover Yuki no
Akebono, which means Snow Dawn, and the other
Ariake no Tsuki, or Dawn Moon. Because of the
demands of English grammar I have had to intro-
duce both of these nicknames into the story long
before Lady Nijō did. She never does reveal the
identity of these lovers, and her reticence presented
an irresistible challenge to scholars. After much de-
tective work these men have all been identified: The
lover of three nights was the regent Kanehira;
Akebono was Saionji Sanekane, a high-ranking aristocrat; and Ariake, though this is less definite, was
probably GoFukakusa's half brother, the prince-
priest Shōjō.

For the sake of comprehensibility I have simplified
the uses of names and titles in the text. Occasionally
Lady Nijō uses personal names, but more often she
refers to people by their titles or ranks. Since these

would change over the years, a single character may have several appellations. When Sanekane appears in his public role he is referred to by his family name, or his personal name, or one of six titles, although in his capacity as her lover he is only called Akebono. Since all this would be overwhelming, I have given each character a single designation, except in the cases of her nicknamed lovers.

There is, finally, the problem of general ambiguity, some of it deliberate on the part of Lady Nijō, some of it a consequence of linguistic structure. In describing the night when Kameyama tried to persuade GoFukakusa to let her sleep between them, Lady Nijō is vague for obvious reasons. In general, however, linguistic features are involved. No distinction is normally necessary between singular and plural in Japanese. Furthermore, there is no grammatical necessity to identify a speaker or to distinguish among direct speech, indirect speech, and unspoken thoughts. This means the translator has to make choices at every turn and that the English version becomes much more specific than the Japanese original.

Fortunately, the manuscript of *Towazugatari* itself presents few problems. Although it is a seventeenth-century copy it is in good condition, and the copyists did not garble many passages. The manuscript is divided into five books, but there are no further divisions of the text. The chapter divisions in the translation are my own, and I am also responsible for the dates used as chapter headings. Lady Nijō was often vague about the specific year in which events occurred, but scholars have pinned down most of the chronology. The Japanese title,

Towazugatari, which may or may not be Lady Nijō's own title, means literally "unrequested tale." In the Kamakura period the phrase also had the connotation of pouring forth something you can no longer keep to yourself.

My translation has been possible only because Japanese scholars have produced carefully annotated texts. I have consulted the editions of *Towazugatari* edited by Yamagishi Tokuhei, Tomikura Tokujirō, Tamai Kōsuke, and the Gochiku Dōbunkai, but I have relied most heavily on the interpretations offered by Tsugita Kasumi, whose edition was published in 1966 as a part of the series *Nihon koten bungaku zensho.* Additional articles by these men as well as by Matsumoto Yasushi and Nagano Jōichi have been very useful. When I first began translating part of *Towazugatari* as a Ph.D. dissertation at Columbia University, my research was supported for two years in Kyoto and New York by the Foreign Area Fellowship Program, and I received helpful advice from Professors Satake Akihiro and Yamamoto Ritatsu, both of Kyoto University, and Professors Ivan Morris and H. Paul Varley at Columbia University. Professor Donald Keene first introduced me to Lady Nijō, and his advice and encouragement have been invaluable in the process of completing this work. My husband, James Brazell, has spent countless hours improving my English style. It is to him that this book is dedicated.

Kyoto, December 1972   Karen Brazell

Major Characters

AKEBONO 1249–1322. An abbreviation of the nickname Yuki no Akebono (Snow Dawn) that Lady Nijō gives to Saionji Sanekane when he appears as her lover. He was a high official in the Kyoto aristocracy.

ARIAKE Died 1281(?). An abbreviation of the nickname Ariake no Tsuki (Dawn Moon) that Lady Nijō gives to Prince-Priest Shōjō when he appears as her lover. He was GoFukakusa's half brother and the abbot of the Ninna Temple.

GoFUKAKUSA 1243–1304. The eighty-ninth emperor of Japan (r. 1246–59). Lady Nijō was in his service.

GoSAGA 1220–72. The eighty-eighth emperor of Japan (r. 1242–46). He was the father of Go-Fukakusa and Kameyama.

HIGASHI-NIJŌ, EMPRESS 1232–1304. Consort of Go-Fukakusa and mother of Yūgi. She was also Go-Fukakusa's aunt and was eleven years his senior.

IINUMA Died 1293. Son of Taira no Yoritsuna. These two men were for a time very powerful in the Kamakura government.

KAMEYAMA 1249–1305. The ninetieth emperor of Japan (r. 1259–74). He was GoFukakusa's younger brother and rival.

KANEHIRA 1228–95. He served as imperial regent and as prime minister and was the progenitor of the Takatsukasa family. Lady Nijō had a brief affair with him in 1277.

KITAYAMA, LADY 1196–1302. The grand old lady of the period. She was mother of Ōmiya and Higashi-Nijō, grandmother of GoFukakusa and Kameyama, and Lady Nijō's great aunt.

KOMACHI, LADY A friend and distant relative of Lady Nijō, she served the Kamakura shogun.

KYŌGOKU, LADY One of GoFukakusa's ladies, who later served his son Emperor Fushimi. Lady Nijō calls her "aunt," but their relationship is not clear.

MASATADA 1223(?)–72. Lady Nijō's father and head of the Koga family.

NAKATSUNA Masatada's faithful steward. His wife was Lady Nijō's nurse, and two of his sons, Nakamitsu and Nakayori, also appear in the story.

NIJŌ, LADY Born 1258. The author of *The Confessions of Lady Nijō*, she was the daughter of Koga Masatada.

ŌMIYA, EMPRESS 1225–92. Emperor GoSaga's consort, mother of GoFukakusa and Kameyama, and the elder sister of Higashi-Nijō.

SANEKANE *See* AKEBONO.

TAKAAKI Born 1243. Uncle and confidant of Lady Nijō. In 1276 he was betrayed by his father Shijō Takachika and retired from court life.

TAKACHIKA 1203–79(?). Lady Nijō's maternal grandfather and father of Takaaki. He was a high-ranking court official.

TSUNETŌ 1233–97. A politically ambitious member

of the Yoshida family who was willing to violate custom to further his own ends.

YŪGI, EMPRESS 1270–1307. Daughter of GoFuka-kusa and Higashi-Nijō. She became the consort of Emperor GoUda.

Book One

1 (1271)

As the mist rose among the spring bamboo herald-
ing the dawn of the new year, the ladies of Go-
Fukakusa's court,[1] who had so eagerly awaited this
morning, made their appearances in gorgeous costumes, each trying to surpass the others in beauty.
I too took my place among them. I recall wearing
a layered gown shaded from light pink to dark red,
with outer gowns of deep purple and light green
and a red formal jacket. My undergown was a two-
layered small-sleeved brocade patterned with plum
blossoms and vines, and embroidered with bamboo
fences and plum trees.

My father, a major counselor, served today's
medicinal *sake*.[2] After the formal ceremonies everyone was invited in, the ladies were summoned from
the tray room, and a drinking party began. Earlier
Father had proposed the customary three rounds of
sake with three cups each time, which meant that
the participants in the formal ceremonies had already had nine cups. Now he proposed the same
again, but His Majesty revised the suggestion: "This
time we'll make it three rounds of nine cups each."
As a result, everyone was quite drunk when Go-
Fukakusa passed his *sake* cup to my father and said,
"Let 'the wild goose of the fields' come to me this

spring.["3] Accepting this proposal with great deference, my father drank the cups of *sake* offered to
him and retired. What did it all mean? I had seen
them speaking confidentially, but I had no way of
knowing what was afoot.

After the services had ended, I returned to my
room and found a letter:[4] "Snowbound yesterday,
today spring opens new paths to the future. I shall
write you often." With the letter was a cloth-
wrapped package containing an eight-layered gown
shaded from deep red to white, a deep maroon undergown, a light green outer gown, a formal jacket,
pleated trousers, and two small-sleeved gowns of
two and three layers. This unexpected gift upset
me, and I was preparing to return it when I noticed
a piece of thin paper on one of the sleeves. It contained this poem:

> Unlike the wings of love birds
> Our sleeves may never touch,
> Yet wear this plumage
> That you may feel my love.

It seemed cruel to reject a gift prepared and sent
with such feeling, yet I returned it with this note:

> Were I to wear these gowns
> In your absence, I fear
> The sleeves would rot away
> From muffling my sobs.
> If only your love does not vanish.

Late that night, while I was out on duty,[5] someone came and knocked on the back door to my
room. The young serving girl who rashly opened the
door told me later that a messenger had thrust

something inside and immediately vanished. It was
the same package with another poem:

> Our hearts were pledged.
> If yours remains unchanged,
> Spread out these gowns
> And sleep on them alone.

I did not feel I could return the present a second
time.

On the third of the month, when Cloistered Emperor GoSaga came to visit GoFukakusa, I wore
those gowns. My father noticed them and said, "The
colors and sheen are especially fine. Did you receive
them from His Majesty?"

My heart throbbed, but somehow I replied calmly, "They are from Her Highness, Lady
Kitayama."

On the evening of the fifteenth, a messenger arrived from my father's house in Kawasaki saying he
was to escort me home.[6] I was annoyed by this
urgent summons, but saw no way to decline it.
When I arrived at my home I could tell that something was about to happen—though I did not know
what—for the furnishings were much more elaborate
than usual. Folding screens, bordered mats, portable curtains, and even hanging curtains had been
arranged with special care. "Is all this just for New
Year's?" I wondered as I retired for the night.

At dawn there was much talk about what should be
served and how the courtiers' horses and the nobles'
oxen should be cared for, and even my grandmother,
a nun, came and joined in the bustle. I finally asked
what all the fuss was about. My father smiled at me:
"His Majesty has announced that he will come here

this evening because of a directional taboo, and since it's the first of the year, we'd like everything to be exactly right.[7] I summoned you expressly to serve him."

"But it's not the eve of a seasonal change. What directional taboo brings him out here?"

"What a naïve child you are," he replied amid the general laughter. How was I to understand?

They were setting up folding screens and small portable curtains in my bedroom. "Such preparations! Is my room going to be used too?" But my questions were met with smiles instead of answers. No one would tell me a thing.

That evening a three-layered white gown and deep maroon pleated trousers were laid out for me to wear, and elaborate care was taken in scenting the house and placing the incense burners where they would be unnoticed. After the lamps had been lit, my stepmother brought me a gay small-sleeved gown and told me to put it on. Later my father came in, hung several gowns about the room for their decorative effect, and said to me, "Don't fall asleep before His Majesty arrives. Serve him well. A lady-in-waiting should never be stubborn, but should do exactly as she's told." Without the least idea what these instructions were all about and feeling bewildered by all the commotion, I leaned against the brazier and fell asleep.

What happened after that I am not sure. His Majesty GoFukakusa arrived without my knowing it, and there must have been great excitement when my father welcomed him and refreshments were served, but I was innocently sleeping. When GoFukakusa overheard the flustered cries of "Wake her

up!" he said, "It's all right, let her sleep," so no one
disturbed me.

I don't know how long I had slept leaning against
the brazier just inside the sliding door, my outer
gown thrown up over my head, but I suddenly
awakened to find the lights dim, the curtains low-
ered, and inside the sliding door, right beside me, a
man who had made himself comfortable and fallen
fast asleep.

"What is this?" I cried. No sooner did I get up to
leave, than His Majesty wakened. Before I could rise
he began to tell me how he had loved me ever since I
was a child, how he had been waiting until now
when I was fourteen, and so many other things that
I have not words enough to record them all. But I
was not listening; I could only weep until even his
sleeves were dampened with my tears as he tried to
comfort me. He did not attempt to force me, but he
said, "You have been indifferent to me for so long
that I thought on this occasion perhaps. . . . How
can you continue to be so cold, especially now that
everyone knows about this?"

So that's how it was. This was not even a secret
dream, everyone knew about it, and no doubt as
soon as I woke my troubles would begin. My worries were sad proof that I had not completely lost
my senses at least, but I was wretched. If this was
what was in store for me, why hadn't I been told
beforehand? Why didn't he give me a chance to discuss it with my father? How could I face anyone
now? I moaned and wept so much that he must
have thought me very childish, but I could not help
myself, for his very presence caused me pain.

The night passed without my offering him even

a single word of response. When at dawn we heard someone say, "His Majesty will be returning today, won't he?" GoFukakusa muttered, "Now to go back pretending something happened!" and prepared to leave. "Your unexpected coldness has made me feel that the pledge I made long ago—when you still wore your hair parted in the middle—was all in vain.[8] You might at least behave in a way that other people won't find too strange. What will people think if you seclude yourself?" He tried both scolding and comforting me, but I refused to answer. "Oh, what's the use!" he said at last; then he got up, put on his robe, and ordered his carriage. When I heard Father inquiring about His Majesty's breakfast, I felt as though I could never face him again. I thought longingly of yesterday.

After GoFukakusa had gone, I lay utterly still with my outer gown pulled up over my head, pretending to sleep, until the arrival of a letter from him threw me into even greater misery. To add to my wretchedness my stepmother and grandmother came in full of questions. "What's the matter?" they asked. "Why don't you get up?"

"I don't feel well after last night," I blurted out, only to realize with dismay that they thought it was because I had shared my pillow with a man for the first time.

In great excitement someone entered with the letter I had no intention of reading. The royal messenger was waiting uneasily for a reply, and my attendants were wringing their hands not knowing what to do, until finally someone suggested, "Go tell her father." This, I knew, would be the most unbearable ordeal of all.

"Aren't you feeling well?" Father asked when he arrived. When they brought up the matter of the letter he said, "What childishness is this? Surely you intend to answer it?" I heard him opening the letter. It was a poem written on thin purple paper:

> Friends for many years,
> Yet now your perfume haunts
> My last night's sleeves
> That never lay on yours.

When my attendants read this they gossiped among themselves about how different I was from most young people these days. Still tense and uneasy I refused to get up. After much fretting they agreed that it would not be appropriate to have someone else reply for me, whereupon they gave the messenger a gift and entrusted him with this message: "She's such a child that she's still in bed and hasn't even looked at His Majesty's letter yet."

Around noon a letter came from an unexpected source. I read these lines:

> I might well die of grief
> If now the smoke trails off
> Entirely in that direction.[9]

To this the writer added, "Thus far I have survived this meaningless life, but now what is there?" This was written on thin, light blue paper, which had as a background design the old poem:

> If I could cease to be
> No longer would these clouds
> Cling to the secret mountains
> Of my heart.[10]

I tore off a piece of the paper where the words "secret mountains" appeared, and wrote:

> Can you not understand?
> My thoughts scattered and confused
> My heart has not gone drifting off
> A wisp of evening smoke.

After I sent this I began to wonder what I had done.

My refusal that day to take any kind of medicine gave rise to idle gossip about my "strange illness." Shortly after dusk fell, I was informed that His Majesty had arrived. Before I had time to wonder what might happen at this meeting, he pushed open the door and entered my room with an air of intimacy. "I understand you're ill. What's the trouble?" he inquired. Feeling not the least inclination to reply, I lay motionless where I was. He lay down beside me and began to talk of what was uppermost in his heart, but I was so dazed that I could only worry about what would happen next. I was tempted to acquiesce quoting the line, "If this were a world without lies,"[11] except for my fear that the person who had claimed he might die of grief would consider my behavior vulgar when he learned that the evening smoke had so quickly trailed off in a certain direction. Tonight, when GoFukakusa could not elicit a single word of reply from me, he treated me so mercilessly that my thin gowns were badly ripped. By the time that I had nothing more to lose, I despised my own existence. I faced the dawn with dread.

> Ties of my undergowns undone,
> The man uncared for—
> Gossip soon will spread.

What surprised me, as I continued to brood, was that I still had wits enough to think of my reputation.

GoFukakusa was expressing his fidelity with numerous vows. "Though from life to life our shapes will change," he said, "there will be no change in the bond between us; though the nights we meet might be far apart, our hearts will never acknowledge separation." As I listened, the short night, barely affording time to dream, gave way to dawn and the tolling of bells. It was past daybreak. "It will be embarrassing if I stay," GoFukakusa said, getting up to leave. "Even if you are not sorry we must part, at least see me off."

Unable to refuse his insistent urgings, I slipped a thin, unlined gown over the clothes I had on, which were damp from a night of weeping, and stepped outside. The moon of the seventeenth night was sinking in the west, and a narrow bank of clouds stretched along the eastern horizon. GoFukakusa wore a green robe, scarlet-lined, over a pale gown. He had on heavily figured trousers. I felt more attracted to him than I ever had before, and I wondered uneasily where these new feelings had come from.

The imperial carriage was ordered by Lord Takaaki, a major counselor, who was dressed in a light blue robe. The only courtier in attendance was Lord Tamekata, an assistant chief investigator. While several guards and servants were bringing the carriage up, some birds sang out noisily as though to warn me of the new day, and the tolling bell of Kannon Temple seemed meant for me alone. Touched by two kinds of sadness, I remembered the line, "Tears wet my sleeves both left and right."[12]

GoFukakusa still did not leave. "It will be lonely," he said. "See me home." Knowing who he was, I could hardly claim to be "unaware of the shape of the mountain peak,"[13] so I stood there in confusion as the brightening dawn spread through the sky. "Why do you look so pained?" he asked as he helped me into his carriage and ordered it driven away. Leaving this way, without a word to anybody, seemed like an episode from an old tale. What was to become of me?

> Dawn's bell did not awaken me
> For I never went to sleep
> Yet the painful dream I had
> Streaks the morning sky with grief.

I suppose our ride might be considered amusing, for all the way to the palace GoFukakusa pledged his affection to me as if he were a storied lover making off with his mistress, but for me the road we traveled seemed so dreary I could do nothing but weep.

After the carriage had been drawn through the middle gate to the Corner Mansion,[14] GoFukakusa alighted and turned to Takaaki: "I brought her along because she was too unreasonable and childish to leave behind. I think it would be better if no one learned of this for a while." Then, leaving orders that I was to be taken care of, he retired to his living quarters.

It hardly seemed the same palace where I had lived for so many years as a child. Frightened and ill at ease now, I regretted having come and wondered blankly what I might expect. I was sobbing when I heard the comforting sound of my father's

voice expressing concern over me. When Takaaki
explained GoFukakusa's instructions, Father replied, "This kind of special treatment won't do.
Things should go on as usual. To be secretive now
will only lead to trouble when word gets out." Then
I heard him leave. After his visit I brooded uneasily
about the future. GoFukakusa interrupted my painful musings and poured out so many words of affection that I was gradually comforted. The thought
that my fate was inescapable began to resign me
to it.

I remained at the palace for about ten days, during which time His Majesty never failed to visit me
at night; yet I was still foolish enough to think
about the author of that poem, which had questioned the direction the smoke was taking. My
father, meanwhile, kept insisting on the impropriety
of my situation, and finally had me return home. I
could not bear to see anyone, so I pretended to be
ill and kept to my own quarters.

GoFukakusa wrote an affectionate letter saying,
"I have grown so accustomed to you that I'm depressed now you are gone. Come back immediately."

> I doubt you yearn for me this much.
> If only I could show you
> The many teardrops on my sleeves.

Although I usually thought his letters disagreeable,
I found myself eagerly reading this one. My answer
was perhaps too artificial:

> Perhaps they were not for me,
> Those drops upon your sleeves,
> Yet word of them makes my tears flow.

Several days later I returned to the palace—this time openly, in the usual fashion—yet I grew uncomfortable when people immediately began to talk. "The major counselor certainly treasures her," they would say. "He's sent her with all the ceremony due an official consort."

The gossip spread, and before long Empress Higashi-Nijō began to be unpleasant. As the days dragged by I became wretched. I cannot claim that His Majesty really neglected me, but I was depressed when days passed between his visits, and although I didn't feel I could complain—as his other ladies did—about who kept him company at night, every time it fell to my lot to conduct another woman to him I understood anew the painful ways of this world. Yet I was haunted by a line of poetry that kept coming to mind: "Will I live to cherish memories of these days?"[15] The days passed, each dawn turned to dusk, and autumn arrived.

2 (1271–72)

In the eighth month of the same year Empress Higashi-Nijō went into confinement in the Corner Mansion. She was somewhat advanced in years and had suffered complications in her earlier deliveries, so there was widespread fear for her condition. Priests performed every possible esoteric rite for her benefit, offering prayers to the Seven Healing Buddhas, the Five Great Guardian Kings, Fugen Bodhisattva, Kongō Dōji, and Aizen-ō. The altar for the Guardian King Gundari was customarily provided by my family's province of Owari; but to show special deference on this occasion, my father also arranged for the prayers to Kongō Dōji.[16] The high priest of the Jōjū Temple served as exorcist.

Shortly after the twentieth there was great excitement over the report that Her Highness was going into labor. We expected the baby to come at any moment, but after two or three days had passed with no results, we grew alarmed and sent word of her condition to His Majesty. When he arrived and saw how weak she was, he ordered the exorcist closer, until he was only separated from Her Highness by a portable curtain. GoFukakusa then called over the abbot of the Ninna Temple from where he was conducting the rites to Aizen-ō and asked him to come inside the curtain to discuss what could be done in view of her apparently hopeless condition.

The abbot said, "The Buddhas and Bodhisattvas have promised that even predetermined fate can be changed. You need not fear for her." He then began his invocations while the exorcist hung a picture of Fudō—it was, I think, the same image that Shōkū had prayed to—before Her Highness and chanted, "He who serves Fudō will have the virtues of a Buddha; he who utters a single secret incantation will have Fudō's protection forever."[17] The abbot fingered his rosary and prayed, "Long ago in my youth my nights were filled with prayer and meditation, and now, in my maturity, my days are spent in strict ascetic practices. Am I then to receive no divine sympathy or aid?"

At signs that the child was about to be born, the prayers grew so fervent they seemed to rise like billows of smoke. The court ladies handed unlined gowns and raw silk gowns under the blinds to the attendants, who presented them to the courtiers. Then imperial guards passed them to the priests reciting the sutras. At the foot of the stairs sat the nobles, hoping the child would be a boy. The masters of divination had set up offeratory tables in the garden and were repeating the purification rite a thousand times. Courtiers passed the purified articles to the ladies, who thrust their sleeves under the blinds to receive them. At the same time royal attendants and junior imperial guards were bringing out the offeratory horses for His Majesty to inspect before they were distributed to the twenty-one shrines.[18] No woman could hope for a more auspicious set of circumstances.

One of the head priests was ordered to chant the *Sutra of the Healing Buddha* with the assistance of three other priests chosen for their fine voices. He had just reached the part that says, "Those who see it are glad," when the baby was born. Amid the clamor of congratulations a rice kettle was rolled down the north side of the roof to indicate it was a girl.[19] Though His Majesty was disappointed, he saw to it that the exorcists received the customary number of gifts.

Cloistered Emperor GoSaga made a great fuss over his new grandchild, even though she was a girl, and the festivities on the fifth and seventh nights after her birth were unusually fine. After the seventh-night ceremonies, at about 2 A.M., the retired emperors were conversing in GoFukakusa's living quarters when we were all startled by a terrifying roar from the inner courtyard. It sounded like waves breaking on a desolate, rocky shore in a storm. GoFukakusa ordered someone to go to see what it was.

Looking into the courtyard where the orange trees grew, I saw a number of apparitions, perhaps as many as ten, darting here and there. They were so bright that my eyes hurt. The creatures were shaped like dippers, bluish-white, with cup-sized heads and long thin tails.[20] I screamed and fled inside. From the veranda the nobles looked on, horrified. "They're the spirits of the dead," someone cried. "Over there, strewn on the ground under that big willow tree, is something that looks like boiled seaweed."

Divination was performed immediately and revealed that GoSaga's spirit had temporarily fled from his body. That very night, services to recall his spirit and prayers to the God of Mount Tai were begun.[21] Soon afterward, in the ninth month, I learned that GoSaga had been taken ill and that despite regular applications of moxa he showed no signs of any improvement.[22] As the year drew to a close his condition rapidly deteriorated, and because of his illness the new year was ushered in with none of the usual gaiety.

Toward the end of the first month, when GoSaga's condition was said to be hopeless, he was carried to his Saga Palace in a palanquin. GoFukakusa promptly followed, with me in attendance. The two empresses, Lady Ōmiya and Lady Higashi-Nijō, rode in a single carriage, attended by the mistress of the wardrobe. Medicine prepared especially for GoSaga to use on his trip had been put into two water jugs in his presence by the physicians Tanenari and Moronari. Then, at Tsunetō's orders,

the jugs had been entrusted to the junior imperial
guard, Nobutomo. Yet when they wanted the
medicine en route at Uchino, they discovered there
was not a single drop in either of the jugs. This
mysterious circumstance must have greatly upset
His Majesty, and I heard he looked much worse.

GoFukakusa was quartered in a hall facing the Ōi
River. He was constantly sending someone, with no
regard for sex or rank, to go and ascertain GoSaga's
condition. Day and night he dispatched these messengers across the long corridors. When the chore
fell to me I became aware of the sound of the waves
in the river, and a feeling of depression stole
over me.

By the beginning of the second month it was
simply a matter of waiting for the end. I think it
was on the ninth that both of the Bakufu's
Rokuhara deputies came to pay their respects.[23]
Major Counselor Sanekane conveyed their condolences. Then on the eleventh there was a brief
flurry of excitement when Emperor Kameyama arrived for a two-day visit, but even his stay could not
dispel the gloom in the palace. Indeed, the sight of
GoFukakusa and Kameyama sitting together without any of the usual entertainments and weeping
continually was enough to bring tears to anyone's
eyes.

About six o'clock on the evening of the fifteenth,
great clouds of smoke could be seen over the capital.
When I asked where the fire was, someone told me
that the Rokuhara deputy Tokisuke had been at-
tacked and killed, and that the smoke was coming
from the remains of his residence. Life is inexpress-
ibly frail! The man who came to visit the dying

GoSaga on the ninth was dead before His Majesty.
That he was not the first to ascend Mount Tai before his time did not make his passing any less
pathetic. His Majesty GoSaga had not uttered a
word since the night of the thirteenth, and of course
he knew nothing of this untimely death.

On the morning of the seventeenth we learned
that His Majesty had taken a turn for the worse.
Both High Priest Keikai and the head priest of the
Ōjō Temple came to instruct him and offer prayers:
"Through virtue in past lives you have risen to the
rank of emperor and are revered by officials throughout the land. Have hope that you will be reborn in
paradise. Quickly ascend to the highest place in the
highest heaven, and then return to guide those left
behind in this world of illusion." They attempted
to comfort and instruct His Majesty, but a love of
worldly things stayed his heart and blocked the road
to repentance. He died at six o'clock in the evening
on the seventeenth day of the second month of
1272, at the age of fifty-three, without any sign that
his heart had been changed by these teachings. His
subjects sank into grief; colorful gowns were
changed to black; the world seemed to be shrouded
in darkness.

On the eighteenth the body was removed to the
Yakusō Temple building within the grounds of the
Saga Palace. The Emperor's representative at the
funeral was the chief chamberlain, Middle Captain
Sanefuyu. Also in attendance were the chief priests
of the Ninna, Emman, Shōgō, Bodai, and Shōren
Temples, all sons of GoSaga. The sorrow felt that
night was more than my brush can record.

Tsunetō had been so close to GoSaga that it was

assumed he would retire from the world, but after the cremation, to everyone's surprise, he wore a court robe instead of the habit of a monk when he carried the urn of ashes.

GoFukakusa wept day and night, communicating his extreme grief to the members of his retinue, who often found themselves in tears. Because His Majesty was mourning the loss of a parent, all periodic announcements of the time, roll calls, and shouts to clear the way when important people passed, were suspended. I felt as if even the cherries on the mountain would "blossom in black."[24]

Although my father received permission to wear a dark shade of mourning,[25] when it was suggested that I too should wear deep mourning, GoFukakusa objected, "She's just a child. She need not wear special mourning; the usual shade is fine."

My father repeatedly petitioned Empress Ōmiya and Retired Emperor GoFukakusa for permission to retire from the world, but they refused him. Feeling deeper grief than anyone else, he continued to visit the imperial grave daily and attempted to plead his case before GoFukakusa, using the good offices of Major Counselor Sadazane to send the following petition: "From the day I first knelt in His Majesty's service at the age of nine I have never been without imperial favor. Even after my father died and I incurred my stepmother's displeasure,[26] my lord continued to bestow his favor upon me, and I in turn served him faithfully. Participation in court affairs has never brought me grief, nor caused me to envy others. On the mornings that promotions are announced I am always content, for my position and rank have risen faster than I had expected, and I have received other honors as well. I have enjoyed life in the palace: the nights of the Toyoakari festival when we drink and cross our sleeves in dance; the many special shrine dances I have attended; and the sight of my formal figure reflected in the waters of the Mitarashi River. I now hold the senior second rank. I am also the head major counselor and chief of my clan. Moreover, I was offered a post as a minister, but because the major captain of the right had submitted a petition suggesting that the post only be conferred upon people who had first been major captains, I was in the act of declining this honor when my lord passed away. Though I still live, the tree that shaded me has died, and so despite my position in society I feel useless. I have already lived for fifty years; how many more remain to me? To cast off mundane affections and follow the eternal way is truly to repay obligation; with your permission I will carry out my intentions and pray for His Majesty's spirit." Such was his earnest plea, but once more the emperor declined to grant permission. His Majesty then talked directly with my father, who was gradually reconciled to the imperial decision, although he did not allow the seed of forgetfulness to take root.

The forty-nine days after GoSaga's death were spent in Buddhist services and other rites, and when these ended we all returned to the capital.[27] After our return, messengers were sent to Kamakura about the political situation, which by the fifth month had grown very complicated.[28]

Was it because of the rains of the fifth month, which left nothing untouched, that my father's spirits were damper than the wettest autumn day? Or was he so thin and worn because he had given up his custom of never spending a night alone and had even stopped going to drinking parties? On the night of the fourteenth, as he was coming home in his carriage from Buddhist services at Ōtani, the outriders accompanying him noticed that he looked sallow and knew something was seriously wrong. The doctor they summoned made a diagnosis of jaundice caused by too much worry and began administering moxa treatments. I began to worry about him when I saw that his health was gradually deteriorating. Then in the sixth month, when I was already at my wits' end, I discovered that my own condition was not normal. But how could I mention it at such a time?

Father did not order any prayers for his recovery. "Since my condition seems hopeless anyhow, I don't want to waste a single day in joining His Majesty," he explained. For a few weeks he remained at his house at the corner of Rokkaku and Kushige streets before returning on the fourteenth of the seventh month to his Kawasaki home. He left his younger children behind so that he could quietly prepare for the end. I alone accompanied him, proud of having such responsibility. Father noticed that I was not my usual self, but at first he supposed I was not eating because of my worry for him. He tried to console me until he recognized my real condition and suddenly began to hope that his life might be prolonged for a while. For the first time he had religious services performed: a seven-day service to the God of Mount Tai at the central hall of Enryaku Temple, seven performances of outdoor *dengaku* dances at the seven shrines of Hie, and an all-day recitation of the *Great Wisdom Sutra* at the Iwashimizu Hachiman Shrine. He also had a stone monument constructed at the riverbed. All these acts of piety were inspired not by any love of his own life, but by concern for my future. I had become, alas, an impediment to his salvation.

Though still seriously ill, my father was out of immediate danger by the twentieth, at which time I returned to the palace. When GoFukakusa learned of my condition, he was especially kind, and yet I was well aware that nothing, not even the so-called "eternal ivy," lasts forever, and I was afraid lest my fate be like that of the mistress of the wardrobe, who had died in childbirth last month. As the seventh month drew to a close my father was showing no improvement, and I was uncertain as to what my own fate would be. On the night of the twenty-seventh, when fewer people were in attendance than usual, GoFukakusa asked me to come to his room. I accompanied him there, and he took the opportunity of our privacy to talk quietly of things past and present. "The uncertainty of life is cruel," he began. "Your father's case seems hopeless, and if worse comes to worst, you will be left with no one to depend on. Who besides me will take pity on you?" He wept as he talked of this. How sad that even consolation brings pain.

It was a moonless night. We were talking alone in the darkened room lit only by a dim lantern when suddenly we heard a voice calling my name. It was very late, and I was puzzled until I learned that it was a messenger from Kawasaki. He announced, "The end is imminent."

I left at once, without any preparations, and feared all the way that I would find Father already dead. Though I knew we were hurrying, the carriage seemed to crawl. When we finally arrived I learned to my great relief that he was still alive.

My father spoke to me, sobbing weakly. "The dew, not yet quite gone, awaits the wind. This life is painful, but knowing your condition I cannot face death without regrets."

Bells were tolling a late hour when GoFukakusa's arrival was announced. This was so completely unexpected that even my father, desperately ill though he was, became excited. I hurried out when I heard his carriage being drawn up, and saw that he had come in secret, accompanied by a single courtier and two junior guards. The late moon had just appeared over the rim of the mountains when I saw His Majesty standing in the brilliant moonlight dressed in a light violet robe with a woven flower design. What a splendid honor it was to receive such a sudden visit from the retired emperor.

Father sent this word: "Lacking even the strength to slip on a robe, I am unable to receive you, but the fact that you have honored me with this visit will be one of my fondest memories of this life."

At this GoFukakusa unceremoniously slid open the doors and entered the room. Father attempted to sit up but could not. "Stay as you are,"

GoFukakusa said as he laid a cushion beside Father's pillow and sat down. Before long, tears were streaming down GoFukakusa's cheeks. "You have served me intimately since I was a child. News that the end is near grieved me so much I wanted to see you once more."

"The joy your visit has brought me is more than I deserve, yet I am so concerned for this child I don't know what to do. Her mother left her behind when she was only two, and knowing that I was all she had, I raised her carefully. Nothing grieves me more than the thought of leaving her in this condition." Father wept as he spoke.

"I am not sure how much I can do, but at least I am willing to help. Don't let these worries block your path to paradise." His Majesty spoke kindly. "You should rest," he said and got up to leave.

It was now past daybreak and the retired emperor, anxious to leave before he was observed in his informal attire, was on the point of departing when a messenger came out to his carriage with a *biwa* that had belonged to my grandfather, Prime Minister Michimitsu, and a sword that once belonged to Emperor GoToba and had been presented to my grandfather about the time of GoToba's exile.[29] A note on light blue paper was attached to the thong of the sword:

> Master and man, our ties
> Span three worlds they say,
> Departing I commit
> The future to your hands.

GoFukakusa was deeply moved by this. Several times over he assured me that I had no reason to worry about anything. Shortly afterward a letter arrived written in His Majesty's own hand:

> The next time we shall meet
> Beyond this world of sorrow
> Under the brightening sky
> Of that long-awaited dawn.[30]

His Majesty's concern was our only pleasure in this sad and painful time.

GoFukakusa sent me a maternity sash earlier than was customary so my father could witness the ceremony.[31] It was formally presented to me by his emissary, Major Counselor Takaaki, on the second day of the eighth month. Takaaki wore a court robe, having been instructed by GoFukakusa not to wear mourning on this occasion, and was accompanied by outriders and attendants. My father, who was immensely pleased by this, ordered *sake* to be prepared. I wondered sadly if this would be the last such occasion. Father made Takaaki a present of Shiogama, the highly prized ox he had received from the prince who headed the Ninna Temple.

Because Father had felt better on this day, I had a glimmer of hope that he might improve. When it grew late I lay down beside him to rest and promptly fell asleep. He awakened me abruptly: "It's useless. I am able to forget the grief of setting out, perhaps even today or tomorrow, on an unknown path, but my thoughts keep dwelling on the one thing that grieves me. Just to watch you innocently sleeping there makes me wretched. Ever since your mother died when you were only two, I alone have worried about you. Although I have many other children, I feel that I have lavished on you alone the 'love due three thousand.' When I see you smile, I find 'a hundred charms'; when you are sad, I too grieve.[32] I have watched the passing of fifteen springs and autumns with you, but now I must depart. If you would serve His Majesty and not incur his displeasure, always be respectful; never be negligent. The ways of this world are often unexpected. If you should incur the ill will of your Lord and of the world and find you are unable to manage, you are immediately to enter holy orders where you can work toward your own salvation, repay your debts to your parents, and pray that we might all be together in paradise. But if, finding yourself forsaken and alone, you decide to serve another master or try to make your way by entering any other household whatsoever, consider yourself disowned even though I am already dead. For the truth is that relationships between men and women are not to be tampered with, inasmuch as they are not limited to this world alone. It would be shameful indeed if you remained in society only to blacken the name of our great family. It is only after retiring from society that you can do as you will without causing suffering." Father spoke at such length that I took these as his final instructions to me.

The bells were tolling daybreak when Naka-mitsu[33] came in with the steamed plantain leaves that were regularly spread under the patient's mat.

"Allow me to change the plantain," he said to my father.

"It doesn't matter now. The end is near," my father said. "Anything will do. First see to it that Nijō eats. I want to watch her. Hurry!" I did not see how I could eat, but my father insisted. I wondered sadly what would happen later when he was no longer around to watch me. Nakamitsu returned bringing a yam dish called *imomaki* in an unglazed pottery bowl. Everyone knows that *imomaki* is said to be an unhealthy food for a pregnant woman, and when the dish was set before me it looked so unappetizing that I merely pretended to eat it.

At daybreak we decided to send for a priest. In the previous month the chief priest of the Yasaka Temple had come to shave Father's head and administer his vows. He had also given Father the religious name Renshō. Therefore, that priest seemed the logical one to summon for the last rites, but for some reason my grandmother, the Koga nun, insisted instead on calling Shōkōbō, the chief priest of the Kawara Temple. Even though he had been informed Father was rapidly failing, he did not hurry.

The end appeared imminent. My father called to Nakamitsu, "Sit me up." Nakamitsu, the eldest son of Nakatsuna, had been raised from childhood by my father and had always served at Father's side. He lifted Father up and then sat down behind him. The only other person present, a lady-in-waiting, sat before Father while I sat at his side. "Hold my wrist," Father said. When I had taken it he asked, "Where is the surplice the priest gave me?" After I draped the surplice over the informal silk robe he wore without trousers, he instructed Nakamitsu to join him in prayer. Together they prayed for about an hour, and then as the sun began to shine into the room Father dozed off, leaning over to the left. Intending to rouse him and help him continue his meditation, I shook his knee. He awoke with a start, raised his head, and looked directly into my eyes. "I wonder what will happen," he started to say, but he died before he could finish the sentence. It was eight o'clock in the morning on the third day of the eighth month of 1272. My father was fifty years old.

Had Father died saying his prayers, his future would have been assured; but as it was I had uselessly awakened him only to see him die with other words upon his lips. The thought of this plagued me. So black was my own mood that when I looked up at the heavens I thought the sun and moon must have fallen from the sky, and as I lay on the ground sobbing, my tears seemed to be a river flowing out of me.

When I was two years old I lost my mother, but at that time I was too young to realize what had happened. However, my father and I had spent fifteen years together—ever since the forty-first day of my life, when I was first placed upon his knee. Mornings, looking in my mirror, I was happy to realize whose image I reflected; evenings, changing my gowns, I thought of my indebtedness to him. The debt I owed him for my life and my position was greater than the towering peak of Mount Sumeru, and the gratitude I felt toward him for taking my mother's place in raising me was deeper than the waters of the four great seas. How could I ever show my gratitude or repay him who gave me so much? Things he said at various times kept coming back to my mind. I could not forget them. Nothing I could ever do would erase the grief of this parting.

My grief extended even to parting from his mortal remains, but that painful moment was unavoidable. On the night of the fourth he was taken to the

mountain called Kaguraoka to be cremated. I
watched the lifeless smoke trail off, troubled by the
futile wish that I could go with him, but I returned
home with only my tears for a memento. I was filled
with anguish at the sight of his empty place and the
realization that we could meet again only in dreams,
and I longed for that face of yesterday. Even the
memory of his urging me to eat filled me with emotions words cannot express.

> Endless flow of tears, stream
> Into the rivers of that world
> And mirror for me there
> The crossing of his shade.

On the evening of the fifth, Nakatsuna called on
me. When I saw him approaching in his dark robes,
I suddenly realized that if Father had lived to be a
minister, Nakatsuna would have become a steward
of the fourth rank. The unexpected sight of him
dressed in monk's garb was indeed a sad change. He
announced that he was going to the grave and asked
if I had any message to be included in his prayers.
His dark, tear-stained sleeves were enough to cause
anyone to weep.

Seven days after Father's death, his wife, two of
his ladies-in-waiting, and two of his retainers took
holy orders. I was deeply moved, my emotions
tinged with envy as I watched the priest from Yasaka give them the tonsure and recite, "Caught in
the vicissitudes of the three realms."[34] I longed to
follow the same path, but since in my present condition that was impossible, I could only weep in
vain. The third-week services were especially elaborate, with a great display of condolences from

GoFukakusa. His messengers continued to come every day or two. "If only Father could see them," I mused.

At about this time Empress Kyōgoku became ill again. Greatly admired for her position and her youth, she was the daughter of Lord Saneo, and the beloved consort of the reigning emperor, Kameyama, as well as the mother of the crown prince; yet despite these many advantages she was continually troubled by some kind of evil spirit. Her illness this time was thought to be her usual malady, but suddenly I heard the frantic announcement that she had died. I was deeply affected, for I could well understand the despair of her father and the heartache of the emperor.

For the fifth-week service GoFukakusa sent a quartz rosary and an artificial branch of gold and silver flowers with a prayer paper attached. He included this poem:

> The drops that wet your sleeves—
> Are they simply autumn dew
> Or tears wept for the past?

I was pleased with the letter, yet uncertain what to do about it. I replied: "Even from his grave, Father is grateful," and added this poem:

> The chill autumn dew dampens
> Sleeves already soaked
> By tears of parting.
> Have pity on me.

As I lay awake those long autumn nights, every sound intensified my anguish, so that when I heard the bleak sound of wooden mallets beating silk tears burst forth to spot the gowns on which I lay alone, thinking of him who was no more.

Following that sad morning when my father had died, all the members of the court, from Their Majesties on down, had come or sent messengers to pay their respects; all, that is, but Senior Counselor Mototomo. His staying away was most unusual.[35]

4 (1272)

Shortly after the tenth day of the ninth month, someone who had inquired about me every day since my father had died came to visit me by moonlight. Because the court was still in mourning,[36] he wore an unpatterned court robe which matched my gowns as well as my mood. Seeing no need for an intermediary, I met him in the southern room.

"When we consider both past and present griefs, this year has had more than its share of sorrows. Our tears have scarcely had time to dry. One snowy night when your father and I were drinking together he said to me, 'Look in on her often,' and I felt very pleased that he honored me with this request." Talking thus, we laughed and cried the night away until we heard bells toll the dawn. Though the autumn night was long, we were kindred spirits, and many words still remained unsaid when the birds began to sing. "I suppose people will gossip about my staying here all night even though things aren't what they seem," he said as he left.

Reluctant to see him go, I wrote a poem and sent a servant out to his carriage with it:

> To that other parting
> Is added today's farewell:
> On sleeves already damp
> Still more dew falls.

He responded:

> Can you find it in you
> To grieve over today's farewell
> When dew from that other parting
> Scarcely leaves room for more.

I was recalling the night we had spent together, amazed that simply being with someone could arouse such feeling, when a messenger in a deep russet robe carrying a letter box knocked at the middle gate. It was an affectionate letter from him:

> I consoled you secretly,
> My arm pillowing your head,
> Your tears dew drops on my sleeves.
> Will we be blamed for this?

It was a period of such universal grief that I found this sort of diversion very appealing, and I replied in a similar vein:

> Autumn dew falls on every tree
> On every blade of grass:
> How could anyone claim
> It's only on our sleeves?

My half brother Masaaki was the chief mourner at the forty-ninth-day services where the priest from the Kawara Temple read the usual phrases comparing the bereaved mourner with a mandarin duck whose mate has forsaken it, and alluding to the leg-

endary one-winged birds; but today these customary
metaphors struck me as trite.[37] There was also a
service led by the priest Kenjichi for the purpose of
dedicating some letters, on the backs of which Father had copied portions of the *Lotus Sutra*. After
the services were over, Takaaki and Father's cousins,
Michiyori and Morochika, came up to me, offered
their formal condolences, and then departed, leaving me with the sad realization that today marked
the close of the seven-week period of mourning, and
that from this day forth everyone would go his own
way. I went to stay at my old nurse's house at the
corner of Fourth Avenue and Ōmiya Street. I could
not stop the tears that continued to fall on my
sleeves; at least while we were together there had
been someone to share my grief, but now that I was
alone, my sorrow was unbearable.

His Majesty had come to see me in secret even
during the darkest days of my grief. "Come back as
soon as the forty-nine days of mourning are over,"
he urged me. "Everyone is in mourning anyway, so
the color of your gowns won't matter." But I felt so
miserable that I remained in seclusion even after
the forty-ninth day, which fell on the twenty-third
day of the ninth month. It all seemed so sad that
even the weakening cries of the insects brought me
to tears. From GoFukakusa came impatient inquiries: "Do you intend to remain there forever?
Why don't you return?" His messages left me unmoved, and the tenth month began without my even
considering when I would return.

Sometime in the middle of the month there was
a message from another quarter.[88] "I have wanted
to write to you every day, but I was afraid that my

messengers would meet His Majesty's and cause him to wonder if your heart had strayed. Now more days have passed than I intended."

On the messenger's way to the house where I was staying, he noticed a place along Fourth Avenue, near the Ōmiya corner, where brambles had been planted to hide a dilapidated section of the wall. Only two of the stalks were of any thickness. The messenger asked if a guard was posted there, and on being told that there was no guard, he reportedly remarked, "Then it would make a fine passage." With this, I was told, he took out his sword, cut down the brambles and left.[39]

I was curious about this, but I certainly did not expect anything to come of it. Shortly after midnight, however, when the moon was bright, someone knocked surreptitiously on the door outside my room. My young serving girl Chūjō said, "That's a strange sound. Do you suppose it's a water rail?"[40] She went to open the door and rushed back to report: "There's a gentleman here. He says he wants to see you for a moment." Caught by surprise, I was attempting unsuccessfully to frame a reply when the gentleman suddenly appeared in the doorway, evidently having found his way to my room by following Chūjō's young voice.

He was wearing a soft, light crimson robe with an autumn leaf pattern and loose trousers that laced at the bottom. I knew at once that he had come in great secrecy, but because of my condition I begged him to defer his visit. I said, "If you care for me, come to see me at Mount Nochise, the 'Mountain of Later Meetings.'" In the strongest possible terms I expressed my desire to avoid him

tonight, but he replied, "Knowing your condition,
I won't do anything rash tonight. It's just that I've
been wanting to have a quiet talk with you and explain how I've felt about you these many months.
If we sleep apart even the gods of Ise will see nothing wrong in our being together." My usual irreso-
lute nature, further weakened by his virtuous promises, made it impossible for me to refuse him, so I
let him into my room.

His eloquence throughout the long night would
have softened the heart of a Chinese tiger, not to
mention my own which is far from adamantine, so
although I had had not the slightest intention of
giving myself to him, I did. I wondered if perhaps
His Majesty would learn of my unexpected new love
in a dream, and I was afraid.

Warned by the morning song of the birds, he left
while it was still dark. His departure upset me, and
I could not get back to sleep. I simply lay there until
his letter arrived sometime before dawn.

> Returning, the way dimmed by tears
> Even the late moon seems cruel
> There in the dawning sky.

"How long has this feeling been building up in us?
Now I don't think I can bear to wait 'till nightfall.
How sad that it must all be kept secret."
   I replied:

> I cannot speak of your return,
> Only of the shadow of your presence
> Lingering here in tears on my sleeves
> As the morning sky grows light.

I could blame no one for the fate I had failed to

avoid, but it seemed that nothing was going as it should. My whole future was in doubt. I grew despondent and began to weep, trying my best to hide it. Then around noon a different letter came saying: "What are you thinking of to have stayed away so long? With so few people around, there is nothing very amusing at the palace these days." This letter, which went on at great length, did nothing to lighten my spirits.

When my lover arrived very early that evening, my nerves were frayed. As if we were meeting for the first time, I could not bring myself to speak.

As a rule there were no men in the house where I was staying, for Nakatsuna, my nurse's husband, had been living with the priest of Sembon Temple ever since he had taken vows on the occasion of my father's death. Tonight however Nakatsuna had come home because, as he said to me, "Your visits are so rare." His children had also come, making it noisy and most annoying. You would never have known that my former nurse had been raised in a royal household, for she was very much like Imahime's foster mother[41]—utterly without refinement, always making a fuss over something.

Determined to keep them from learning of my guest, I hid him in my bedroom, extinguished all the lamps—I told them I was viewing the moon— and sat down against the brazier by the sliding door. Then, to my vexation, Nurse came to the door. "Since it's a long autumn night, Nakatsuna has suggested we all play some games. Come and join us." She spoke in a demanding tone that was most irritating. "I just don't know what we're going to do. So-and-so has come, and of course so-and-so is here too." She proceeded to rattle off the names of her stepchildren and her own children, and then started talking about a party, droning on until I was afraid she was going to bring up more topics of conversation than there are boards around the hot springs in Iyo.[42]

I declined her invitation with the excuse that I felt indisposed. "As usual you don't pay the least bit of attention to what I say," she complained as she left.

From my quarters facing the garden we could hear every word said among the family. They were speaking informally: "She's so conceited! Do you suppose she'll be an empress soon?" In my mortification I recalled how Genji had heard the vulgar sound of the threshing mills and the workmen from Yūgao's house.[43]

Events were not going at all the way I had planned, and I saw our opportunity slipping away. Confronted with this frustrating situation, we decided to go to sleep in hopes that things would quiet down soon, and we had just dropped off when we were awakened by someone pounding noisily on the gate. "Who could it be?" I wondered. It turned out to be Nakatsuna's youngest son, Nakayori.

"The imperial meal was late tonight," I heard him explain. "By the way, did you know that there is a distinguished-looking wicker carriage drawn up at the corner of Ōmiya Street? I looked in and found the attendants all asleep. The ox is tethered to the axle. I wonder where the owner could be?" I continued to listen in dismay as Nurse—one might have expected it of her—insisted that he go to find out whose carriage it was.

Then I heard Nakatsuna's voice: "Why bother to ask since it's none of our business? It's best not to intrude. If someone is taking advantage of Lady Nijō's visit here to call on her secretly, he probably came in through that gap in the wall hoping the guard was asleep. You just can't be certain of any woman, no matter what her rank or age."

Nurse complained, "This is disastrous. Who can it be? There wouldn't be any reason for His Majesty to come secretly." We could hear every word she said. "I'll be the one who will be blamed if he's some presumptuous man of the sixth rank."[44] How miserably unhappy that woman made me!

Now that another of their sons had arrived, the house was much too noisy for us even to think of sleeping. The party she had told me about seemed to be starting. I heard someone shout, "Tell her to join us." When Nurse came to call me, the attendant in front of my door explained that I wasn't feeling well. There was a fierce knocking on the sliding door to my room, and although I knew who it was, I reacted as if it were a complete stranger. My heart was pounding.

"What's the matter with you? Come see what we've prepared. Come on, come on," she said as she rapped on the door near my pillow.

It would not have done to remain silent, so I replied, "I'm afraid I'm not feeling well."

"I came to invite you because we have some of that white stuff you like so well. When we don't have any you ask for it, and now that we have some you aren't interested. Such fickleness! Well, if that's the way you feel. . . ." Muttering to herself, she left.

Under normal circumstances I would have thought of some witty remark, but now I just wanted to die.

"What is the white stuff you ask for?" my companion inquired.

I thought of making some elegant reply like frost, snow, or hail, but knowing he would not be content with that I told the truth: "It may seem strange, but occasionally I ask for a little white *sake*. She was exaggerating just now, of course."

"It's a good thing I came tonight. I'll be sure to have some white stuff when you visit me, even if I have to go to China for it!" How he laughed then. There have been other embarrassing moments in my life, but none of them, either before or since, has left such an indelible memory.

Thereafter we spent many nights together, and I grew so fond of him that I did not feel at all like returning to the palace. Around the twentieth of the tenth month I learned that my maternal grandmother, Gondainagon, was ill. A few days later, almost before I had had time to wonder how she was, word of her death reached me. For some years she had been living apart at a place called Ayato, near the Zenrin Temple in Higashiyama, yet I felt sad to lose even such a distant link with the mother I had known only in my dreams. My grief continued:

> First autumn dew, now the rain
> Of winter, chill and soaking
> On sleeves already damp.

I had not heard from His Majesty recently and was beginning to fear that he had learned of my misconduct when a message arrived. It began, "It has been a long time, and I have been wondering how you are." He concluded the rather long letter by saying he would send for me that very evening.

"The other day I received word that my aged grandmother had passed away," I wrote in reply. "I'll return to you after the period of defilement has passed."

> Take pity on me!
> After the dew of autumn,
> A rain of winter tears
> Upon wet sleeves.

He answered with this poem:

> I knew not of your added grief
> In the wake of autumn's sorrow,
> Now my sleeves too are damp.

On the first day of the eleventh month I returned to the palace. I had begun to feel at this time that I needed to change my way of life. Too many things depressed me: I was obsessed with thoughts of my father, and my own undefined position made it difficult to know how to behave when Empress Higashi-Nijō chose to be unpleasant. GoFukakusa had instructed my grandfather Takachika and my uncle Takaaki to see that I continued to be as well cared for as I had been when Father was alive. He even made the fine gesture of ordering that my clothes be selected from among those presented to him as tribute. This was splendid treatment indeed, but all I really wanted was to have my baby quietly and then go off to some quiet spot where I could give up this illusory world and pray for my parents' happiness in the next life. Toward the end of the month I left the palace again.

With the purpose of hearing some Buddhist teachings I went to stay with a relative of mine, the nun Shinganbō, who lived at the Shokutei Convent at Daigo Temple. The winter there was lonely. Nuns gathered firewood in the bleak hope that the fire had not died out or that there would at least be some smoke; and even the trickling of water through the bamboo pipes was stopped by ice.

End-of-the-year preparations—quite different from those at court—were under way when one night, just as the late moon was rising, His Majesty came in secret to visit me. He arrived in a plain wicker carriage, accompanied by Takaaki. "I'm staying at the Fushimi Palace," he told me, "and I suddenly thought of you." I wondered when he had learned I was here.

He spoke with particular kindness tonight, and left me only after being roused by the tolling of the dawn bell. The morning moon lingered in the west, while along the eastern hills streaked clouds were breaking up. White blossoms of snow swirled softly down. GoFukakusa's unfigured court robe with matching silk trousers resembled my own dark gray gowns.

The nuns coming out for the morning services, having no idea who was visiting their temple, appeared with surplices slipped on informally over simple gowns and called to each other casually as they walked by: "We're late for the services, sister. Oh, good morning, sister." I envied them. Then they caught sight of the gray-robed guards bringing up the imperial carriage and scurried off in embarrassment.

"I'll see you again soon," His Majesty promised as he left me with tears of parting on my cheeks and the scent of his perfume which had penetrated deep into my sleeves. I listened attentively to the morning service and heard the nuns chant the line: "Even the most virtuous king must follow the three rivers of the afterworld." But my affection for him still remained even after the service had finished.

Shortly after daybreak a letter arrived: "The reluctance I felt at leaving you this morning was something I have never known before."

I replied:

> Even you, my lord,
> Felt the strangeness of this dawn.
> Traces of you linger still
> As you might know by my sleeves.

One evening I was sitting with the nun Shinganbō. There were only three days left in the old year, and I was feeling unusually melancholy. "When will I ever have such peace and quiet again?" I wondered aloud. Thinking I was bored, she decided to cheer me up by calling in several of the older nuns and having them tell stories about times past. In the garden before us the water in the bamboo pipes leading to the cistern had frozen silent, and from the distant hill came the forlorn sound of someone chopping wood. It was like a scene from a fairy tale. In the gathering darkness I watched the lamps as they were lit one by one and listened to the early evening service.

I had just decided to go to bed when someone

knocked quietly on the door outside my room. This
was indeed unexpected, and I had no idea who was
there. Soon I learned it was Akebono. I spoke to him
sharply. "This is outrageous! If anyone should see
you or hear about your visiting me here, I would be
humiliated. I came here to worship, and if my devotions are to have an effect, I must remain pure.
I can't prevent His Majesty from visiting me, but
how can I defile myself merely for the sake of
pleasure? Please go back."

Outside it was snowing hard, and the wind was
fierce. He begged for shelter. "How cruel you are!
At least let me come in until it stops snowing."

Shinganbō and the others had been listening.
"How unkind!" I heard them say. "That's cruel!
Whoever he is, he came here especially to see her.
Mountain storms are dangerous; how can she turn
him away?"

Taking advantage of the unlatched door and the
lighted lamps, he marched in. As though it were
deliberately providing him with a pretext, the snow
piled up on mountain peaks and temple eaves, and
the wind continued its dreary howling all night long.

He made no preparations to leave even after day
had dawned, and indeed made himself so much at
home that it frightened me, although there was
nothing I could do but worry. When the sun was
high in the sky, two retainers came with a great
number of packages. "How inappropriate!" I
thought as I watched them divide up the gifts and
distribute them among the nuns.

One nun said, "This will help us forget the cold
winter winds." Another said, "Your kindness in offering us these surplices and gowns makes us feel as

though light at last shines on our humble mountain retreat." They tried to outdo each other in expressing their thanks.

Except for being received into paradise by Buddha, what should be more desirable than an imperial visit? Yet when the nuns caught a glimpse of Retired Emperor GoFukakusa the other day, none of them thought it auspicious or even very significant. But now, at Akebono's questionable visit, every single one of them was overcome with admiration—simply because of his opulent gifts. What was this world coming to?

The New Year's costume he gave me was subdued, light blue in tone, and included a multilayered gown and a three-layered white gown with small sleeves. We spent the day drinking together, although I was uneasy for fear the wrong people would hear of this.

When dawn broke the next day, he finally prepared to return. "At least come to see me off," he urged, so I got up and went outside. The snow-covered peaks glowing against the faintly dawning sky gave an unearthly aspect to the scene. Two or three attendants dressed in plain robes accompanied him. I was sad, unbearably sad, when he left. How very fickle of me!

On the last day of the year a messenger came for me with a note from Nurse: "In your condition it isn't good for you to remain deep in the mountains." Reluctantly I returned with the messenger to the capital, and the year came to a close.

New Year's activities were dreary even at court, for it had been an unhappy year throughout the realm; my own tears flowed afresh, and I saw no hope in the new year. I customarily set out early each year for our clan's shrine at Iwashimizu, but this year a visit to the shrine was inappropriate, so I went only to the outer gate where, as I stood praying, I saw a face in a vision—but I have recorded that elsewhere.[45]

5 (1273-74)

Toward evening on the tenth day of the second month there were signs that my labor was beginning. It was not an auspicious time. GoFukakusa was troubled,[46] and I had worries of my own, although Takaaki had been taking good care of me, and GoFukakusa had already instructed the abbot of the Ninna Temple to perform a service to Aizen-ō, the God of Love, in the main hall. Prayers were also offered to Fugen Bodhisattva at Narutaki, and the high priest of the Bishamon Temple conducted a service to the Healing Buddha. These were all formal services conducted in the main halls of the temples. In my own quarters the high priest Shingen performed an informal service to Shokannon, the goddess of mercy, and the high priest Dōchō, who had just returned from a mountain retreat, came to pay his respects and told me how well he could recall my father's great concern for my welfare.

After midnight I went into painful heavy labor. My aunt, Lady Kyōgoku, who had come as GoFukakusa's representative, merely added to the confusion. Takachika was also present; but tears came to my eyes when I thought of how matters would have been handled if my father were alive. Leaning back against someone,[47] I dozed off and dreamed that my father, looking as he always had, was standing directly behind me with a worried air. It was not long after this that the birth of an imperial prince was announced. I was amazed that the baby had been delivered safely, and I now began to worry about the results of my misconduct and felt, as though for the first time, the full force of my acts. Without any fanfare GoFukakusa sent a sword to his son,[48] and Takaaki distributed unpretentious gifts to all the exorcists.

I longed for the past. I longed to be back at Father's house in Kawasaki. Such thoughts filled my mind as I watched Takaaki hurry off to present clothes to the wet nurse while bowstrings were twanged to ward off evil spirits. From this point on a seemingly endless round of ceremonies took place, and the entire year passed quickly, as though it were but a dream.[49]

In the twelfth month, GoFukakusa was so occupied with the customary year-end religious services and other activities that he had no leisure. I too was planning to perform some type of religious observance when Akebono, guided by the supposedly unromantic moon of the twelfth month, came to see me. As we sat talking the night away we heard what we thought was only the hoarse cry of the night-singing widow crow, but in fact dawn had already broken. Since Akebono would have been too conspicuous leaving then, he remained for the day with me, although it made me uneasy. We were together when a letter arrived from GoFukakusa. His Majesty wrote with extraordinary tenderness and included this poem:

> Dimly in a dream
> I perceived the sleeves
> Of another's gown on yours.
> Could this be but a dream!

I was astonished. What did he know, and how had he learned it? Thoroughly shaken, I tried to reply with a poem that would imply I was brooding.

> Alone I spread my gowns
> For sleep each night,
> Moonbeams sometimes lie
> Upon my lonesome sleeves.

Only too aware of my shamelessness, I attempted to mislead him.

Akebono and I passed the day together quietly. Of course the people of the house and my own ladies knew of this, and I was acutely uncomfortable at not being able to explain his presence. That night I dreamed Akebono gave me a silver hair-oil jar, which he proffered on a cypress-wood fan bearing a pine tree design. I had accepted this and concealed it in the bosom of my kimono when I was awakened by the dawn bells. As I was pondering this extraordinary dream, Akebono told me of the dream he had had; to my amazement it was identical to mine. What did this signify?

Immediately after New Year's, GoFukakusa went to the Sixth Avenue Palace,⁵⁰ where he put twelve scribes to work copying the *Lotus Sutra*. He recalled with regret the events of the past year—they appeared more like dreams—and did not levy any contributions for the imperial ceremonies, taking instead the necessary supplies from his own store of goods. From the first of the year he began to draw blood from his fingers to write out the *Lotus Sutra* in his own hand. He remained in religious retreat from the beginning of the first month until the seventeenth of the second month, and during this time he saw no women.

Toward the end of the second month I lost my appetite and began to feel out of sorts. At first I thought it was merely a cold. Gradually, however, I came to suspect it was that strange dream coming true. My sins were catching up with me, for there was no way to deceive anyone about this. Unable to soothe my own conscience, I wondered if I would have to confess my condition. I stayed at home a great deal, offering the excuse of religious observances, but Akebono, who visited me often, soon noticed my condition and asked me about it. He treated me with great kindness and agreed that the truth should be kept from His Majesty.

I exhausted myself offering one prayer after another, even though I knew I had no one to blame but myself. I was still brooding over my plight when, at the end of the second month, I began to see Go-Fukakusa again. Naturally enough, by the fifth month, GoFukakusa believed me to be four months pregnant, when actually I was already six months along. I was afraid that the discrepancy would soon be discovered.

On the seventh day of the sixth month, Akebono urged me to leave the palace. I left, curious about what he wanted, and discovered he had prepared a maternity sash for me.

"I especially wanted you to have this," he said. "It should have been presented two months ago,[51] but I was afraid it would attract unwanted attention, so I waited until today. When I learned that His Majesty plans to give you a sash on the twelfth, I decided to present this now." His extraordinary kindness, however, did little to allay my anxiety about the future.

He remained with me for three days. A sudden illness on the tenth delayed my return to the palace for several days, and during this time, on the evening of the twelfth, Takaaki came to present me with a maternity sash from His Majesty, as he had done once before. His arrival brought back memories of that earlier occasion when my father had nervously wondered what to do. The teardrops that covered my sleeves like dew were—as an old poem reminded me—"Not necessarily a sign of autumn."[52]

Had the discrepancy between the length of my actual and supposed pregnancy been only one month instead of two, I would not have worried so frantically about how to explain it. Bad as matters were, however, they were not desperate enough for me to consider drowning myself, and so despite constant worry I managed to pass the time until the ninth month. Fearing other people then, I made up some excuse and hurriedly left the palace on the second day of the month. That very night Akebono came, and we talked about what I should do.

"First let it out that you are seriously ill, and then announce that a master of divination says you have a contagious disease," he advised. I did as he said. I stayed in bed all day, permitted no outsiders to come near me, and had the two attendants who were in on the secret announce that I was not even able to sip warm water; yet no one went out of his way to come to visit me. In sadness I thought of what might have been had Father lived.

We sent word to GoFukakusa begging him not to go to the trouble of sending messengers, but he sent them occasionally anyway. I feared that our story would be uncovered and my future ruined, but for the moment everyone believed it.

Takaaki came often. "Is she all right? What do the doctors say?" he would ask, but he had been told to be careful because my illness was highly contagious, and he only tried to see me once. That time he said he was worried and, to my horror, forced his way in. When I lay utterly silent under my gowns in the darkened room, he left thinking I was really ill. No one else came to call.

Akebono remained with me. He had announced that he was going into religious retreat at the Kasuga Shrine and had sent someone else in his stead, even instructing his substitute to reply as best he could to any letters. I found such elaborate stratagems most distressing.

On the morning of the twentieth I felt the time of my confinement approaching and alerted the few people who knew the secret. While they busied themselves with preparations I mused on the sort of reputation I would leave behind should I die in childbirth. Such thoughts were banished, however, by Akebono's extraordinary kindness. The day drew to a close without anything happening.

After the lamps were lit I suddenly felt that my time was very near. Yet there was no twanging of bows on this occasion; unaided I suffered under my gowns until, when the late-night bell tolled, I could stand it no longer and tried to get up.

"I'm not sure, but isn't the woman supposed to be held around the waist?" Akebono asked. "Perhaps it's taking so long because I'm not doing that. How should I hold you?" I clung to him as he pulled me up, and the baby was safely delivered.

Akebono's first words were, "How wonderful!" Then he ordered, "Bring her rice water at once." The women assisting at the birth were impressed by his knowledge of such things.[53]

He lit a lamp to look at the child, and I got a glimpse of fine black hair and eyes already opened. It was my own child, and naturally enough I thought it was adorable. As I looked on, Akebono took the white gown beside me and wrapped the baby in it, cut the umbilical cord with a short sword that lay by my pillow, and taking the baby, left without a word to anyone. I did not even get a second glimpse of the child's face.

I wanted to cry out and ask why, if the baby must be taken away, I could not at least look at it again; but that would have been rash, and so I remained quiet, letting the tears on my sleeves express my feelings.

"It will be all right. You have nothing to worry about. If it lives you'll be able to see it," Akebono said on his return, attempting to console me. Yet I could not forget the face I had glimpsed but once. Though it was only a girl, I was grieved to think that I did not even know where she had been taken. I also knew it would have been impossible to keep her even if I had so desired. There was nothing for

me to do but wrap my sleeves around myself and
sob inwardly.

At dawn a message was sent to His Majesty:
"The baby was aborted this morning because the
mother's condition was deemed critical. Its devel-
opment was sufficient to indicate that it was a girl."

GoFukakusa replied by sending medicine and a
note that said: "My physicians tell me that this is
normal procedure when there is a very high tem-
perature. Take care of yourself. I wish you a speedy
recovery." I felt afraid.

The following days were uneventful. Akebono returned home—he had been staying with me—and I
was due to return to the palace after my one hundred days passed.[54] In the meantime, however, he
came to visit me every night of my retirement, although neither of us was ever free from the fear that
we would become objects of gossip.

It was at this time that I learned of the illness of
the son I had borne to GoFukakusa last year, who
was now being raised quietly by Takaaki. Hardly
did I have time to ponder the evil consequences that
might flow from my misconduct when I heard, on
the eighth day of the tenth month, that my son had
died, vanishing like a raindrop after a winter rain.
I had tried to prepare myself for this, but its swift-
ness left me grief-stricken. Now to my sorrow at being separated from my daughter was added the bitter grief of my son's death. In my childhood I lost
my mother, in my prime my father was taken from
me, and now I had to suffer anew. Would anything
be able to comfort me?

I continued to see Akebono. Our partings in the
morning were hard to bear, and I would go back to

bed and weep afterward; at night while waiting for him my sobs mingled with the sounds of the bell tolling the hours; and I worried, when we were together, that there would be talk about us. When I was in my own residence, however, I also longed to see GoFukakusa, and when I was at the palace I begrudged the nights he spent with others and feared that his regard for me might be lessening. Suffering is the nature of human existence, but I felt as though the myriad sufferings said to exist in a single day had all fallen to my lot. I wanted to forsake worldly bonds of affection and become a disciple of Buddha.

I remembered looking at a scroll when I was only nine years old called "Records of the Travels of Saigyō." It contained a particular scene where Saigyō, standing amid scattering cherry blossoms, with deep mountains off to one side and a river in front of him, composed this poem:

> Winds scatter white blossoms,
> Whitecaps breaking on rocks;
> How difficult to cross
> The mountain stream.[55]

I had envied Saigyō's life ever since, and although I could never endure a life of ascetic hardship, I wished that I could at least renounce this life and wander wherever my feet might lead me, learning to empathize with the dew under the blossoms and to express the resentment of the scattering autumn leaves, and make out of this a record of my travels that might live on after my death. But I could not escape the grief of the three paths a woman must follow:[56] First I obeyed my father, then I served my

Lord, but my life left something still to be desired, and with each passing day I grew more averse to this sad world.

That autumn the ways of the world also brought grief to GoFukakusa. Greatly humiliated by the fact that Kameyama had established a retired emperor's office, he decided to relinquish the title of Retired Sovereign and enter religious life.[57] He summoned his bodyguards, and having rewarded them, announced that thereafter he would require only the services of Hisanori. The guards took leave of him with tears in their eyes. From among the court ladies Lady Genki and I were selected to take religious orders with His Majesty. This sorrow, I thought, might prove to be the means to my own higher happiness. At this point the Kamakura government tried a course of appeasement: GoFukakusa's son by Lady Genki was named crown prince. This so revived GoFukakusa's spirits that he decided not to enter religious orders. The Corner Mansion, which had been serving as the repository for a picture of GoSaga, was made into the residence of the crown prince, and the picture removed to the Ōgimachi Palace.

Lady Kyōgoku, a court lady and former palace attendant, was sent to serve the crown prince, and although I was not especially close to her, she was a relative of mine, and her going cast gloom upon my world. My mind kept wandering to a place beyond the mountain, and I bemoaned the fate that had made my fleeing there impossible. This year drew to a close with GoFukakusa summoning me so often that I knew I could not give up this life. I returned to the palace.

In the palace I was provided with clothes and other necessities by Lord Takachika, who looked after me out of a sense of duty rather than affection. I ought to have been content, but after my son's death a sense of Akebono's guilt and my own misdeeds preyed on my mind. That child's innocent, smiling face had borne a striking resemblance to GoFukakusa's. I can still recall how, when he came to visit his young son, GoFukakusa had exclaimed: "It's just like looking into a mirror!"

Dwelling on such memories, I grew disconsolate as the days passed. Then, to cap my misery, I learned that for reasons which she did not explain—there was no specific misdeed she could accuse me of—Empress Higashi-Nijō had forbidden me to enter her presence and had stricken my name from her list of attendants.

"Despite everything, you still have my affection," GoFukakusa said, trying to console me; but I was so depressed by these misfortunes that I wanted to withdraw from the world. And yet I clung instead, desperately, to His Majesty's love and continued at court.

During this period one of GoSaga's daughters was the high priestess at the Ise Shrine. She had remained at Ise for three years after her father's death before being relieved of her duties, and had only this fall returned to the capital, where she had taken up residence at Kinugasa, an area near the Ninna Temple. I had pleasant memories of the time

she went to Ise, for then Father was alive and serving at court and had gone out of his way to help her
because she was related to him. Her present residence was such a lonely place that GoFukakusa felt
sorry for her and often sent me to cheer her up. On
the tenth day of the eleventh month she was to go
to Saga to visit Empress Ōmiya. The dowager empress sent a note to GoFukakusa saying: "It will be
rather boring if I am the only one to entertain her.
Why don't you come too?"

This was a time of conflict over the issues of political power and the order of succession, and Empress Ōmiya and GoFukakusa had not been on
good terms.[58] Recently, however, the dowager empress had been sending conciliatory messages, and
GoFukakusa felt he could not refuse her invitation.
Because of my relationship with the high priestess
I accompanied His Majesty. For this occasion I selected a light silk scarlet gown lined in violet, beneath which I wore a three-layered gown running
from green to yellow. Completing my ensemble was
a red formal jacket of the type we had worn regularly since GoFukakusa's son had been designated
Crown Prince. No other ladies went—not even any
serving ladies.

Upon arriving, GoFukakusa went to the dowager
empress' quarters, where they talked quietly together. His Majesty took advantage of this opportunity to discuss my situation: "I have raised this
child ever since she was very young, and I am so
accustomed to her attendance that I often have her
accompany me. Empress Higashi-Nijō has misinter-
preted this, however, and has removed Nijō's name
from her list of court ladies. For my part, I can see

no reason to abandon her, for both her mother, the late Sukedai, and her father, Masatada, served me faithfully and besought me to care for her."

"Really, why should you give her up? When you are used to having someone attend you it is most inconvenient if she is gone for even a short time," Her Highness replied, and turned to me to say in a kind voice: "Feel free to come to me whenever you are troubled." I was skeptical about how long such kindness would last.

They passed the evening together talking. GoFukakusa even had his dinner brought to Empress Ōmiya's rooms. It was quite late when GoFukakusa retired to his quarters, which overlooked a courtyard sometimes used for games of kickball. There were only a few notable people in attendance: Sanekane, Takaaki, Nagasuke, Tamekata, Kaneyuki, and Sukeyuki.

The next day, when the high priestess was to arrive, oxen handlers, messengers, and imperial guards were dispatched by the dowager empress to meet her. GoFukakusa took special pains with his costume. He wore a yellow informal robe lined in green, with a design of burnet flowers worked into it, over a light violet gown bearing gentian-flower crests. His light violet trousers were lined in green, and everything was carefully scented.

At dusk her arrival was announced. The doors on the south side of the main room had been opened and dark gray curtained screens set out with smaller curtain stands inside. Soon after Empress Ōmiya received her, a court lady came to tell us: "The former High Priestess has arrived. This is an out-of-the-way place and I'm afraid our hospitality is sadly lacking,

so please come to visit with her." GoFukakusa went
at once, and as usual I accompanied him, carrying
his sword.

Empress Ōmiya wore a light-gray gauze nun's
habit, bearing a crest, over a darker gray gown the
same shade as the smaller curtains. The high priestess' costume—a three-layered gown shaded from
pink to dark red over a green undergown—did not
quite suit her. The court lady serving her wore a
five-layered purple gown but was not in full court
dress. The high priestess was in her twenties and
had matured so beautifully it seemed natural that
even the gods would be reluctant to part with her.
Her beauty, which might aptly be compared to that
of a cherry blossom, was such that one waited im-
patiently for some slight parting of the sleeves that
hid her face. I was frankly worried as I wondered
what seeds of trouble might take root in His Majesty's passionate heart.

In the conversation that followed she spoke halt-
ingly of her experiences at Ise. GoFukakusa then
suggested that because it was late she might want
to retire. "Perhaps tomorrow you would enjoy going
to view the bare trees on Mount Arashi before you
leave," he said as he bade her goodnight. No sooner
was he in his own quarters than he turned to me
and asked, "What should I do? What should I do?" I
had foreseen this turn of events, but I was nevertheless amazed when he said, "You have been with me
since you were a child. Now you can prove your
devotion by conveying my feelings to her."

Immediately I was sent with a message. After ex-
changing the usual pleasantries—"How nice it is to
see you!" "Isn't it depressing to sleep in a strange

place?"—I was secretly to hand her a note written on glossy white paper:

> You cannot possibly know
> How the vision of someone
> Just met clings to my heart.

It was very late, and the high priestess' ladies were all asleep outside the small screens surrounding her bed when I approached and gave her the message. She blushed deeply and put the letter aside without replying, without even looking at it.

"What shall I tell His Majesty?" I asked.

"I have no idea how to reply to such an unexpected message," she said, and went back to sleep.

Irritated, I returned to GoFukakusa and reported what had happened. "Show me where she's sleeping. Take me there," he urged.

It was a simple matter to escort him there, and even though it upset me, I led the way with GoFukakusa following stealthily behind in his undertrousers—he felt his court robes would have been conspicuous. Sliding open the door, I went in and found her sleeping just as I had left her. Her attendants also seemed to be asleep, for no one made a sound as GoFukakusa stooped and crawled beneath the curtains.

I wondered about the outcome of this affair. Feeling I ought not to go off and leave His Majesty, I lay down beside one of the sleeping attendants, who at that moment awoke with a start and mumbled, "Who's there?"

"There are so few of you on duty I thought you might be worried. I decided to keep you company," I replied. She believed me and started to chat. I was annoyed at her insensitivity. To cut her off I said, "I'm afraid it's late, and I'm very sleepy," and pretended to fall asleep. I was not far from the curtains surrounding the high priestess' bed. It was a pity, I thought, that she required so little persuasion. How much more interesting it would have been if she had held out till dawn.

GoFukakusa returned to his own quarters before daybreak. "The cherry blossom is beautiful to behold, but too easily broken," he commented, and I had to agree.

He slept until the sun was very high; in fact, it was almost noon before he awakened. "Oh dear, I really overslept this morning." Only then did he send his letter. Her answer, I gather, was simply, "How can I forget the dream I had last night?"

GoFukakusa sent a message to Empress Ōmiya asking what she had planned to entertain her special guest today. "Nothing in particular," was the reply.

Takaaki was then instructed to plan a gathering, and toward dusk he announced that the preparations were complete. The dowager empress was invited and came. I was to serve the *sake* because I was intimate with all of them. The *sake* cups remained empty until after the third course, when Empress Ōmiya took the cup from the high priestess and filled it for GoFukakusa. Sanekane and Takaaki were summoned to the veranda, where they sat down just outside the portable curtains. I received GoFukakusa's cup and offered it to Sanekane, who tried to yield to Takaaki, tonight's official host. Takaaki, however, countered by saying, "She's chosen you, how can you refuse?" Whereupon Sanekane drank first, then Takaaki.[59]

The dowager empress remarked, "There has not been any really good entertainment since the demise of the late retired emperor, so please relax and enjoy yourselves tonight." At her order the court ladies played their *koto*, both GoFukakusa and Sanekane played their *biwa*, and Kaneyuki entertained us on the *hichiriki*.[60] All in all, the time passed most pleasantly. Two lords intoned sacred music, and Takaaki sang that song about the village called Seryō.

Upon hearing that the high priestess refused to drink, no matter how much she was urged, GoFukakusa picked up the *sake* jar to serve her himself. This prompted Empress Ōmiya to say, "If you're going to serve *sake*, you'll have to provide something to go with it—if not seaweed from the shore of Koyurugi, at least a song."[61]

His Majesty sang:

> Pity the charcoal seller:
> His coat so thin and yet
> He gathers wood
> And longs for winter.
> A wretched plight.[62]

He had a nice voice.

"I'll have some this round," Empress Ōmiya said. She drank three cupfuls and passed the cup to the high priestess. Then GoFukakusa took it again and returned to his seat.

"It is written that the august person who is emperor has neither mother nor father, but surely I am responsible to some extent for your ascending the throne," Empress Ōmiya remarked meaning-fully. She requested another song.

His Majesty answered, "I have constantly recog-nized my debt to you from the day of my birth to the time I ascended the throne and even to the pres-ent when I hold the title Retired Sovereign. How can I treat your orders lightly?" Then he complied by singing another song:

> A group of cranes gather
> To play in the pond
> Near tortoise hill.
> Longevity for you,
> Peace throughout the realm.[63]

He sang this three times and offered Her Highness three cups of *sake*.

Next he declared he would drink a round. When he had finished he offered the cup to Takaaki and remarked, "Sanekane received his from a beautiful woman. Aren't you envious?" The cup was then passed down to the courtiers, and the party was over.

I was sure GoFukakusa would go to the high priestess again tonight, but he surprised me by saying, "I drank too much, and I feel terrible. Rub my back." He went to bed and slept till dawn.

The next day the high priestess returned home, and His Majesty went to the Imabayashi Mansion to call on Lady Kitayama, who was down with a cold. He spent the night there and returned to his palace in the capital the next day.

On the evening of GoFukakusa's return, Lady Chūnagon brought him the following message from Empress Higashi-Nijō: "I terminated Lady Nijō's service because her behavior was unacceptable, and yet you persist in treating her with special favor. When she wears a three-layered gown[64] and rides in your carriage, people naturally think she is an empress. This is more than I can bear. I am constantly humiliated. With your permission, therefore, I shall go into retirement at Fushimi and enter religious orders."

His Majesty replied: "I have received your letter. I can see no point, however, in bringing up the question of Nijō's position at this time. Her mother, Sukedai, was an outstanding woman, and I was exceedingly fond of her. When she was Nijō's age she served me day and night, and I hoped to do a great deal for her, but unfortunately she died young. Her dying request—to which I agreed—was that I look after her daughter. Nijō's father, the late major counselor, also spoke of this in his final hours. It is said that a master rules because of his subject's loyalty, and that a subject serves because of his master's kindness. Therefore, I willingly consented to Masatada's last request, and he died confident that this worry would no longer impede his progress in the next life. Promises cannot be retracted. Surely her parents are watching us from beyond their graves; how could I, then, expel her when she has done no wrong and has nowhere else to turn?

"It is by no means improper for her to wear a three-layered gown. When she first came to me at the age of four, her father said, 'My own position is a humble one. I am sending her to you as the adopted daughter of her grandfather, Prime Minister Michimitsu.' Consequently she was entitled to ride in carriages with five hanging straps on the blinds and

to wear double-weave gowns. Furthermore, Nijō
has inherited all the rights of the adopted daughter
of an honorary empress since her mother, Sukedai,
was adopted by Prime Minister Saneuji and the
honorary empress, Lady Kitayama. At the ceremonial donning of trousers, when Nijō was still a child,
it was Lady Kitayama herself who tied the sash.[65]
Nijō has publicly been granted permission to wear
thin silk gowns and white pleated trousers anytime.
She has even been granted permission to board her
carriage at the door.[66] So I do not understand why
these rights should be questioned now, since they
were determined years ago. If I had treated some
insignificant person from the ranks of the junior
guards in this way, then I would listen carefully to
what you say and attempt to come to a just decision.
But even in such a case, I would certainly not expel
a woman from the palace when there was no place
for her to go. Rather, I would have her serve in some
low-ranking position.

"It is no secret that when Nijō was given that
name her father refused it. Therefore, although people call her Nijō, I do not. Her father argued that because his own position was so humble, even though
she had been sent here as Michimitsu's daughter,
she should not be given a street name.[67] I told
him that for the time being I would call her 'my
child,' and that when—as was expected—he became
a great minister, she would be given an appropriate
name.

"As the adopted daughter of a prime minister,
she is of course permitted to wear thin silk, but
there is more to it than that. Although every family
boasts of its lineage, even such families as the Kasan

and Kan'in are many generations removed from
their illustrious founders—both are descended from
Fujiwara Fubito. The Koga family, however, is not
very far removed from its imperial progenitor, Prince
Tomohira, seventh son of Emperor Murakami and
younger brother of the Emperors Reizei and En'yu.[68]
Even now the women of that family do not choose
to serve at court, but in Nijō's case, because her
mother served me and especially requested me to
look after her daughter, I have had her with me since
she was very young. I was certain that you understood all this, and consequently I was taken aback
by your message.

"As for your talk of taking religious vows, such
desires grow within one as a result of accumulated
virtue. No one else can decide this for you."

After this exchange of letters, my situation went
from bad to worse. The only consolation I had was
GoFukakusa's deep affection for me.

As for the high priestess, I could well imagine her
distress, inasmuch as His Majesty had made no effort to approach her since that night at Saga. Uneasy about my own failure as a go-between to keep
the affair alive, I also felt truly sorry for her, and so
I suggested to GoFukakusa that he should do something before the end of the year. He agreed and
wrote a letter to her in which he said: "You must
plan to visit me at the earliest opportunity."

When I went to deliver the message I was met
immediately by the nun who served as the high
priestess' foster mother. With tears of reproach
streaming down her cheeks, she began to complain:
"The high priestess had thought she would never
be attached to anyone except the gods. But now

what troubles she has, and they have all sprung out
of her infatuation that night."

To my consternation, she went on and on, but I
finally managed to state my business: "I have come
on His Majesty's behalf to ask if the high priestess
might find some time to visit him."

"There's nothing to prevent her going anytime."

I reported what she said to His Majesty who replied, "When the road of love is barred by mountains of difficulties, one grows eager and impatient;
but this road is too easy to be interesting."

Nevertheless, sometime in the twelfth month he
summoned a nobleman's carriage and secretly sent
it for her. It was a long trip, and she arrived late that
night. The private quarters facing Kyōgoku Street
had been taken over by the crown prince,[69] so her
carriage was drawn up to the corridor leading to
the Great Willow Hall, and she was shown into a
small room beside the main sitting room. Since I
was on duty on the other side of the screens, I heard
her express her quite understandable bitterness at
being neglected ever since that single dreamlike
night. Day broke and she departed, her sobs min-
gling with the tolling of the bells. The sadness of
her going would have moved anyone to the point of
tears.

The last day of the year came around with no
prospect of relief for my own worries: I was not
even free to go home. It appeared that Lady Genki
would spend the night with GoFukakusa, so as soon
as supper was over I complained of a stomachache
and went to my room. It was quite late when I
heard a knock on the door. Afraid of gossip, I wondered if I should let him in, yet we had not seen

each other for so long that it did not seem right to refuse him. I secretly admitted him. He departed before dawn, and my regret at his leaving far exceeded my regret at seeing the old year pass—how foolish I was. Even now these memories bring tears to my eyes.

Book Two

7 (1275)

This year, having turned eighteen, I felt that my years had passed as quickly as a racing horse glimpsed through a crack, as irrevocably as water rushing over rapids. The new year began on a balmy spring day, yet neither the sunshine nor the singing birds could dispel the worries that clouded my heart; and so in a season of gaiety, I was unhappy.

The ceremonial *sake* was served this year by Michimasa, the prime minister who had been appointed chief of Kameyama's retired emperor's office last year. GoFukakusa had been distressed by that arrangement, but the selection of his own son to be the crown prince had mollified him, and it was with a view to ending the dispute that he invited Michimasa to preside over the ceremony. All the court ladies, even those from the tray room, took great pains with their gowns, and selected color combinations with the utmost care. I remembered how my late father had served the ceremonial *sake* a few years earlier, and even though it was a new year, tears for the past streamed down my cheeks.

The crown prince had us divided into two competitive teams, and for fifteen days we were kept busy. As usual, GoFukakusa and the crown prince headed the teams, and the men were paired

off with the women by lots. Assisted by Nijō
Morotada, the crown prince led the men, while His
Majesty captained the women. We drew for oppo-
nents, and I found myself matched with Morotada.
We were urged to put our imaginations to work and
come up with ideas for prizes.[1]

On the day of the Full-Moon Gruel Ceremony,[2]
events occurred that were almost more than we
women could bear: Not only did His Majesty beat
us severely, but he then summoned his attendants
and had them strike us too. This annoyed me, and
so I connived with Lady Genki to retaliate on the
eighteenth by beating His Majesty in return. On
that morning, while GoFukakusa was finishing his
breakfast, we assembled the ladies in the tray room
and assigned each of them to a station. The ladies
Shindainagon and Gonchūnagon were placed at the
door to the imperial bathing room; Bettō and
Kugo remained outside; Chūnagon went to His
Majesty's living room; and Mashimizu was stationed
in the corridor. Lady Genki and I stood chatting in
one of the end rooms.

"His Majesty is certain to come in here, isn't he?"
she asked nervously. Then, just as we had expected,
he entered the room, dressed informally in wide-
legged trousers. His Majesty was blissfully unaware
of what was about to happen.

"What's this? There doesn't seem to be anyone in
my room. Is anybody here?" At this moment Lady
Genki seized him. "Oh, that hurts. Is nobody here?
Someone help!" he called, but no one came.

Morotada was immediately outside the room and
made an effort to come to GoFukakusa's aid, but
Mashimizu, who was standing guard in the corridor,

told him that we were busy and that he would not be allowed in. Seeing that she was armed with a stick, he turned and fled.

While this was going on I beat His Majesty so soundly that he apologized profusely and made a solemn vow: "Never again will I order others to strike you."

I was still congratulating myself on our success when, later in the day, the nobles arrived at GoFukakusa's quarters to be in attendance for the evening meal. He spoke to them at once: "This year I am thirty-three, but judging from today's misfortune it might well be an inauspicious year.[3] Something terrible has happened to me. I accumulated such great virtue in former lives that I was reborn to be master of all things, and yet someone has dared to beat me with a stick. I can't imagine such a thing has ever happened before. Why is it none of you noticed what was going on? Were you all in it together?" Being scolded in those terms, each man attempted to make excuses for himself.

Morotada, Michiyori, Takaaki, Sanekane, and Morochika were all of the same opinion: "The offense of striking Your Majesty, even though it was perpetrated by a court lady, cannot be dismissed lightly. In former times not even persons hostile to the court and emperor would have committed such an outrageous act. We would not even dream of stepping on Your Majesty's shadow. The actual striking of Your Majesty with a stick is a gross violation of decency and cannot be ignored."

As usual, Takaaki felt the need to distinguish himself by speaking out. "What is the name of the guilty court lady?" he asked. "When we have this information we shall be able to decide together on a condign punishment."

"I don't think the lady ought to be punished singly. Shouldn't her relatives share the burden of responsibility?" His Majesty asked.

"They should indeed," was the reply. "All her near relations should be punished." On this everyone was agreed.

"The person who actually struck me was the daughter of Masatada, the granddaughter of Takachika, and the niece of Lord Takaaki. It is my understanding that you, Takaaki, have been acting as her foster father, and I would assume from this that it is only fair to call her your daughter. This affair being the work of Lady Nijō, shouldn't you be held more responsible than anyone else?" When GoFukakusa made this pronouncement, the nobles in attendance roared with laughter.

Someone said, "It would be too much of a nuisance to banish a court lady at the beginning of the year, and accusing all of her relatives would be even more tiresome. Why not take advantage of precedent and demand immediate reparations?"

In the midst of the clamor I spoke up. "I never looked for this to happen. On the fifteenth of this month His Majesty not only belabored us severely himself but called in nobles and courtiers to assist him. Deplorable as it was, there seemed to be nothing an insignificant person like myself could do about it—until, that is, Lady Genki suggested that I join her in an attempt at revenge. I agreed to help, and I struck His Majesty. But I should not be the only one found guilty."

"What you say may indeed be true," I was told,

"but the person who actually wielded the stick against His Majesty is by far the guiltiest." They decided on reparations.

Takaaki went to report what had happened to Lord Takachika, his father. "What a stupid trick!" Takachika said, "We had better make amends immediately. It won't do to delay." He urged Takaaki to expedite the preparations.

On the twentieth Takachika came to the palace bringing elaborate gifts: a court robe, ten light green small-sleeved gowns, and a sword for GoFukakusa; a sword each for Morotada and five other ranking nobles; and one hundred sheaves of fine mulberry paper for the court ladies. Takaaki arrived on the twenty-first with more ordinary gifts. He presented GoFukakusa with a miniature *koto* and a tiny *biwa* fashioned out of purple brocade, and with a lapis lazuli *sake* cup in a silver box. For the nobles he brought horses and oxen, and for the court ladies, ten baskets made from dyed silk each containing balls of silk thread made to resemble melons.

Just as the sumptuous banquet was about to begin, the high priest Ryūben arrived. His Majesty at once invited him to join the party. When the carp was brought in, he turned to Ryūben and said: "The high priest of Uji has set an example. How can you, who were born into that illustrious family, bear to sit idly by? You should carve."

Ryūben firmly declined,[4] yet His Majesty kept insisting. Takaaki placed the cutting board in front of the high priest and laid a carving knife and cooking chopsticks alongside it.

GoFukakusa persisted. "Is there anything else

you require?" he asked. His *sake* had already been served.

Since no other alternative was left to him, we were treated to the rare sight of Ryūben slicing the fish in his priestly robes. After making a few cuts he protested, "I cannot cut off the head."

"What do you mean?" asked His Majesty, continuing to prod.

Ryūben deftly severed the head and hastily departed from the presence of the retired emperor, who was so filled with admiration that he had the lapis lazuli cup, still in its silver box, presented to the priest outside the gate.

Sometime after this, Takaaki saw fit to raise an important point. He said, "Lady Nijō's grandfather and I, her uncle, have been duly punished, but we are both related on the maternal side. I have heard that a paternal grandmother is still alive, and also an aunt.⁵ What about them?"

"They aren't blood relatives," His Majesty replied, "and so to ask them to make amends would be somewhat awkward, and not especially entertaining either."

"I think it would be quite all right, and I stand ready to deliver the order," Takaaki said. "But another possibility might be to seek restitution from the Honorary Empress Kitayama, who has watched over Nijō ever since she was a child, and who cared for her mother Sukedai before that."

GoFukakusa turned to Sanekane. "Aren't you guiltier than the honorary empress?"

"This conversation is getting entirely too farfetched," said Sanekane, trying unsuccessfully to ward off the coming attack. But the other courtiers saw no reason to drop the matter, and in the end he had to capitulate. He helped Lady Kitayama with the reparative gifts,[6] which were of the usual sort. The retired emperor received a robe and a toy boat carved out of wood that carried a boatman made of three musk sacs; Morotada was given an ox and a sword; oxen went to the other nobles involved; and for distribution among the court ladies there were one hundred sheets of mulberry paper, variously decorated—in gold leaf, silver leaf, gold and silver dust, or dyed plum red.

Takaaki was still convinced that Nijō's grandmother should not be spared, and acting on this belief, he sent her the following message: "An outrageous act was perpetrated, and we have acknowledged our responsibility for it by making amends. For your part, what may one expect?"

She answered him thus: "This is my view of the matter. Nijō was only two when her mother died. Taking pity on her, her father raised her carefully. But when she was hardly more than a babe in arms His Majesty summoned her to his palace, and we permitted her to go, thinking that she would receive a better upbringing than we could ever give her. We had no inkling that under His Majesty's tutelage she would turn into the kind of woman who would play such stupid pranks. This, I submit, is due to His Majesty's negligence. Is she incapable of distinguishing differences in rank, or is she simply spoiled by too much attention from His Majesty? I do not know about such things. Begging your pardon, I suggest that if I am to be accused it is only proper that I hear about it directly from His Majesty. This is actually no affair of mine. If

Masatada were alive he would, I have no doubt, take pity on Nijō and make reparations, but I feel no pity for her. If His Majesty ordered me to disown her, I would obey."

Takaaki brought this letter to the palace and read it before His Majesty. "The Koga nun's position is by no means unreasonable," he began. "What she says about Lady Nijō's having been reared in the palace is obvious enough. Besides, it is said a woman's first love must even help her cross the rivers of the underworld."

At this, GoFukakusa spoke up. "What is the drift of your remarks? Remember that it was my own complaint that led to these proceedings. How, then, can you ask me to make amends?"

The argument against him took this line: If superiors undertake to judge the guilt of their inferiors, it does not seem illogical for inferiors to want to do the same. It was agreed that GoFukakusa himself should make a suitable gesture of conciliation. Tsunetō was put in charge of the arrangements. Accordingly the nobles were each presented with a sword, and the court ladies with sets of gowns. It was all vastly amusing.

8 (1275)

On the third month of this year the customary eight lectures on the *Lotus Sutra*, given in memory of Emperor GoShirakawa, were delivered in the temporary Chōkō Temple at the Ōgimachi Palace, the temple at the Sixth Street Palace having burned down.[7] While GoFukakusa was attending the final

service on the thirteenth, a visitor[8] arrived at his
palace, announced he would await His Majesty's return, and retired to a side veranda.

I went to welcome him. "His Majesty will return
shortly," I assured him, and turned to leave.

"Please stay a while," he urged.

Because he was not the kind of person who
normally would have aroused my suspicions, I remained and listened to him talk about the past,
even though I doubted he had anything important
to discuss. His recollections of the things my father
always used to say made me nostalgic, and I found
myself having a cozy chat with him when he most
abruptly changed the subject. He said, "I wonder if
the Buddha knows with what a tainted heart I perform my services."

Flustered by this astonishing outburst, I attempted to go, but he seized my sleeve and demanded, "At least promise that we can meet!" To
make matters more complicated, tears of sincerity
glistened in his eyes. I pulled free and escaped only
because His Majesty's return was announced. His
wholly unexpected behavior was like an extraordinary dream.

After the retired emperor and his visitor had exchanged greetings, they called for *sake*. I served
them, wondering if anyone could have imagined
what was going on in my mind.

About this same time the Kamakura government
revealed its official displeasure over the breach between the two retired emperors and suggested a conciliatory visit, with Kameyama calling upon
GoFukakusa. This prompted an elaborate discussion
as to whether Kameyama should view the gardens

or watch a kickball game. GoFukakusa turned to Lord Kanehira and asked, "How shall we entertain him? What would be appropriate?"

"*Sake* might properly be served before matters are too far along," he replied. "Then, in the middle of the kickball game, when he is resting, some persimmons in *sake* would be appropriate. It would be suitable for one of the court ladies to serve."

"Which lady?" GoFukakusa inquired.

"Lady Nijō is about the right age," came the reply. "She would be a far from unfortunate choice." And so I was assigned the task.

For the occasion I donned raw silk pleated trousers, a seven-layered gown in various shades of red, two outer garments—one crimson, one yellow lined in green—and a light green formal jacket. Underneath I wore two sets of small-sleeved gowns: a three-layered set in red and pink shades of brocade and a two-layered set in Chinese brocade.

Upon his arrival Kameyama inspected the seating arrangements, which had the two retired emperors carefully placed in positions of equal honor. "Inasmuch as these matters were already decided in our late father's time, this arrangement is incorrect," he said, and ordered his place moved to a lower level.

GoFukakusa entered and remarked on this. "When Emperor Suzaku visited Genji he gave instructions that his host's seat be moved into a position of equality. Today, our guest has seen fit to move his own seat down. How extraordinary!" Everyone commented on the elegance of this response.

After the welcoming banquet and the usual round of ceremonial toasts, the crown prince arrived, and

the kickball game began. During the interval between halves, when Kameyama had retired to an
inner room, I placed a ceramic cup in a wicker box
and poured some persimmon *sake* into a metalwork
pitcher; then, in order that I might serve His
Majesty, I handed them both to Lady Bettō to carry
in. She was dressed in a five-layered garment in
shades of green and purple under a white gown
lined in green; over this gown she wore a yellow formal jacket. Kameyama insisted that I have the first
drink. The kickball game lasted until dusk, so
torches were lit for His Majesty's return.

The following day Nakayori[9] brought me a letter
from Kameyama written on crimson paper and attached to a willow branch:

> What has happened to me?
> That image cannot be real—
> Merely a dream I'm convinced
> Yet I still cannot awaken.

It would have been highly improper not to reply to
this, so I wrote a poem on pale blue paper and tied
it to a cherry branch:

> Reality or a dream
> What does it matter?
> Cherry blossoms bloom but to fall
> In this fleeting world.

After this I continued to receive pressing letters, until at last I decided to send for a carriage and go to
the home of my relative Morochika.

In the fourth month, when the Chōkō Temple
reconstruction was completed, His Majesty moved
to the Sixth Street Palace. The dedication service

for the hall, a mandala ceremony, was conducted by High Priest Kōgō, assisted by twenty chanting priests. The Jōchō Hall in the palace was dedicated by High Priest Kenjichi after the move had been accomplished. During His Majesty's move I rode in the seat of honor, on the left-hand side of the first of five carriages of court ladies, with Lady Kyōgoku seated on my right. My costume consisted of a light blue gown, pink-lined, worn over a seven-layered gown shaded from plum red to green, while Lady Kyōgoku wore a five-layered gown with shades running from violet to blue. For the three days of ceremonies after the move I donned a deep crimson jacket and a train to go over my white gown and pleated trousers.[10]

His Majesty, having decided that we should have a miniature garden contest, assigned plots to the nobles, courtiers, and court ladies of the two highest ranks. My plot was a square on the east side of the living quarters just in front of the Jōchō Hall. I put in a pretty little bridge that arched over a stream, but in the middle of the night Takaaki crept up and stole it to use in his own garden—a stunt that struck me as genuinely comical.

Sometime in the eighth month GoFukakusa began to feel unwell, but his symptoms did not point to any recognizable illness. He did not eat for several days, and he sweated profusely. With mounting concern, we summoned a doctor, who began a course of moxa applications, but when His Majesty's condition remained unchanged after ten treatments, we had services for his long life offered to the Bodhisattva Fugen on the eighth day of the ninth month. Another week passed with no change for the better.

In the midst of our general concern and bewilderment a certain priest arrived—the one whose tear-filled eyes had revealed the depth of his feelings for me the previous spring. On the occasions thereafter when I had gone to him bearing messages from GoFukakusa, he took advantage of every opportunity to declare his love, a tactic that invariably caused me to withdraw in confused embarrassment. But lately I had also received affectionate letters begging for some sort of reply. In his presence once, deeply troubled, I tore off a piece of my paper hairband and wrote the single character for dream on it; then, instead of handing it to him properly, I put it down and left. On my next visit he threw me a fragrant star anise branch from the altar. Taking it aside, I discovered he had written on one of the leaves:

> Gathering altar branches at dawn
> Sleeves thoroughly damp—
> My dream left hanging—
> O that I might see its end!

Moved by this, my heart softened, and I began to enjoy being sent to him with messages, and even obliged him by responding amicably to his questions. Such was the situation when he arrived at the palace to minister to GoFukakusa.

His Majesty lamented, "I cannot go on this way."

The priest then advised him, "Tonight before the services begin, dispatch a messenger to the audience hall bearing something you have touched."[11]

When it was time for the early evening service to

begin, His Majesty ordered me to take one of his
robes to the audience hall. I arrived just after the
assisting priests had retired to don their ceremonial
vestments, so no one was in the dim hall except the
priest I knew, Ariake. Approaching him I asked,
"Where shall I put this robe?"

"Take it to the small room beside the sanctuary,"
he replied.

Going there, I found the room open and the
lamps lit. I was taken aback, however, when I saw
that the priest had followed me in, still dressed in
his ordinary robes. What could have entered his
mind?

"Even when we walk in paths of darkness, we are
guided by the Lord Buddha,"[12] he said in a burst of
sobbing before he embraced me.

For his sake I bore the outrage without crying for
assistance; certainly he had not appeared to be a
person who would act in this way. I whispered,
"Some things are embarrassing even to Buddha,"
but my words were wasted; the moment had the un-
reality of a dream remembered. Suddenly the other
priests trooped into the hall for the service, forcing
Ariake to leave by a sliding door at the back.

"Return again after the final service," he urged
me as he left. "Don't fail me."

I could not imagine he would be able to appear
for the service, and yet there he was when it began,
acting as though nothing had happened. I was
afraid, for our meeting had occurred in the light of
sacred lamps, light that leaves no shadows. How
terrifying to think about the darkness of the world
to come.

My heart was not entirely possessed by love, and

yet late that night, seen by no one, I slipped out
and went to him. The service was already over, so
our time together was unhurried. There was a disconcerting edge of sadness in his voice, and it was
not without mixed feelings that I left him at the
first sounds of dawn. He did have an undeniable way
about him, a manner that was both pathetic and
appealing. Forcibly he had seized the small-sleeved
gown I wore next to my body, giving me his in return as a memento of our love.

Back in my room I was composing myself for
sleep when I noticed something in the hem of his
gown. It was a slightly torn piece of paper, on
which this poem was written:

> Reality? A dream?
> Still I cannot discern
> In my lingering anguish
> The moon this autumn night!

When had he found time to write this? I understood
now how deeply he felt, and from that moment we
took advantage of every opportunity to meet, being
together practically every night. This meant that
Ariake was offering prayers with an impure heart. I
was ashamed of what the Buddha must think. Yet
toward the end of the second week His Majesty
showed improvement, and so the services were
scheduled to be discontinued—and the priests to depart—at the end of the third week.

I spent the night before he was to leave with
Ariake. "How can we dare hope to meet after I leave
the palace?" he asked. "I have allowed dust to
accumulate on the floor of the meditation hall and
the sacred altar fires to go out. If only you felt as I

do, we could don the dark robes of hermits and retire deep within the mountains, never to worry
again about this insubstantial world." Yet for my
part, I was fearful of taking this step.

As the bells tolled dawn he expressed his grief at
our parting in moving language—so beautiful that I
wondered where he had learned the phrases. Yet
I was genuinely moved, and it worried me that our
tears might become the subject of gossip. After the
final service was performed he departed from the
palace, leaving me despondent. Now I was burdened with yet another futile worry.

In the ninth month there was a splendid flower
service at the new Sixth Street Palace attended by
Retired Emperor Kameyama himself. The court
ladies who were to offer the flowers this year were
in a flurry of self-conscious preparation; but amid
all the excitement I could not rid myself of my
anxieties. I remained shut up in my quarters as much
as I could.

After the flower service both of the retired emperors proceeded to the Fushimi Palace to select
young pine trees. Lord Kanehira, unexpectedly prevented from accompanying them, sent a poem instead:

> Today a new beginning
> For the small green pine
> From Mount Fushimi:
> May it flourish forever.

The poem GoFukakusa wrote in reply was:

> Here at Mount Fushimi
> It would grow forever,

> May it flourish now
> A thousand years beyond.

Their Majesties remained at Fushimi for two days,
visiting the pavilion by the river and enjoying festive
banquets before they returned.

9 (1275)

In the seventh month of the year before last when
I was preparing to return to the palace after a brief
visit to my home, I sent some unmounted fan paper
along with a frame of camphor wood to a fanmaker's
house, where they were to be pasted together. The
paper was decorated with flecks of gold dust on
the top and bottom, and the phrase "smoldering
ashes"[13] was written in white on the blue wave-
like design in the center. Seeing this quite ordinary
fan paper, the daughter of the house, who painted
beautifully, was inspired to design a new fan with
an autumn landscape and the line "Though you
view the moon from a distant shore."[14] She pasted
her fan paper on the frame in place of the paper I
had sent.

Upon my return to the palace at that time
GoFukakusa observed that the style of painting on
the fan differed from anything else I had and asked
who had given it to me, questioning me with such
persistence that I finally told him quite plainly what
had happened. It came as no surprise that the beauty
of the fan led him to become enamored of the artist,
and on several occasions after that I conveyed messages for them. Finally it was somehow arranged for

the girl to come to the palace on the tenth day of the tenth month.

That evening His Majesty was tense and nervous. He was still fussing over his costume when Middle Commander Sukeyuki arrived to announce that he had escorted the young lady to the palace. "Then have her carriage pulled up near the Fishing Pavilion at the south end of Kyōgoku Street," His Majesty ordered. "Tell her to wait there a moment."

The bells were striking eight at the arrival of the young woman who had remained unseen for three years. For the occasion I had selected a red formal jacket to go over a deep crimson gown and a two-layered green and orange undergarment with an ivy design embroidered in purple thread. Since Go-Fukakusa had instructed me to escort her in, I went to the place where her carriage was waiting. As she descended from her carriage the rustling of her gowns was unusually loud and coarse. I led her to a small room, carefully decorated and elaborately scented, beside His Majesty's living quarters. She appeared uncomfortable in her stiff costume, which consisted of a gown embroidered with huge fans, two undergowns lined in green, and crimson pleated trousers. From the back she looked bulky, her collar drawn up as high as a priest's. But she was without question a beautiful woman—her face delicate, her nose finely molded, her eyes vivid—despite the fact that she was obviously not of aristocratic birth. She was a well-developed girl with a fair complexion and had the advantage of being both tall and plump; had she been a member of the court, in fact, she would have been perfect in the principal female role at a formal ceremony of state, carrying the sword, with her hair done up formally.

When he learned that she had entered the room, GoFukakusa made his appearance, attired in a pale violet robe decorated with woven chrysanthemums, and wearing wide-legged trousers. His clothes were so heavily scented that the fragrance preceded him; it was even wafted to my side of the screens. They talked together, and her responses were so glib and wordy that I suspected his displeasure and was amused. After they retired I went to my customary place near the bedroom. Saionji Sanekane stood guard on the lower veranda on the other side of a paper screen.

Before long—indeed, before it seemed possible that anything could have happened—it was all over. To everyone's astonishment, His Majesty hurriedly left the room and summoned me to his quarters. "That was as sad as Tamagawa Village,"[15] he muttered, and even I felt sorry for her.

The young woman also left the room before the late bells were rung. His Majesty was depressed: He changed his clothes and refused to eat anything, then fell asleep while I was massaging his back. There was a heavy rainstorm that night, and I thought about the hapless girl on her way home. At dawn I turned to His Majesty and said, "I wonder what became of the girl Sukeyuki brought."

"Oh dear," he said, "I had forgotten all about her. Go and see."

The sun was already shining when I arose to investigate the matter. In front of the fishing pavilion of the Corner Mansion I discovered her carriage, which was soaked through after the night's down-

pour. Dismayed, I told the attendants who were just
then emerging from the shelter of the gate to draw
it over to me. Peering inside the carriage, I thought
for a moment that she had carelessly painted a picture on her two-layered gown.[16] Then I realized
that the carriage had leaked, soaking her entire
costume and causing the flower design from her undergown to show through. What a terrible mess!
That she had spent the night weeping only added
to the dampness of her sleeves, and her hair was so
wet, whether from tears or from rain, that it looked
freshly washed. "I look too frightful to be seen," she
said, refusing to get out of the carriage.

It was all quite unpleasant. "There is a new gown
in my room," I told her. "Put it on and go see His
Majesty. He had some important business last
night." She responded by weeping, wringing her
hands, and begging pitifully to be allowed to leave.
It was already day, and so not knowing what else
to do, I sent her home.

I duly reported this to His Majesty, who agreed
it had been a wretched affair and immediately wrote
a letter to the young woman. Instead of replying
formally, she sent something wrapped in blue paper
and placed in the cover of an ink box. The cover
bore as a design the desolate phrase, "a spider lost
among reeds." The blue paper, which had for its
design the line "about you, I am lost," contained a
lock of hair[17] and this rather ordinary poem:

> My worthless self becoming
> Gossip for this world
> Bothers me far less
> Than this broken dream.

We all agreed it had been a most unsatisfactory affair and were curious to know if she actually became a nun. His Majesty occasionally made inquiries about her, but we were unable to learn of her whereabouts. Only a year later did we hear that she had indeed entered a religious order at the Sarara Temple in Kawachi province where she was observing the five hundred precepts[18] befitting a nun. Her sorrow thus resulted in joy, for it led her to the true way.

10 (1275–77)

To my surprise I began receiving letters from the priest Ariake, delivered by one of his page's relatives. It disturbed me to find that his feelings were deeper than I had supposed, and although I answered him occasionally I must confess how relieved I was that during the remainder of the year we had no opportunities to meet.

The following spring I was too busy to have time for any secret affairs. Among other things there was a contest between GoFukakusa and Kameyama to see who could gather the loveliest blossoms, an event that required us to search for flowering trees in the depths of unfamiliar hills. I could only record my loneliness.

When autumn arrived I was spending my time exclusively in the company of His Majesty. In the middle of the ninth month there was a long letter to me from Takaaki, which said in part, "By all means pay me a visit, for there is something I very much want to discuss with you. I am at Izumoji,[19] and the ladies here would also like to see you."

And so I went, thinking that Takaaki was a sympathetic friend who shared my views. I discovered, however, that this was Ariake's stratagem to see me. As a child he had been intimate with Takaaki and knew of Takaaki's close relationship with me—a fact that he exploited to his own advantage. By going to such extraordinary lengths he revealed the strength of his passion, but his dogged persistence also left me unhappy, bitter, and even a little frightened.

That night I sat in the middle of the bed refusing to say a single word to Ariake. Suddenly I was struck with the comical thought that my plight resembled that of the person who wrote the poem "When Love Pursues from All Sides."[20] How could I not be amused? Throughout the night Ariake wept and pledged his love to me, but I continued to feel like an outsider looking in, and I vowed privately that it would be my last night with him. When the morning bird songs urged us to part, Ariake expressed boundless grief; but my unrelenting heart was glad. Then Takaaki murmured a warning and Ariake started to leave, but as he did so he turned and said that the least I could do was to see him off. I replied that I did not feel well, refusing even to rise. I watched his departing figure—he was shaking with sobs—and I felt that he had left part of himself with me. It was then that I knew the full extent of our sin.

Aware that Takaaki would be troubled, I nevertheless said that I had something to attend to and hurried back to the palace in the early light of dawn.

In bed in my own room I was haunted by a vision of Ariake's earnest face hovering beside me. At noon there was a long and apparently sincere letter, with this poem:

> The sorrow, the heart's hurt—
> Words cannot render this.
> I saw her so briefly,
> The woman of my dreams.

Although my feelings were unchanged, it would have been heartless not to reply at all. I wrote:

> Will your heart change?
> I do not know.
> Indifferently I watch
> Chrysanthemums fade.

I sent only the poem, for I had no idea how to respond to the many other things he had mentioned, and I did not answer the letters he wrote to me after that. I was determined never to see him again and made excuses to prevent our meeting. Toward the end of the year, startled to realize that we had not met again, he wrote another letter. It arrived inside of a letter from Takaaki, who wrote, "I am enclosing Ariake's letter. Although your present situation is highly unfortunate, I see no need for you to avoid this affair with such obvious repugnance, for surely an inescapable fate is causing him to love you so fervently. Hence my grief at your cruelty, which is causing him to suffer immensely, so much so I fear what will happen should you ignore this letter too."

Ariake's letter, folded in the official manner and formally pasted together top and bottom, contained paper charms from Kumano Shrine and several major temples, on the back of which he had listed all the gods and Buddhas of the sixty-odd provinces of Japan, starting with Bonten-ō and Taishaku. He also wrote:

"Ever since I decided when I was seven to become a monk and follow Buddha, I have diligently lit sacred fires, devoted days to ascetic practices, and prayed for the long life and prosperity of the emperor and his realm and for the general diminution of evil and augmentation of good. Two years ago I was just beginning to think that the multitudinous gods had granted me a sign of enlightenment, when for no reason—perhaps it was the influence of an evil spirit—I fell in love with you. Night after night I wept out of longing for you; every time I faced the holy image to read a sutra your words came to mind; I placed your letters on the altar of sacred fires and made them my private sutra; I opened them by the light of holy candles and let them soothe my heart. Desperate to find some relief from this unbearable passion, I consulted Takaaki, thinking then that you felt as I did. Now I know it has all been in vain. It had been my hope that we could exchange letters and converse together, but now I have relinquished all hope for this life. What I forget now will not be forgotten in later incarnations, however, for I shall certainly fall into one of the three lower realms,[21] though I doubt the realm exists that could purge me of bitterness. A lifetime of religious observances, all I did from my first initiation to my final ordination, my ascetic practices, my sutra reading, I now dedicate to hell. This will surely be my guarantee of a long, fruitless life here and rebirth in a worse state.

"As far back as I can recall, at least since I cut my

hair and donned monk's robes at seven, I had
never thought about love, much less dreamed that I
would share my bed with a woman. It shall never
happen again. But perhaps you think I say such
things to every woman who comes along. How vex-
ing all this must be to Takaaki."

Below this he had written the names of a forbid-
dingly large number of gods, starting with
Amaterasu and Hachiman. Seeing all this made my
hair stand on end and struck terror and grief into
my heart. But even so, what could I do?

I gathered up the letter and the charms in order
to return them and wrote the following poem on the
wrapping paper:

> Your brush marks tell me,
> "After this, no more!"
> My silken sleeves
> Are wet with tears.

I refolded the paper as it had been, and sent it back.
There was no further word from him, and what
more could I say? The year drew to an uneventful
close.

Ariake customarily visited the palace early in the
new year. This spring he came and quietly drank
sake with GoFukakusa. They were, as usual, in His
Majesty's informal living quarters, and since no
other guests were present it was impossible for me
to slip away unobtrusively. When I appeared His
Majesty asked me to serve the *sake*, but as I was
carrying it in, my nose suddenly began to bleed and
everything went black before my eyes. I was helped
away, and for the next ten days lay seriously ill,
afraid to ponder why.

During the second month Kameyama visited GoFukakusa, and the two of them struck upon the happy
idea of an informal archery competition, with the
understanding that whoever lost would show the
other retired emperor all of his court ladies. When
GoFukakusa lost, he promised to advise Kameyama
as soon as he was ready to make good on the wager.
After Kameyama's departure the lay priest Sukesue
was summoned for a consultation. "How shall we
manage this affair?" GoFukakusa asked. "Can't we
think of a truly original approach?"

"Of course we could always have the ladies line
up in the tray room, as they do for the New Year's
festivities, but that would be far from unusual,"
someone said. "It would be different if we had the
ladies appear before His Majesty individually, as if
each were visiting a fortune teller." Each of the
nobles offered a suggestion.

GoFukakusa had an idea. "Why not build a boat
with a prow shaped like a dragon's head and the
stern like an osprey and then furnish each of the
ladies with a water jug in imitation of that famous
spring party."[22] His suggestion was not followed
because of the difficulties involved in preparing such
a boat.

The lay priest Sukesue then offered his proposal.
"Let's select eight court ladies from each of the top
three ranks and dress them in the attire of the three
classes of kickball players. Then we can set out the
traditional trees[23] in the garden and have the ladies

act out a kickball game. That certainly would be a rare sight." All readily agreed, and the matter was decided.

Each of the ladies was assigned a man to assist with her preparations: Nobles were assigned to the upper-class ladies, courtiers to the upper middle class, and senior imperial guards to the middle class. We were instructed to wear our robes tucked inside of our pleated trousers, to carry swords, and to put on the shoes and stockings customarily worn to play kickball.

"This is too much to endure," we complained. "It's not even going to be held at night, but in broad daylight!" We were abashed, but having no real choice, we began our preparations.

Saionji Sanekane was appointed my assistant. The costume I wore was intended to represent the poem, "I heard the waterfall."[24] My robe and pleated trousers were lined in light blue, and I wore a layered crimson undergown. On my left sleeve I fastened balls of fragrant aloe wood carved to look like rocks, and over them sewed a tiny waterfall of white silk thread. I attached a twig of cherry blossoms and scattered petals on my right sleeve. The motif of blossoms, rocks, and waterfalls was carried out in the designs on my trousers as well.

The lay priest Sukesue assisted Lady Gondainagon. Her robe and trousers were lined in light green. On her left sleeve was a model of a Chinese turret; on her right, cherry blossoms. To her left trouser leg she secured a piece of bamboo, and on her right, a miniature lamp stand. Her layered crimson undergowns were not lined. Each of the court ladies devised a costume along similar lines, and it provided a delightful spectacle when all twenty-four of us were dressing in the large central hall, which had been divided up with screens.

A brightly decorated ball was originally to have been placed in front of Kameyama, but then it was decided to have one of the ladies in the garden kick the ball in the air while the rest of us would try to catch it in our sleeves. Then we would remove our shoes and present it to His Majesty. Everyone dreaded being given the role of kicking the ball, a task that fell to Lady Shin'emon no Kami, one of Empress Higashi-Nijō's ladies and a member of the first team. She was said to be talented at such things. Under the circumstances this was an honor, though certainly an unenviable one. I was the captain of the eight ladies who were to try to catch the ball and present it to Kameyama. It was to be a deliberately ostentatious affair.

The bamboo blinds facing the southern garden were raised, revealing the two retired emperors and the crown prince, with the court nobles seated below on either side and the courtiers standing in the background. We trooped in through a gate in the fence and crossed the garden accompanied by our male assistants, dressed in variously colored robes. Kameyama demanded that our names be announced—he had arrived shortly after noon and had begun drinking early.

Our director, Tamekata, kept pressing us to hurry up and get on with the game, but we delayed until it was necessary to light the torches. At last, with our escorts holding small torches and calling out our names, we each turned to face His Majesty, drew our sleeves around us, and moved off to one side. It was acutely embarrassing. We then filed out onto the field, the lowest-ranking team first, and took up our appointed positions under the trees. If this show dazzled our eyes, how much more it must have appealed to the men of every rank. After I had placed the ball in front of Kameyama I tried to hurry away, but he told me to remain for a while and asked me to serve *sake* in my costume, which I felt was a real imposition.

Several days before this event the court ladies had all gathered in the palace, for we wanted to accustom ourselves to the different hair styles, robes, and shoes we would be wearing. The men assigned to us helped with these preliminaries, until each came to look upon the woman he assisted as his special property. No great amount of imagination is necessary to picture the things that went on.

Following this occasion there was another archery match, won this time by GoFukakusa. In due course we were all invited to the Saga Palace, where Kameyama's thirteen-year-old daughter, who was being raised by Lady Azechi, danced the numbers usually performed at the Dais Rehearsal,[25] with her senior court ladies taking the roles of the special attendants and girl assistants. Nothing was omitted in Kameyama's imitation of these festivities: The men even paraded through the northern guard house, the nobles wearing robes with padded hems, the senior courtiers and men of the sixth rank going with their outer robes slipped off their shoulders. They then performed the traditional *gosechi* men's dances on a roofless stage, and danced other numbers at royal request. It was all indescribably delightful.

We so regretted having to end the party that yet another match was held; and when GoFukakusa went down in defeat once again he invited everyone to the Fushimi Palace. There, plans were under way to present a concert modeled after one in *The Tale of Genji*.

As was only proper, the leading role of Murasaki no Ue was to be played by Lady Genki; but the secondary role of Onna Sannomiya[26] was, to my dismay, awarded to Takachika's daughter, a newcomer to the palace. To make matters worse, an easy-to-play thirteen-string *koto* was substituted for the more difficult seven-string *koto* actually played by Onna Sannomiya in the novel. When I learned that Takachika had specifically requested this role for his daughter, I was so upset that I did not want to appear; but I was ordered to take the minor role of Lady Akashi no Ue and play the *biwa* because Kameyama knew me by sight and had spoken to me personally at the kickball game.

I had begun *biwa* lessons when I was seven, learning two or three pieces from my uncle Masamitsu, although I never put my heart into it. When I was nine I continued for a while under GoFukakusa's tutelage, and while I did not get as far as the Three Secret Airs, I mastered all the usual court pieces; and when I was only ten I played the *biwa* at the Shirakawa Palace rehearsal for GoSaga's fiftieth birthday party. GoSaga found my playing charming enough to present me with a *biwa* made from Chinese quince with rosewood pegs and a red brocade case. Since then I had not put much effort into practicing, and the order to perform for this occa-

sion made me uneasy, yet I took no special care with
my preparations.

I was told to wear light blue and crimson gowns
under a yellowish green gown and a russet and yellow short robe; but I still smarted from resentment
at having to take the lowly role of Akashi no Ue. For
this occasion Lady Genki had taken special pains to
learn to play the six-string *koto*, even though the
newcomer was substituting a thirteen string *koto*
for the proper seven-string one.

As for our positions onstage, the place immediately behind Murasaki no Ue was reserved for
Nyogo no Kimi,[27] played by the daughter of Prime
Minister Michimasa. My seat was arranged to the
right of the leading lady's, and in front of the newcomer's. I was told that this was because our positions were to be the same as they had been at the
kickball game. Yet I wondered how this could be,
for if the newcomer was to play the important role
of Onna Sannomiya she ought by rights to have
been seated in front. Still, these were His Majesty's
orders.

I had accompanied GoFukakusa to the Fushimi
Palace early, and hence on the day of the performance I was present to see a shadow of my own past
when the new girl arrived in a carriage embellished
with crests, followed by her retainers. What memories flooded over me! Then Kameyama arrived, and
the drinking commenced immediately.

When it was nearly time for the concert to begin,
one by one the ladies entered the concert room,
each carefully placing her instrument in front of her
and arranging her cushions exactly as it had been
done in *The Tale of Genji*. GoFukakusa himself was

to play Genji, with Kameyama taking the part of
Yūgiri; I think that Kanetada and the Tōin middle
commander were to sit on the steps playing the
flute and the *hichiriki*.

Just as we ladies had completed our preparations
and GoFukakusa was expected to enter momentar-
ily from the room where the men were drinking,
Lord Takachika came in. When he saw the arrangements of our seats he declared, "This won't do at
all. The lady playing Onna Sannomiya should be in
front. Besides, she is Nijō's aunt, Nijō is merely her
niece. The aunt should certainly take precedence.
My rank is higher than that of the late Masatada.
Why should my daughter take the lower seat? Re-
arrange the places!"

He spoke in such a loud voice that Takaaki and
Sanekane heard him. They came in and pointed out
that His Majesty had specifically ordered it done this
way. But he would not listen. "It's not as it should
be, is it?" he cried.

They remonstrated with him, but there was no
one present who could back them up with authority.
GoFukakusa was still in the other room, where it
would have been most improper to interrupt him,
and so I had to watch as my seat was moved to the
inferior position. Suddenly I had a vivid, painful
recollection of a carriage ride, wide gown sleeves
hanging down over the side.[28] What possible difference can it make if she is the aunt and I am the
niece? Should the many people who are born of
humble mothers be specially honored when they
happen to be aunts or grandmothers? The whole
affair seemed disgusting, for no matter how I be-
haved, it did not appear that I could avoid dishonor.

At that thought I arose and made my way out. Back in my room I wrote a letter and told my attendants to give it to His Majesty should he inquire.

I decided to go to a small residence near the cemetery of the Sokujō Temple in Kobayashi where my nurse's mother, known as Lady Iyo when she was in the service of Princess Sen'yō, had been living as a nun since the death of Her Ladyship.

The letter I left for GoFukakusa, written on thin white paper and tied with a cut *biwa* string, contained this poem:

> Aware of the meager worth
> Of my wretched self,
> I abandon forever
> The *biwa* strings.

"If His Majesty inquires, tell him I have gone to the capital," I instructed the attendants as I left.

It was not until the drinking bout was past the halfway mark that GoFukakusa made good on his promise to come to the concert room. When he saw that there was no Akashi no Ue at the *biwa* he questioned Lady Genki, who related exactly what had happened. On hearing the story he had to agree that my actions were warranted, and he sent a messenger to my room to look for me. The messenger came back with the report that I had departed for the capital. "She wrote this letter and told her attendants to be sure that Your Majesty received it," he said. The messenger's words caused surprise and disappointment, and the entertainment seemed to lose its sparkle.

Kameyama read the poem I had written and remarked, "She is a person of remarkable sensitivity.

It's too bad about the concert. I believe I'll leave now, but I would like to keep this poem." And with that he departed.

Thus the newcomer missed her chance to perform on the *koto*, and the party ended with much idle talk, the gist of which was that Takachika's behavior had been utterly absurd, that he must be advancing in senility, and that Lady Nijō had come through it all beautifully.

Early the next morning GoFukakusa dispatched messengers to make inquiries at my nurse's home at Fourth Avenue and Ōmiya and at my grandmother's residence at Rokkaku and Kushige; but at both places they were informed that my whereabouts were unknown. Determined to find me, he sent messengers far and wide—to no avail.

I realized that this was an excellent opportunity for me to renounce this sad life; but I was faced with the fact that my condition had not been normal since sometime in the twelfth month. This also meant, of course, that I did not feel well, so I decided to remain in hiding and hope that I could become a nun after my time had passed and the baby was born.

Having vowed never again to take up a *biwa* plectrum, I made an offering of the instrument GoSaga had given me to the god Hachiman, presenting it along with some of my father's letters, on the backs of which I had copied out sections of the *Lotus Sutra*. I tied the letters in a bundle and wrote on the wrapper:

> Resolved never again
> To pluck these strings,

I offer them with sutras
Written over traces of his brush.

I reflected on my situation: Two years ago this
spring, on the thirteenth day of the third month,
Ariake had confessed, in effect, that he could "not
pass by without plucking";[29] and last year in the
twelfth month I received his letter containing those
awesome vows. How much had happened! This year
on the thirteenth day of the third month I was not
even in the palace that had been my home for so
long. I had given up the *biwa* and incurred the displeasure of Takachika, though ever since my father's
death I had thought of him as a parent. Takachika
had reportedly barred his house to me for as long as
he lived, on the grounds that I had challenged his
authority and then fled. I felt that all paths were
sealed off from me and wondered fearfully what
would happen next.

GoFukakusa's messengers were searching high
and low for me, and Akebono had left no place un-
visited, inquiring at many temples deep in the
mountains. Word of their efforts left me unmoved.
In the hope that I might improve my prospects in
future lives by attending Buddhist services, I decided to go into retreat at the Shokutei Convent in
Daigo Temple, where the nun Shinganbō resided.

12 (1277)

At the Kamo Shrine Festival in the fourth month
the two retired emperors shared a viewing stand
provided for them by Takachika, but the reports I

heard of this lively affair failed to stir my interest.
The coming-of-age ceremonies for the young emperor and the crown prince were also held in the
fourth month.[80] It was necessary to have a major
counselor well advanced in years participate in these
ceremonies; a retired counselor would not have
been appropriate. For this reason, Major Counselor
Takaaki agreed to lend his title for one day to his
father Takachika, who had served the imperial family
for many years. It was understood that Takachika
would accept the title, perform in the ceremonies,
and return the position to his son, who had won
the acclaim of everyone for such an admirable gesture. Things took a wholly unexpected turn, however, when Takachika proceeded to confer the title
on Tsunetō. Takaaki was of course deeply embittered at being deprived of his rightful position by his
own father's duplicity. The reason for this unpro-
voked betrayal, it seems, was the ambition of Middle
Commander Takayoshi—Takachika's son by his
present wife—to become an imperial adviser. By giving the post of major counselor to Tsunetō, Takachika was hoping to promote his younger son's in-
terests at Takaaki's expense. Knowing this, Takaaki
could no longer continue living with his father, and
so he went into seclusion at the home of his father-
in-law, the Kujō middle counselor.

When I heard this dismaying news I wanted to
pay a consolation visit to Takaaki, but thinking of
the gossip that would surely follow I wrote a letter
instead, telling him where I was and asking him to
visit me.

He wrote in reply: "How happy I am to hear from
you! I cannot tell you how worried I was when I

learned you had disappeared without a trace. I'll come as soon as it's dark, and we can discuss the events of these unhappy days." He arrived at dusk.

It was a night toward the end of the fourth month. The blossoms of a late-blooming cherry shone white against branches tipped by new leaves, and among the tree shadows cast by the brilliant moonlight, deer were wandering. If only I could have captured the scene on paper! Bells in nearby temples suddenly tolled the opening of evening services, and as we stood in a corridor beside the meditation hall we heard the chanting of Buddha's name. I was touched by the pathos of the nuns in their rough hempen robes leaving the hall after the service, and even Takaaki, normally unmoved by such things, was deeply affected. The glossy sleeves of his informal robe were damp with tears.

"I intend to leave this world of human love and attachments and enter the true way," he said, "but I am detained by my worries about you. Your late father transmitted to me his deep concern for you, and now I am the only one left to look after you."

It was true. Who else did I have? The thought of parting from him filled me with such anguish that I burst into tears. I said, "After my time has passed, I too plan to retire deep into the mountains. Then we will share the same plight."

That night we talked about the painful things that had occurred. "I saw the letter Ariake wrote you some time ago," he said. "Even though it did not concern me directly, it terrified me, and I feel now that the suffering that has befallen you and me is retribution. One day Ariake called on GoFukakusa when His Majesty was searching everywhere for you with no inkling of your whereabouts. On his way home Ariake asked me if what he had heard was really true, and I had to tell him that even I had no idea where you were. I believe I know what he felt at this reply, for he hesitated at the middle gate and stood without a word, hiding his tears behind his cypress fan. Then as he was parting from me he murmured, 'The restless world of unenlightened men is like a burning house.' It is pathetic enough to see an ordinary man overflowing with yearning, pain, wretchedness, and grief, but it is so much worse for me to see him in this condition. I can well imagine his feelings when he turns to the altar to pray."

Takaaki's words revived memories of the moon-lit night when Akiake wrote the line "in my lingering anguish."[31] Why had I treated him with such cruelty? Stung with remorse, I used my sleeves to brush away my tears.

In order to forestall the malicious gossip that would begin if he remained until dawn, Takaaki prepared to leave. "It looks as though I'm going after an eventful visit," he joked, and then quickly added, "When you enter holy orders, try not to forget the deep feelings we shared last night, and our reluctance to part this morning." He composed this poem:

> The transitory nature of this world
> Is easily forgotten!
> Yet again pain and tears.

I replied, "I know that sorrow is inherent in all things, but is grief always like this—with so much anguish?"

> Am I to believe
> This pain is but the suffering
> Inherent in all life?

At this time Akebono, in grief over my disappearance, was spending two weeks in retreat at the Kasuga Shrine. There on the night of the eleventh day of his retreat he dreamed he saw me standing unchanged in front of the second shrine. Immediately he headed back toward the capital, and at the spot known as Wisteria Woods he met one of Takaaki's servants carrying a slender letter box. Acting on a shrewd guess, Akebono refrained from questioning the messenger directly. He merely said, "You must be returning from the Shokutei Convent. Have you heard when Lady Nijō will take her vows?"

The messenger assumed that Akebono knew all about the situation and replied, "Last night Lord Takaaki came here from the Kujō family mansion, and I am serving as his messenger this morning, but I have not heard when she will take her vows. Apparently she has decided to enter religious orders."

In his delight at what he had discovered, Akebono took the horse his attendant was riding back to the Kasuga Shrine, where he presented it as a gift to the gods. Then, aware of the disconcerting rumors that would spread if he visited me in broad daylight, he went to visit a priest he knew at the nearby Upper Daigo Temple.

Unaware of this I spent the day viewing the summer scenery and learning of the true way from the head nun. Toward dusk, when someone came up on the veranda without any warning, I assumed it was one of the nuns until I heard the soft rustling of court robes. As I turned to look, the sliding door right beside me was pushed open a crack, and a voice said, "You are determined to hide, but the gods have guided me to you." It was Akebono.

The surprise of his unexpected visit caused my heart to leap, but there was nothing to do now except go out to him. "I left the palace embittered by everything," I said. "Should I have given special treatment to some?"

He spoke to me with his customary elegance, and I must confess I was deeply affected, yet having determined my course, I felt no desire to return to the palace. Who would take pity on me even in my present condition?

Akebono assured me that His Majesty's feelings for me had not changed. "Was Takachika's senile prejudice reason enough to behave like this?" he asked. "Do as His Majesty commands, just this once."

He spent the following day with me and sent a letter of condolence to Takaaki. "I was surprised to discover Lady Nijō in hiding here," he wrote. "I am paying her a visit, and it would be a pleasure to see you." Then he added warmly, "I do hope you'll come."

Takaaki arrived at dusk, and we spent the night drinking to console ourselves. As dawn approached and Takaaki prepared to leave, the men discussed my situation and agreed that GoFukakusa should be informed of my whereabouts. Akebono was also going to leave, and the thought of parting with them both was difficult to bear.

I went out to see them off. Takaaki wore an informal crepe robe with an embroidered design of moonflowers on a cypress fence. He departed before daybreak lest he be seen en route. The light of the setting moon flooded the veranda where Akebono, dressed in a vermilion costume, stood alone waiting for his carriage to be readied. He turned to the head nun and remarked how happy he was to have had this unexpected meeting, and she replied, "In this simple place of retreat, where we chant the Tenfold Invocation and await the coming of the Three Holy Ones,[32] it is as though a brilliant light shines on our mountain abode when the presence of our un-expected guest lures such illustrious visitors as your-self."

"After we had unsuccessfully scoured the moun-tains in search of Lady Nijō," he replied, "I went to the Kasuga Shrine to seek the guidance of the gods, and there I was granted a vision of her." As Akebono was relating all this he reminded me of the Sumiyoshi captain.[33]

The tolling of the dawn bells summoned him to leave, and as he left he uttered a parting verse in such a low voice that I had to ask him to repeat it.

> I ponder life's sorrow:
> Sound of tolling bell,
> Moon in the dawn sky—
> What grief they bring.

Having said this, he left me to grieve after him.

> The tolling of the bell
> Evokes sadness and grief;
> The regret of parting lingers
> With the moon at dawn.

That day I was afraid that my plan was in danger of being thwarted again, so I consulted the head nun. "They will definitely inform GoFukakusa," she said. "When imperial messengers have come searching for you I have insisted that you were not here, but I hardly dare continue that now. You had better go back to Kobayashi."[34] She was undoubtedly right, I thought.

I requested a carriage from Takaaki and went to Kobayashi in Fushimi. That night and the following day passed uneventfully. Lady Iyo, my nurse's mother, said to me, "The number of messengers that have come from GoFukakusa's palace searching for you has been extraordinary. Kiyonaga himself appeared several times."[35]

Although I heard her words, my mind was preoccupied with visions of Ariake as he must have appeared when he said, "The restless world of unenlightened men is like a burning house." How terrible that anyone could be so burdened with grief. It was a dreary, rainy day in the fourth month, yet I heard the song of the first cuckoo from its leafy perch among the trees on Mount Otowa:

> May the cuckoo's first song
> Banish my tears and ease
> My burdened heart under
> A lowering sky at dawn.

The nuns regularly arose before daybreak for their predawn service, and the next morning, awakened by the bell of the nearby Sokujō Temple, I too got up early to read sutras. The sun was already high when a letter arrived from Yuki no Akebono. After expressing his sorrow at our parting, his letter went on to discuss the child I had borne him—the child who had never been more than a dream to me. I had never laid eyes on her after the night of her birth, and I had accepted this as my fate. Yet now Akebono was writing to me about her. "She has been ill since this spring. When her condition grew serious I consulted a diviner, who pronounced that her illness was attributable to your suppressed anxiety about her.[36] The bonds of parental love must indeed be indissoluble. I shall arrange for you to meet her when you have returned to the capital."

Until this time I had never thought of her with either affection or sorrow, yet perhaps my case was like the one in the poem, "I did not consider the mountain peak evil."[37] Occasionally I thought about how old she would be, but it puzzled me that I could never recapture the longing I felt when I glimpsed her that first night. Were our disentwined strands of love the cause of this misfortune? The thought of this possibility made me more wretched than before. I answered Akebono that I was prepared to meet her should the right occasion present itself. From this time forth she too would weigh upon my conscience, for I feared what I might learn.

At dusk when the early evening services were in progress I entered a private chapel to pray, and discovered an ancient nun already there reading the sutras. I heard in the distance the words "Bodhisattva's promise," and my heart filled with hope. Just then there was the sound of the folding doors being opened, a sign that someone had arrived. Curious as to who the unexpected visitor might be, I opened the sliding door beside the Buddha and peered through the crack. There I saw GoFukakusa in a palanquin, accompanied only by a few junior imperial guards and several servants. Before I could recover from my astonishment and slip away to hide somewhere, he had caught sight of me and had his palanquin carried over to where I was. I struggled to maintain my composure as His Majesty descended and said, "How fortunate I am to have found you." I refrained from answering.

"Return the palanquin and bring a carriage," he ordered, and then while he was waiting he turned to me. "I have come because I learned you are determined to give up this world," he began. "Must your bitterness toward Takachika extend to me as well?" He continued at some length in an attempt to reason with me, but I stubbornly reiterated my desire to take this opportunity to escape from this world of sorrow.

"I was at the Saga Palace when I suddenly learned of your whereabouts," he explained. "Not content with hearsay I determined to see for myself how you were, so I announced that I would proceed to Fushimi and came here instead. I would like to know what you have been thinking recently. Why don't we quietly discuss all that's happened?" He went on in this fashion until my weak will succumbed and I went to his carriage.

We spent the night talking together.[38] He assured me that at the time he had known nothing about Takachika's rudeness to me, and I listened with trepidation as he pledged to the gods Amaterasu and Hachiman that no matter what happened he would never value me less than the others. As a result, I consented to return to his palace, though it pained me to realize that the next opportunity to escape this world might lie in the distant future. He prepared to go at daybreak. "Accompany me," he said. "Come now, quickly." And because I had already promised him that I would go eventually, I accompanied him then.

All the furnishings from my quarters in the palace had been sent back to my home, so I went to Lady Kyōgoku's apartments. Worldly ways now depressed me more than ever, and the palace ceremony in which I received my maternity sash toward the end of the month awakened countless old memories.[39]

About this time I was invited to see the daughter I had borne to Akebono. The meeting was not to be at the place she was living—I was told it would have been inappropriate for me to visit her there—but at a rather unexpected place. I suggested the fifth day of the fifth month as a possible date, for then I could cover my absence with the excuse that I was visiting my mother's grave. The fifth month proved inconvenient for the others involved, however, and it was pointed out besides that it would be highly inauspicious to see my daughter the same day I visited a grave. I ended up going to the appointed place on the last day of the fourth month.

The child was dressed in a plum red, small-sleeved gown, and her hair, which had been allowed to grow since the second month,[40] reminded me of how much she had had the night she was born. One of the children of Akebono's wife had been born at about the same time, but it had died, and she had taken my daughter in its stead. Everyone believed it was her own child.[41] I learned that the child was being raised carefully with the hope she would one day be sent to the palace and become an empress, and it made me uneasy to realize that my child was another's treasure. His Majesty knew nothing of my duplicity, and I hoped that he would never learn the truth.

13 (1277)

In the eighth month Kanehira[42] visited the palace. He was a regular caller, for GoSaga on his deathbed had requested him to look after GoFukakusa, and His Majesty always received him warmly. On the day he arrived they were drinking and chatting in GoFukakusa's living quarters when Kanehira noticed me. "What have we here?" he asked. "I understood that Lady Nijō's whereabouts were unknown. Was she hiding in some mountain retreat?"

"Without the aid of diviners I would never have found her," His Majesty replied. "She was on Mount Hōrai."[43]

Kanehira was indignant at what he called Takachika's "senile tricks." He said, "It is shocking that Takaaki was retired. I fail to understand how such things can happen. Do you suppose Tsunetō requested the post of major counselor? And what's this about Lady Nijō's renouncing the biwa?"

When I did not reply, GoFukakusa answered, "She has sworn a vow to the god Hachiman that neither she nor her descendants will ever touch a biwa again."

"Isn't it rash for her to give up the biwa at such an early age?" Kanehira asked. "Hers is an unusually

noble heritage. The Koga family alone has preserved
its court status since its family name was bestowed
by Emperor Murakami. There is a story that my
brother, Lord Kanetsune, once offered to do a favor
for a man named Nakatsuna, whose family had for
generations served as retainers of the Koga. Kanetsune offered to take him on as his retainer also, but
Nakatsuna said, 'I am in the service of the Koga.
How could I serve you too?'[44] To this Lord Kanetsune replied with a note in his own hand: 'The
illustrious Koga family is unlike the others, and
therefore I see no reason for you not to serve us
both.' In view of Lady Nijō's paternal lineage,
therefore, her maternal grandfather Takachika was
unjustified in giving his own daughter precedence
over Nijō just because she was Nijō's aunt."

He continued in a similar vein. "Just recently my
son, the former regent Morotada, had a long talk
with Kameyama, and he repeated His Majesty's comments to me: 'The most important accomplishment
for a beautiful woman is the ability to write poetry.
And in the midst of great afflictions Lady Nijō composed a memorable poem indeed.[45] She belongs to
a line of poets extending eight generations back to
the imperial family, and though still young, she dis-
plays exceptional ability. From an attendant of mine
named Nakayori, whose family are retainers of the
Koga, I have learned that Lady Nijō is missing and
that people are searching everywhere for her. I am
worried about what might befall her.' These were
His Majesty's own words."

Kanehira then changed the subject, saying to
GoFukakusa, "My son Kanetada has some talent

for contemporary songs.⁴⁶ Would you be kind enough to teach him the secrets of that art?"

"Of course, why not? It might prove difficult to do here, though, so I'll do it at Fushimi." They agreed to meet there two days hence; and on the appointed day, with a minimum of fuss and only a few people in his retinue—it was, after all, an un-announced visit—GoFukakusa set out for Fushimi. Only the chief steward of the dining room went along to prepare informal meals.

When GoFukakusa informed me that I was to accompany him to Fushimi, I was at a loss what to wear, for with all my recent moving about, my ward-robe was in a sorry state. It was unthinkable to ask Takachika for help after what had happened. I was fretting over my predicament when, to my great de-light, Akebono sent me a parcel that included an un-lined layered gown shaded from yellow to green with an autumn scene embroidered on the sleeves; to go with this was a scarlet jacket, a small-sleeved gown of raw silk, and pleated trousers.

With Kanehira at Fushimi were his two sons, Morotada and Kanetada; GoFukakusa was accom-panied on the journey there by Sanekane, Michiyori, and Morochika. Takaaki, staying nearby at his in-laws' Ninth Street mansion, no longer held a posi-tion at court, but he was invited anyway, since it was not a formal occasion. He refused to come, how-ever, even after being summoned several times, claiming that attendance would be inappropriate for one in seclusion. Finally, Kiyonaga was sent to fetch him. At this Takaaki not only came, but brought two *shirabyōshi*⁴⁷ entertainers with him. He left them in a carriage at the upper palace, for the activities were being held in a large hall in the lower palace, and he wanted to keep them as a surprise.

When the festivities were well begun, Takaaki mentioned the girls, and since His Majesty expressed interest, they were immediately called in. The elder, a girl slightly over twenty, was called Harugiku; her younger sister's name was Wakagiku. Harugiku wore a plum red, unlined layered gown with pleated trousers, while Wakagiku was dressed in wide-legged trousers and a yellow and green robe with a bush clover design embroidered on the sleeves.

After they had sung a few songs, GoFukakusa asked them to dance. "There is no one to play the drum for us," they replied, whereupon a drum was produced, and Takaaki was prevailed upon to play it. After Wakagiku had performed, His Majesty requested her elder sister to dance, but Harugiku excused herself by saying she had given up dancing long before. When GoFukakusa urged her repeatedly, however, she put her sister's dancing robe on over her pleated trousers and performed for us. Her style was distinctive and good. Having been instructed not to do too short a number, she danced a congratulatory piece. As the evening wore on, His Majesty became very drunk, and at a late hour the girls were sent home without his knowledge. The rest of us were to spend the night at Fushimi and return to the capital in the morning.

While GoFukakusa slumbered I left quietly on a personal matter of my own, walking past the Tsutsui Pavilion on my way.[48] Later that night, as I was returning to my own room in the main part of the palace, the wind rustling through the pines chilled my body, and the cries of the insects, chirping as though they had been waiting for me, joined the sounds of my own weeping. The long-awaited moon had risen, and the scene was extraordinarily moving.

I was dressed only in a simple gown, for when I started back I had assumed that everyone had retired, this being such a rural palace. But as I was walking along the veranda just in front of the Tsutsui Pavilion, someone suddenly reached out from between the blinds and took hold of my sleeve. Certain it was a ghost, I screamed in terror.

"Don't shout," a voice scolded, "for if you raise your voice at night, tree spirits will appear."[49] I thought I recognized the voice,[50] yet in my fear I struggled desperately to escape, nearly ripping my sleeve off—but to no avail. The area was deserted, and my assailant managed to pull me behind the blinds into an empty room.

"Why are you doing this to me?" I sobbed helplessly.

"I have loved you for so many years," he declared, and then to my dismay he went on to repeat all the conventional phrases and to give numerous pledges of his love; but all that he said fell on deaf ears, for my one desire was to escape as soon as possible.

"It's been a long night for His Majesty. He's awake now and calling for me," I lied and attempted to leave.

"Promise me you'll find a way to return," he demanded, refusing to let me go until I had sworn by numerous shrines that I would come back. At last I got away, frightened by what might come of my vows.

His Majesty had awakened wanting more to drink, and people were reassembling in his quarters. From his extraordinarily drunken state he expressed his disappointment that Wakagiku had gone home, and ordered our stay to be extended an extra day so she might be summoned back. Satisfied that this would be done, he lapsed into drunken slumber. But I could not sleep a wink the rest of the night, and daybreak found me still brooding over the event that had occurred.

The next day GoFukakusa was the host at a sumptuous banquet prepared under the direction of Saketaka. The entertainers were again present, food and drink were bountiful, and GoFukakusa's liberal hospitality enlivened the atmosphere. Harugiku, the elder sister, received three musk sacs in a silver cup on a sandalwood tray; Wakagiku, her younger sister, was given a single musk sac in a lapis lazuli cup on a silver tray.

We were still enjoying ourselves at the party when the late-night bells tolled. Wakagiku, required to perform again, sang the song about Priest Sōō, whose fervent prayers caused an image of the god Fudō to split in two.[51] When she reached the line, "Did High Priest Kakinomoto no Ki still have an attachment to this world?" Takaaki's sudden glance revealed that he shared my thoughts. In the midst of sad and frightening memories I forced myself to sit impassively. Much later, after more lively singing and dancing, the party came to an end.

His Majesty had retired, and I was massaging his back when the man who had accosted me at the Tsutsui Pavilion the previous night came to the door. "I would like to speak with you a moment," he called.

Not knowing how to escape, I remained perfectly still.

"Just for a short time, while His Majesty is sleeping," he pleaded.

GoFukakusa then whispered to me, "Hurry up, go. You have nothing to worry about." I was so embarrassed I wanted to die. Then His Majesty reached out, and seizing my hand—I was near the foot of his mat—he pulled me up. Without intending it, I was compelled to go.

"From here you can easily go in to attend His Majesty," my would-be lover said. We were separated from GoFukakusa only by a frail sliding door, and though he feigned sleep I was wretchedly aware that he was listening. I wept, but my accoster was very drunk. Finally, at dawn, he let me go. I knew I had done no wrong, but as I lay back down beside His Majesty I was filled with anguish, and his pleasantries were more than I could bear.

We were scheduled to return to the capital that day, but Kanehira had a suggestion. "Let's stay one more day. The entertainers are still here and say they are reluctant to leave. I'll volunteer to host a banquet." And so our stay was again prolonged.

Although there were no proper quarters for ladies, I had withdrawn to a room to rest and was pondering what might happen next when a letter was brought to me containing this poem:

> I cannot awaken
> From that brief dream.
> Your image lingers in my heart,
> Your perfume on my sleeve.

There was also this comment in the letter: "This morning I am embarrassed by the thought that His Majesty might have been awake in the very next room."

I replied:

> Was it but a dream?
> I cannot be sure, yet
> Secret tears have darkened
> The color of my sleeves.

His Majesty summoned me several times before I reluctantly appeared. Realizing then how unhappy I was, he treated me with such elaborate kindness and consideration that I grew more despondent than ever.

It was not yet sunset when we commenced the evening's activities by proceeding to the Fushimi Pavilion in a boat. As dusk settled, the cormorant fishermen were summoned to get into boats alongside ours and set their cormorants to work.[52] After the fishing the three cormorant masters made their obeisances and received a set of unlined gowns. We returned to shore, *sake* was served, and His Majesty again proceeded to become incredibly drunk.

Late that night the same man came once more to His Majesty's bed chamber. "Sleeping in a strange place for several nights in a row is very depressing," he said. "It's especially difficult to sleep here at Fushimi. Come and light a lamp for me. Some kind of insect is annoying me." I grew more and more uneasy as he rattled on.

His Majesty simply said, "Why don't you go?" His remark was most disquieting.

The intruder then said, "Won't you let an eccen-

tric old man have his way? You might think it unusual, but actually there are many precedents for a
man like me becoming the benefactor of a young
woman." All this was said to me practically from
His Majesty's pillow. I did not reply, for words
could not possibly have expressed my mortification.

In his normal cheerful manner GoFukakusa advised us, "Don't go too far away. I don't enjoy sleeping alone either." We slept where we had on the
previous night.

Very early the next morning everyone scurried
about so that we might leave before daybreak. As
we departed I felt that only an empty husk of my
former self remained. When I got into the back of
His Majesty's carriage for the return trip I was surprised to discover Sanekane also riding there.

All the carriages remained together until the
Kiyomizu Bridge was crossed, then just beyond
Kyōgoku Street the imperial carriage I was in headed
north, while the others turned west. For some reason I gazed after my visitor's carriage as though I
regretted our parting. When, I wondered, did such
feelings arise in my own heart?

Book Three

14 (1281)

I was at this time so worried about my affairs, which were proving to be unending sources of trouble, that I longed in my weariness to go and live beyond the mountains. Yet the difficulties of giving up this life barred the way. I fell asleep at night angry with myself, and in my dreams there appeared a deep rift separating me from His Majesty. Nor could I see any way of altering the situation.

By the middle of the second month petals were unfolding everywhere and breezes carried the scent of plum blossoms. Yet I was discontented, for I had no means of assuaging my growing loneliness and grief.

One day at His Majesty's summons I went to the room beside the bathing room, where he was standing alone. I was curious to know what he wanted. He complained of being lonely because so many of his court ladies had gone home on visits, and then he added, "And you remain continually closeted in your own rooms. Who has stolen your heart?" I was groping awkwardly for an answer when someone announced the arrival of Ariake, who was immediately shown to His Majesty's living quarters. Not knowing what else to do, I assumed an air of indifference.

GoFukakusa had summoned him to perform a

service to the god Aizen-ō for the recovery of Empress Yūgi—then known as Princess Ima Gosho—who had been ill for a long time. He also asked that a ceremony to protect his own welfare be performed to the stars of the Big Dipper, but this was to be undertaken by a priest from Narutaki.

The talk between GoFukakusa and Ariake was more subdued than usual, and as I sat with them I became uneasy about what Ariake was actually thinking. Word came that the princess had taken a turn for the worse, so GoFukakusa hurriedly left to go to her. "Please wait here until he returns," I said to Ariake.

The two of us were alone. Turning to me, Ariake began talking about the long and dreary days that had passed, and how he felt now. He wept so profusely he could not hide the tears with his sleeves. At a loss for a response, I simply listened—unaware that His Majesty had returned soon after he had left us and was standing on the other side of the sliding door, where he could surely hear Ariake's oft-repeated laments. We had no way of knowing he was there, and of course he understood the situation at once. When His Majesty finally entered the room, Ariake tried to pretend that nothing was wrong, but tears had spotted his sleeves. I feared what GoFukakusa would think at seeing them.

When it came time to light the torches Ariake left, and the night was quiet and lonely. His Majesty retired and asked me to massage his legs. He said as he lay there, "I have certainly heard the most extraordinary revelation. Now please explain what this all means. Ariake and I have been intimate since childhood, and I thought I knew him well enough to say that he would never have become involved in an affair of this nature." He dwelt so insistently on the subject that I soon decided it would be pointless to deny any part of it, and I related everything that had happened from the time we met until our separation.

"It is truly an astonishing relationship," GoFuka-kusa responded. "First, Ariake was so overwhelmed by passion that he persuaded Takaaki to act as go-between; then you did your best to elude him; and after this you felt the malicious effects of his passion. None of this bodes well for the future, for events from the past teach us that passion respects neither rank nor station. For example, the spirit of the high priest Kakinomoto pursued Empress Some-dono relentlessly, and it was beyond the power of the Buddhas and Bodhisattvas to prevent her from yielding to his malevolent spirit. The holy man of the Shiga Temple was also smitten by passion, but he was luckily returned to the true way by the sympathy and skill of the lady he loved.[1]

"Ariake's passion is unusually strong, and I advise you to keep what I have said in mind when dealing with him. I will help you, but no one must know of it. Now that his duties bring him to the palace regularly, we have an opportunity to make him forget the malice he bears toward you. The fact that he is conducting religious services may present difficulties, but I have a simple stratagem that may succeed." He spoke to me with genuine kindness. "I am willing to do this only because you have never allowed anything to come between us. Try not to worry, and do what you can to keep his malice from increasing."

I wondered why he was not feeling aggrieved.

"I was the first to love you," he continued, "and through the years, no matter what has happened, my devotion to you has not wavered. Yet somehow matters have not turned out as I expected them to, and unfortunately, I have great difficulty expressing my love. I first learned of love from your mother, the late Sukedai, and I was secretly very fond of her, but I was still an adolescent timid in the ways of the world. So while I let the days slip by, Fuyutada and Masatada stole her away, leaving me ignobly to seek unguarded moments with her.[2] I was anxious about you even before you were born, and after you came into my care I eagerly looked forward to the time when you would be mine." Hearing these things about the past, I was overcome with deep emotion.

As dawn broke attendants were busy readying the hall where the esoteric services were to begin that day. I avoided everyone I could, fearful that my face would reveal the grief in my heart; and when Ariake's arrival was announced I attempted to maintain my composure in front of His Majesty. But I was worried, knowing as I did what he must have been thinking.

By now I was accustomed to carrying messages to Ariake, so that evening when GoFukakusa handed me a note to deliver just before the evening service, I had no reason to refuse even though I had qualms about doing it at this particular time. The note contained a question about an obscure aspect of esoteric Buddhism. Few people were around when I delivered it to Ariake, who was intoning prayers leaning on an armrest with the dim light of the hazy spring moon shining in on him. "I have asked Buddha to

help me accept my forlorn condition ever since that
sad autumn night,"[3] he said, "but it is more than I
can endure. Perhaps I must yield up my life for this
passion. Despite prayers that I might be taken from
the world you inhabit, 'the gods do not accept my
ablutions.' "[4]

He would not hear of my leaving, and I worried
all the while that we might be discovered, to the
damage of our reputations. Before we had quite enjoyed our love's dream, however, a voice announced
the evening service. In the ensuing confusion I
managed to slip out through a door at the back, feeling somehow estranged from him. Despite Ariake's
fervent promises to meet me after the late service,
I had no desire to make a bad situation worse. And
since there was no reason to remain, I returned to
my own quarters, though his image lingered in my
mind even more vividly than it had on that far-off
night when he had written, "in my lingering anguish." Tears fell onto my sleeves. Surely this affair
was caused by an inevitable bond of fate, I thought,
and I wondered what my former lives had been.

I lay down to sleep, but dawn broke before I had
a chance to dream of him. Little as I wanted to, I
was obligated to attend His Majesty. He took advantage of a time when few people were around,
to say to me, "Last night I acted with a purpose,
though I hope he doesn't realize that. Don't let on
that I know, for I wouldn't want him to feel constrained." I could find no words of reply.

Perhaps His Majesty was disturbed to think that
the religious services were being performed by a person with an impure heart. Still, he astonished me by
what he said one night. It was late in the evening

of the sixth day of the services—the eighteenth day of the second month—and His Majesty was admiring the plum blossoms in front of the Great Hall, which were particularly lovely and fragrant this year. When he heard the night service end he said, "This is the final night of services, and it's already quite late. Take this opportunity to go to him." Then, after the bells were silent again, he called for Lady Genki and retired with her to a room beside the Orange Garden.

I went to see Ariake in his room, not simply to do His Majesty's bidding, but out of genuine regret that this was to be the last night. Ariake was waiting, apparently hoping that I would appear. Later we might have cause to rue our love, but now with the scent from his sleeves permeating mine, I remembered every word he had ever spoken to me. At the same time I knew that when I next burst into tears of anguished yearning, there would be no one for me to turn to.

Ariake's tearful behavior showed that he thought we were parting forever. I deplored his attitude, and as I had on that night when we parted in sorrow, I longed to have our affair concluded. But such thoughts were futile. Never had there been a briefer night—more fleeting, it seemed, than a sunbeam shining on a drop of dew. We parted at daybreak wondering if we would ever meet again, for it seemed a remote chance.

> Once with bitterness I parted
> From him whose image now
> Lingers in quite different tears.

It would not do for me to dwell on my thoughts,

for the princess had improved and Ariake was due
to depart, yet I could not banish him from my mind.
Then a strange thing occurred. I was resting in my
own room, having left Ariake before dawn, when
Kiyonaga brought word that His Majesty wanted
me at once. Lady Genki had spent the night with
him—why this urgent summons to me? Greatly agitated, I went to him.

"It was late last night when I realized how anx-
iously Ariake must have been awaiting you," GoFukakusa began. "Were this merely an ordinary affair
I would never have become involved, but he is such
an exceptional person that I have permitted it. Last
night, however, I had a bewildering dream: I
dreamed that you received a *goko*[5] from Ariake.
Wanting to hide it from me, you thrust it into your
gown, but I grasped your sleeve and cried, 'Why
are you doing that when you know you have my
sympathy?' You wiped a tear from your face and
held out the *goko* for me to inspect. It was made of
silver and had belonged to the late Emperor Go-
Saga.[6] Seeing this, I said I would receive it as mine,
but as I stood there waiting for it, the dream ended.
I regard this as a sign that something happened last
night. Circumstances suggest that this will be another case of 'the pine tree by the cliff.'"[7] Despite
what GoFukakusa said, I saw no reason to believe
that his dream would come true.

For the remainder of that month GoFukakusa did
not send for me. This was my own fault—or so I
believed—and I felt no bitterness toward him. As
the days passed I began to suspect my condition,
but I was unable to imagine what the future held
in store.

One evening early in the third month Go-Fukakusa took advantage of a lull just before his dinner when few people were around to call me into a small side chamber. I feared the worst when I went, but he plied me with gentle assurances of his love until I did not know whether to be happy or sad. Then he said, "I've purposely avoided sending for you since my dream. I wanted the month to end, but it has been lonesome without you." And so, to my astonishment, I learned that he had had a motive for his actions. My condition was definitely not normal; in fact, there was no doubt that his dream was true. It was useless to regret it now.

At the beginning of the fifth month I went home to pay my annual visit to my mother's grave and to gather iris.[8] Now, it happened that ever since that regrettable incident at Fushimi[9] I had the feeling that Akebono was drawing away from me. We had once enjoyed such a deep relationship that I might term him my first lover, and so it was not unnatural that I worried about his coolness. While I was at home I received a letter from Akebono with this poem:

> Grows there an iris root
> Deep as the sorrow rooted
> In my heart? I search
> Until my sleeves are damp.[10]

At the end of his long letter he wrote: "I'll drop by for a visit while you are at that house where no one guards the gate."[11]

I wrote a simple answer:

> The iris I arrange
> Have shallow, floating roots—

> Unexpected sorrows,
> Sleeves that never dry.[12]

"I thought our love would endure all misfortunes."
It seemed a futile gesture to reply, yet late that
night he visited me. But no sooner had we begun to
talk, recalling our many adversities, than a flurry of
confusion broke out in the house. There was reportedly a fire in the vicinity of GoFukakusa's palace,
and Akebono—who had no business being with me
in the first place—rushed off. Before he could return, the brief night turned to dawn. At daybreak
he sent a letter. "Last night I was aware our bond
had weakened. It saddens me to realize that the interruption probably foreshadowed our future." He
included this poem:

> Has it dried up?
> The hidden current
> Flowing in our hearts—
> We never seem to meet
> Despite our pledge of love.

I too believed that last night's interruption was
more than a coincidence, and I replied:

> Our pledge may end,
> But the stream of tears
> My heart calls forth
> Will never cease to flow.

That very evening GoFukakusa dispatched a carriage for me, sending word that I was to return to
the palace immediately. I had only been at home a
short time and had not meant to return so quickly,
but I did as I was told.

By early autumn I was feeling considerably better. One day GoFukakusa suggested it was time for me to have a maternity sash. Then he asked, "Does Ariake know of your condition?"

"No, he doesn't. When would I have had an opportunity to inform him?"

"Until now, Ariake has never been hesitant about confiding in me, but lately he has become withdrawn and formal. I think I shall tell him there is nothing for him to conceal, for his relationship with you is an unavoidable bond of fate against which he is powerless."

I did not know what to say. I knew how profoundly this would affect Ariake, but if I requested GoFukakusa to say nothing I would appear defensive, and my motive would be suspect. With this in mind, I murmured, "Whatever you think is best," and said no more about it.

Soon afterward there commenced a series of discussions on esoteric Buddhist doctrine, with Ariake among the priests summoned to the palace to explain various tenets. After four or five days of meetings, and at the conclusion of a lecture on the sutras, GoFukakusa ordered some *sake*. As I was serving it he began to talk: "After thinking about the subject at great length, I have concluded that there is nothing sinful in the relationships between men and women inasmuch as they are usually caused by bonds from former lives and thus defy our resistance. Numerous examples from the past illustrate what I mean, as in the case of the ascetic known as Jōzō and the girl from Michinokuni. To escape from the bond Jōzō even attempted to kill her, but without success, and finally he yielded to his passion. In

another case, the holy man of the Shiga Temple was
attracted by the Empress Somedono. Unable to endure such passion, he turned into a blue ghost. Or
again, a story tells of a lovesick woman who turned
into a rock, which was known ever after as 'the rock
of longing for one's mate.'[18] Relationships with animals are also the result of karma from former
lives."

I knew that what he said was directed at me in
particular, and I could feel beads of sweat on my
face, and tears.

That night the party was not elaborate, and before long, people began to leave. Ariake rose to depart along with the others, but GoFukakusa detained him. "Let's take advantage of the stillness of
the night to discuss religious doctrine at our leisure,"
he suggested. At this, I got up and returned to my
quarters. I had no idea what might happen, but I
could not bear to be present.

After midnight His Majesty summoned me to his
chamber. "I took the occasion to explain to Ariake
everything I have been concerned about," he said.
"Parents are supposed to love their children with
blind devotion, but I doubt that any parental love
can rival my own devotion to you." As he spoke,
tears glistened in his eyes.

Before I could reply, I found myself weeping un-
controllably. GoFukakusa resumed speaking. "You
heard me say that people sometimes experience
overpowering affinities for each other. After you left
I told Ariake that I had learned something wholly
unexpected. I said, 'I realize, of course, that you are
hesitant about mentioning the subject. Yet this is
a deadly serious matter, which ought not separate

us. Of course I realize that if word of this affair were to spread, your position would be difficult indeed.

"'I am convinced that this unbearable passion is simply the working out of some karma from the past, so there is no necessity for laying blame. Last spring it became evident that Nijō's condition was not normal. A bizarre dream forewarned me of this, and curious about the strength of your bond, I decided to test the validity of my dream by deliberately refraining from sending for Nijō until the third month—a decision whose difficulty you can appreciate. If what I say is untrue, may the gods of Ise, Iwashimizu, Kamo, and Kasuga, indeed, all the gods that protect this country, withhold their aid. There is no reason to isolate yourself from me. Despite all that has happened, my own feelings have not changed a bit.'

"After I had said this, Ariake wept and was unable to speak for a time. Then he wiped away his tears and began to confess: 'Now that you have spoken out, there is no reason for me to keep anything hidden. The working out of my fate has indeed been cruel. My debt to you for this kindness cannot be repaid in a single lifetime, nor shall I forget it for many lives to come. A fate like mine is unendurably bitter! For the past three years I have struggled to escape from it, yet even when I meditate or read the sutras I discover that I am thinking only of her. Once in an excess of passion I swore an oath and transcribed it for her in a letter, but even that did not curb my heart. I loathe my body for its inability to resist being drawn to her again: It is like a cart dragged about by oxen.

"'I regard what has happened as a sign. I shall

relinquish my position to the young prince,[14] don the dark robes of a hermit, and retire deep into the mountains. Your kindness to me has been unstinting over the past years, but in the ages to come my source of joy will be your sympathy in this affair.'

"Having spoken, Ariake departed in tears, still deeply in love with you. He rouses my fullest sympathy."

I wept as I listened to GoFukakusa report the conversation, though like Genji I could not say whether my tears expressed bitterness or gratitude.

Late that night, wanting to know how Ariake felt before he left the palace, I used the pretext of delivering a message to go to his quarters. A young serving boy, already fast asleep, was the only other person around. Ariake came into the room where we usually met.

"I try to remember that grief can turn to joy," he said, "but still my heart is overwrought, and I feel sorry for myself."

His words recalled to me my feelings on that sad night in the past when I wanted only to escape, yet now I was filled with regret that the religious discussions would end tomorrow, making tonight our last opportunity to meet. I spent the night with him, and he wept so much that I even forgot my own worries about the future. He repeated what His Majesty had already told me about their talk, adding his own reaction: "When I learned that His Majesty knew our secret, I feared we would never be able to communicate again, and this made me realize how much I really love you. In view of your present condition we cannot treat our relationship lightly, for it will endure more than a single lifetime.

His Majesty's promise to look after our child over-whelmed me with joy—and with sadness too. I am anxious now for the child to be born."

We talked together through the night, laughing and weeping until the bells sounded at dawn. When I rose to leave, I saw Ariake choked with tears, struggling with the thought that we might never meet again. I was moved by the depth of his feelings.

> On my sleeves, reflected
> In tears, the dawn moon.
> If only it would remain
> Here, after daybreak.[15]

I kept this poem to myself. Had I also surrendered my heart to love?

Back in my own quarters I lay pondering our ap-parently inescapable bond when my rest was inter-rupted by a summons from GoFukakusa. "All night I have waited in vain for you to come," he com-plained. "You have just left him, haven't you, and you are still so affected by the remorse of parting that the dawn sky seems cruel." He went on in this vein, leaving me utterly speechless. I thought of the vast number of people in the world who are never confronted by such dilemmas, and I wondered why I was always singled out. Then I burst into tears. I did not know how GoFukakusa would construe my behavior, but I did not really care.

"You probably wish you could go back to bed and dream peacefully of him," he said. To my great an-noyance he persisted in misinterpreting events. Yet I ought to have expected that this was how things would finally turn out. The thought of my wretched

situation caused me to weep even more. GoFukakusa, however, was convinced that I was weeping
only for Ariake and that I resented his summons,
and so he abruptly broke off in midsentence and
left the room. More disturbed than ever, I made my
way back to my quarters.

All that day I felt unwell and did not attend His
Majesty until evening. I was nervous about what he
might say, and as I went on duty I felt a powerful
urge to leave this sad world behind—to flee at once
to the far side of the mountain. Apparently the final
religious lecture was over, for Ariake and GoFukakusa were chatting together. Feeling uneasy in their
presence, I slipped out and went to the room beside
the bathing room, where I came upon Akebono. He
greeted me with a complaint. "I'm on duty today,
but you won't even bother to speak to me, even
though I'm right here."

I listened to him with the feeling that I was under
attack from all directions. Just then GoFukakusa
summoned me back. I was worried that something
else had happened, but he merely wanted me to
serve the *sake*. Only a couple of ladies were in attendance in his room, and it was quiet—too quiet
for His Majesty. When he heard that Morochika and
Sanekane were in the palace, he called them in and
embarked on a lively party.

When the gathering reluctantly broke up, Ariake
went to Lady Genki's apartments to perform the
evening service, departing from the palace immediately thereafter. I was left disconsolate, and nothing
in the palace could revive my spirits.

In a quiet ceremony GoFukakusa presented me
with a maternity sash, although it must have been a

painful experience for him. That same night I attended him, and he chatted with me until dawn, as if nothing had ever come between us. How did he manage not to become permanently embittered?

Preparations were under way well in advance for the ninth month flower service, which was to be unusually elaborate this year. I asked to be excused from taking part on account of my condition, but GoFukakusa refused, saying, "It's not that noticeable. You had better appear with the others."

For the festival I wore a red formal jacket over gowns that were light violet and green; my unlined gowns ranged in shades from reddish-brown to yellow. I was on night duty when I heard with considerable misgivings that Ariake had arrived and gone to the hall where he was to perform the concluding Buddhist service. He had no way of knowing that I was nearby. Just then, however, one of GoFukakusa's attendants came up to me and said, "His Majesty thinks he dropped his fan in the hall where the service is to be held, and he would like you to retrieve it."

Though this request was strange, I duly slid open the door to the hall and peered in, only to discover that the fan was nowhere in sight. I quickly slid the door shut again and told the messenger it was not there, whereupon he returned to His Majesty. The door opened again, and I heard Ariake's voice. "It is scandalous that in my misery I am reduced to this. I'll send a letter to you by a person no one suspects, for our affair must never be discovered."

How did he think it would be discovered? Certainly I had no interest in damaging his reputation. I checked my impulse to rebuke him sharply and

merely said that if he did not want the whole world
to know about it, he had best close the door.

After the service was concluded and Ariake had
gone, I returned to GoFukakusa. "How did you like
my message about the fan?" he asked with a laugh.
It had apparently been another of his little ruses.

15 (1281)

In the tenth month the weather was as damp and
cloudy as my spirits. Lonesome, unhappy—never
had I felt so downcast—I went to Saga, the residence
of my stepmother, and began a retreat at the Hōrin
Temple. On Mount Arashi the autumn leaves
whirled by the sweeping wind fell into the rapids
of the Ōi River, where they floated on the waves
like shreds of brocade. Memories of past events,
both public and private, crowded my mind: I could
recall, for example, precisely what everyone had
worn and what offerings had been made on the occasion long ago when GoSaga dedicated some sutras
he had copied.[16] I thought of the poem, "Enviable
indeed the returning waves,"[17] and my melancholy
deepened when deer cried in the near distance. For
whom were they crying?

> This self of mine
> Never free of tears
> The deer too cry out,
> What do they long for?

One especially dreary evening an important-
looking courtier arrived. I was surprised to see that
it was the Yamamomo middle commander, Kane-

yuki, and that he was approaching my quarters with a message. "Empress Ōmiya was suddenly taken ill," he reported, "and this morning His Majesty came to the Saga Palace to visit her. He asked where you were and sent me to escort you to him. His trip was so hurried that no ladies were able to accompany him, and your presence is required at once. If you are fulfilling a vow, you can finish your retreat later."

Having been in retreat for the past five days, I was reluctant to leave with only two more days left; but GoFukakusa had dispatched a carriage for me, and Kaneyuki told me that His Majesty had deliberately not brought any other ladies because he knew I was nearby. It seemed there was no other choice open, so I went immediately to the Ōi Pavilion of the Saga Palace. There I discovered that indeed no other women were in attendance. GoFukakusa's ladies were visiting their homes, and trusting that I would be available, he and Kameyama had come in a carriage without any ladies-in-waiting. Sanekane had accompanied the two retired emperors, and when I arrived they were all enjoying a meal that had been carried over from Empress Ōmiya's apartments.

Their Majesties were in a cheerful frame of mind, for the empress's illness had proven to be mild, and they had decided to celebrate this by holding a party. GoFukakusa, who was acting as host, placed Sanekane in charge of the arrangements.

At the party, ten brightly painted wooden boxes filled with rice and delicacies were placed before each of Their Majesties; then the other guests were served in similar fashion. After three rounds of *sake* the trays were removed and polished rice was served, followed by still more delicacies to go with additional *sake*.

Empress Ōmiya was presented with a miniature replica of a *biwa* made of purple and pink cloth, along with a plectrum of glossy silk; she also received a toy *koto* fashioned from dyed cloth. Kameyama was given an imitation set of gongs; the frame was wrapped in purple cloth, and the gongs were made of tiny rectangles of speckled cloth, each one a different color, hung on the frame with silk cords. The sticks were carved from aloe wood and decorated with bits of quartz.[18] A hundred quires of fine paper and various mementos made from dyed goods were distributed among Empress Ōmiya's ladies, and sections of harnesses and dyed skins among the men.

It was an elaborate party lasting most of the night, and as usual I had the task of serving *sake*. GoFukakusa played the *biwa*, Kameyama the flute, Tōin and a princess living with Empress Ōmiya both played the *koto*, Sanekane the *biwa*, Kinhira the reed pipes, and Kaneyuki the *hichiriki*.

As the night deepened, the mountain wind moaned through the pines and sounded in the halls of the palace. The nearby bell of the Jokongō Temple tolled and GoFukakusa began to sing, "On the tower gate of headquarters."[19] This was so appropriate and moving that for a while all amusements stopped. Then Empress Ōmiya inquired where the *sake* cup was.

"It is in front of His Majesty Kameyama."

"Then he should sing while I have a cup," she said. Kameyama agreed to this, but it was GoFukakusa who took the cup and *sake* jar to the empress, who was seated behind a bamboo blind in the main room. He offered her a cup of *sake* and sang the song, "Days of good fortune, auspicious months."[20] Kameyama joined in the singing.

"Permit me the ramblings of an old lady," Empress Ōmiya began. "It is painful to be born in the final stage of this degenerate world,[21] but I have had the good fortune to ascend to the rank of empress and, as your mother, to serve for two reigns as mother of the realm. I am past sixty, so not much time remains to me in this world. My only desire now is to be reborn in the highest realm of supreme heaven. Will the music accompanying the dawning of that paradise be like the music I have heard here tonight? Surely the birds of paradise cannot sing more beautifully than you have. Please sing again while I have another cup of *sake*."

Kameyama was invited inside the blinds, and Sanekane was asked to come to the edge of her enclosure, where he set up several portable curtains and raised the bamboo blinds halfway. Then the two retired emperors began to sing:

Deeply moved, I cannot forget,
It has penetrated my being—
The nights I waited secretly for you,
The vows of love exchanged between us,
Being together beneath the moon at dawn:
Thinking of all this I feel sharp grief.

Nothing could compare with the beauty of their singing.

By the end of the party we were all drunk and weeping, for someone had begun talking about past times, and a mood of dejection had settled on us. GoFukakusa returned to the Ōi Pavilion accompanied by Kameyama. Sanekane said he did not feel well and went elsewhere, but there were still two or three young courtiers around to serve on duty.

I was told that because so few people were available I should remain in attendance for the night. While Their Majesties were preparing to retire together, GoFukakusa asked me to massage his legs. I did not like the idea, but there was no other lady to whom I could pass down the order. While I was massaging His Majesty, Kameyama spoke up. "Have her sleep between us," he said.

GoFukakusa demurred. "She was resting at home on account of her condition, and I only summoned her because we departed too suddenly to bring any other ladies. The fact that she came doesn't mean that the situation is any less difficult for her. Under different circumstances, perhaps I would agree to it."

"But she would be right beside you. I don't see anything wrong with that. Suzaku gave Onna Sannomiya to Genji, and there is no reason why such an act cannot be repeated.[22] I once offered you any of my ladies that struck your fancy. That was certainly a useless pledge."

Their talk shifted to the former high priestess who was staying at Lady Azechi's house.[23] It was Kameyama's suggestion that GoFukakusa pay a call on her. Perhaps it was because he became so engrossed in this conversation that GoFukakusa forgot to order me to remain by his side before he fell into a heavy, drunken slumber. No other court ladies were on duty when Kameyama led me around to the other side of the screens. I felt wretched, but GoFukakusa had no idea what was going on. Toward dawn Kameyama returned to GoFukakusa's side and awakened him. Opening his eyes, GoFukakusa said, "I must have slept very soundly. Even Nijō has fled."

"She was here until this very moment," Kameyama replied. I was frightened and could only rely on the fact that "I had not committed any real offense."[24] No further questions were asked.

That evening it was Kameyama's turn to sponsor a banquet. Kagefusa was put in charge, much to the chagrin of some people who held it was not fitting to give a person of his rank the same responsibility Sanekane had had on the previous night—even if he was acting on Kameyama's behalf.

The customary food and drink were provided, and Empress Ōmiya received the gift of a tray with a wave design containing tiny rocks made of dyed goods and an aloe wood boat filled with clove incense. GoFukakusa was presented with an aloe wood pillow in a silver box. For the empress's ladies there were miniature waterfalls made of cotton and thread, and for the men, persimmons made out of colored skins and dyed cloth. Then, probably because GoFukakusa had made such a point of my coming as his only lady, I was given a set of fifty-four little books, each made of ten pieces of Chinese twill and ten of purple silk, and labeled with the title of a chapter from *The Tale of Genji*. We had so exhausted ourselves at last night's party that the affair tonight was dull by comparison.

Claiming he had a cold, Sanekane had not ap-

peared all day; there was general suspicion that the
illness was feigned.

Tonight Their Majesties also retired to the Ōi
Pavilion, where they had a late meal, which I served.
Again they slept in the same room, and although
I did not relish the idea of staying with them, there
was no way to avoid it. And so once more I was
made painfully aware of this world's trying ways.

Wanting to go directly home, I excused myself
when Their Majesties set out for the capital, claiming that my condition made me very uncomfortable,
and that I had to continue my retreat at the Hōrin
Temple. The retired emperors departed together,
Sanekane attending GoFukakusa, the Tōin major
counselor going with Kameyama. After their departure it was so lonesome that Empress Ōmiya asked
me to spend the day with her. While I was there, a
letter arrived from Empress Higashi-Nijō, which
piqued my curiosity.

Empress Ōmiya read the letter over and remarked
with surprise that she could hardly believe the
writer was serious.

"May I inquire what it is?" I asked.

"She complains that I am publicly treating you as
though you were an empress, and then goes on to
say, 'I am envious when I hear of all the parties
you've been having. I may be old and worn, but I
do not feel I should be completely discarded.'"[25]

I was upset, but Empress Ōmiya laughed off the
entire matter. I departed and went to Nurse's
house at Fourth Avenue and Ōmiya Street.

Soon after this, Ariake wrote to say he was at the home of his favorite page, not far from where I was, and I began visiting him secretly. Apparently my visits became a source of rumor, for I learned to my chagrin that gossip about us was rampant. Ariake felt it did not matter if his reputation were ruined. "I'll simply retire to a thatched hut in some remote mountain village," he said. But instead of doing this, he continued to see me regularly.

Toward the end of the tenth month, growing discomfort and anxiety made me desolate. Takachika was under orders from GoFukakusa to provide for me, but I was only too aware of the dewlike frailty of my status, and I often worried about it.

Late one night a carriage arrived quietly, and there was a knock on the gate, followed by the announcement of the arrival of Lady Kyōgoku from the Tomi Street Palace. Mystified by this, I watched the gate open and saw a plain wicker carriage enter with His Majesty inside. His surprise visit perplexed me.

"There is something I must talk over with you," he said in a kind way. "Your affair with Ariake is no longer a secret, and I am given to understand that some of the wild rumors even involve me. It is all most deplorable. Just now, however, it was reported to me that a person whose welfare I am very much concerned about suffered from a stillbirth tonight. I gave orders that they are to say nothing and to pretend that the baby has not yet been born. When you give birth, we will give the child to her

and claim yours was stillborn. If we do this the rumors about you will probably die down. I was driven
to this scheme by the terrible things I have heard."
Having related all this, he was warned of dawn's
approach by the singing birds and left hastily.

I felt cheered up by his concern for me, which
seemed to belong in a fairy tale, yet at the same time
I faced the inevitable sorrow of separation from a
child, coupled with the painful knowledge that this
was not the first time.

His letter was brought almost at once. "Last
night's memorable circumstances can never be forgotten," he wrote. He included this poem:

> Desolate and wild,
> A house with wooden eaves;
> Yet how could I forget
> The feelings it has held?

I was concerned with how long his solicitude would
last, and I wrote in reply:

> How much longer will pity
> Lead you to this garden,
> As choked with weeds
> As my thoughts with pain?

That evening I received word that Ariake was
again in the neighborhood, but I made no plans to
go to him because I had been feeling ill since noon.
I suspected that my time was approaching. Late
that night he surprised me by coming to my house,
and since the few people around already knew about
us, I admitted him and told him what had happened
the previous night.

"No matter how one views the situation, I cannot possibly take the child, but it's really too bad that you can't raise it. These matters are sometimes settled in a different way, but what can we do in the face of His Majesty's plan?" He spoke with sincere regret.

At the tolling of the dawn bells I gave birth to a boy. Of course we had no way of knowing what he might become, but he was a lovely baby. Ariake put him on his knees and said, "For this to have happened, our bond from a former life must be extremely potent." He talked to the infant as though it were an adult, tears streaming down his cheeks all the while. Dawn brightened the sky when Ariake at last made a reluctant departure.

Following His Majesty's instructions I surrendered the baby, and since no announcement was made concerning its birth, people assumed the child had died. After that the worst of the rumors died down; and thanks to GoFukakusa's meticulous attention to detail, everyone concerned was spared embarrassment. I was worried for a while, however, that the secret would be revealed when the few people who knew about it sent gifts to the child.

After our child's birth on the sixth day of the eleventh month, Ariake visited me with alarming frequency. Late on the night of the thirteenth, he arrived bringing news that the realm was filled with anxiety. "Last year the sacred tree of the Kasuga Shrine was taken to the capital,"[26] he explained, "and now there is an outcry for its return to the shrine because of an epidemic ravaging the country. One dies within a few days of contracting the disease, and I have just learned that someone especially close to me has perished from it. I fear that it will not be long before I am numbered among the dead, and I have come to prepare myself."

He was depressed and weary, even as he pledged his love. "I ask only not to be cut off from you as our forms change in reincarnations yet to come. Even in the highest realm of heaven, it would be unbearably sad to live without you. If only we can be together, it does not matter how poor the hut."

We stayed up all night talking, and were so absorbed we did not realize the time until it was well past daybreak. He had planned to return, but to leave he would have to pass the main house, where prying eyes would easily have spotted him even though he was simply dressed; and so he decided to spend the day in my quarters, although I feared the consequences. Only his trusted page knew where he was, but who could tell what people here might make of it? This was of little concern to Ariake, and I did not voice my own fears.

We passed the day in quiet conversation. He said, "Sometime after our sorrowful parting on that faraway dawn I learned that you had gone into hiding, and having no one else to turn to, I began copying out five of the Mahayana sutras. In each chapter I inserted a phrase from one of your letters with the plea that we might be united in this world, so deep are my feelings. The sutras are copied now but not dedicated. I shall dedicate them after we have been reborn together. If I store the more than two hundred chapters in the treasure hall of the dragon king, I will certainly be reborn to this life, and then I shall dedicate them to Buddha. To accomplish this I plan to take the sutras with me after death by having them added to the fuel of my funeral pyre."27

His futile attachment to this world distressed me. "Just pray that we may be born together in paradise."

"I cannot, for I am unable to relinquish my love for you. That is why I wish to be reborn as a human. When I die, as all creatures must, my smoke rising to the vast and empty sky will surely drift toward you." He spoke with a grave sincerity which touched me deeply.

Later, after sleeping for a time, he awoke with a start. He was in a cold sweat, and I asked him what the matter was. "I just dreamed that I turned into a mandarin duck and entered your body," he said. "I am sweating like this from excessive passion. Do you suppose my spirit has lodged in your sleeves?"

As he was leaving he expressed doubt that he should have stayed with me so long. To the west, the clouds along the rim of the mountains glowed in the light of the sinking moon; the mountains in the east brightened faintly. Never had we felt such regret. The dawn bell sounded, deepening our sorrow, and we parted.

His letter came from the nearby home of his page.

> My yearning spirit
> Attached itself to you.
> What then remains,
> To cause me such distress?

I hardly knew how to respond to such depths of grief.

> If I could compare
> Sleeves stained by tears

> Of fretful worry, yours and mine
> Whose would be damper?

I wrote this out in a flood of emotion without pausing to compose it carefully.

Later I learned that Ariake had gone to the palace that same day; then I heard that on the eighteenth he had come down with the epidemic disease, that doctors were attending him, and that he was steadily failing. I felt utterly helpless. On the twenty-first a long letter came. "Little did I realize we were meeting for the last time in this life," he wrote. "I have contracted the disease and shall probably die. My sins are deep, for my attachments to this world are excessive. What will be the outcome of the vision I beheld in my dream?" With the letter was this poem:

> Body thus consumed by passion
> May the smoke it leaves
> Drift through the sky in your direction.

Reading this remarkably calm letter, it suddenly came over me that we had perhaps spent our last dawn together.

> Consumed by passion you say—
> Must I live to see
> The smoke that once was you?

I did not attempt to express all my feelings, for the occasion called for restraint; nor could I face the thought that the end was near.

On the twenty-fifth day of the eleventh month I learned that he had died. Life is more fleeting than a dream within a dream, I realized then, but I also knew the depth of my sin. It had all begun when he had pleaded with me in the poem that mentioned his "dream left hanging," and in the way he had looked the night he wrote "in my lingering anguish." Would I not have fewer worries now if we had parted forever that sad night?

That night it rained intermittently, and the clouds had an eerie cast about them, almost as if the sky were grieving in sympathy. His last letter, containing the poem about the smoke from his body drifting through the sky, lay in my letter box, and his scent clung to my pillow. Regrets haunted me. Were I to carry out my long-held desire to enter holy orders, there would be ugly rumors damaging to his reputation, which lived on even though he was dead. It was mortifying to be thus prevented from acting.

Toward dawn, as if in a dream, I learned that Ariake's page had arrived, and I hurried out to meet him. He wore a short yellow tunic with a green lining and a pheasant design. The sleeves were spotted with his tears. We talked and wept together in a flood of emotion that neither brush nor spoken words can convey.

The boy told me how Ariake had folded up the small-sleeved gown he had taken from me on our first night together and had placed it on his meditation mat. He continued, "On the night of the twenty-fourth he put it on next to his skin and told me he wanted to be cremated in it. You can imagine how painful it was to hear him say this." The boy then handed me a large letter box with an inlaid design of a *sakaki* tree. "I have come to deliver this to you, as Ariake instructed me," he said.

The box contained a letter, but the brush marks looked more like bird tracks than writing. At the beginning was the phrase "of one night," and elsewhere the words "while I am still alive"—although I cannot be at all sure that I made them out correctly. As I pondered the letter, I longed to be swept away by the same stream that had taken him.

> Now I'm afloat, now sinking.
> If the streams of the afterworld
> Had shoals where we might meet,
> I would hurl my body in to see you.

I was on the verge of breaking down completely.

The page recounted the manner of Ariake's cremation, telling how he had been wearing my gown and how the five Mahayana sutras he had copied were burned in his funeral pyre so as to accompany him. After giving the sorrowful account there was not a dry corner on either of his sleeves when he finally departed. I stared after him, my spirits darkened by intense anguish.

GoFukakusa also experienced profound grief, for he had been very close to Ariake. He sent me a solicitous letter, which did little to assuage my grief, containing this poem:

> The image of the dawn moon
> Now obscured by clouds
> Must linger with you still.
> How sorrowful a parting.

"Sorrow is the way of this world; yet how regrettable that his love was so extreme, his grief so deep."

Unable to find words for a proper reply, I merely sent this poem:

> I count for nothing, yet
> My sorrows are far from trite,
> Nor has the image faded
> Of dawn's moon.

I am unable to describe my feelings as the year drew to a close with each day and each night blurred by tears, so distraught that I was "unaware of the passing of spring."[28]

The messages that arrived from His Majesty now simply asked why I did not come back without demanding my immediate return, as in the past. Not once did he refer to it, but from this time on I was aware that His Majesty's affection for me was waning. This came as no surprise, for I had committed many indiscretions, however unintentionally; and realizing this, I was reluctant to return to the palace of my own accord.

Two days before the end of the year I recalled the line "the year and my own life ebbing to their close."[29]

The turn of the year found me copying out the *Lotus Sutra* on the backs of his letters. I was lamenting our sin—a sin so deep that Ariake would not pray to be reborn in paradise—and dreading the future.

17 (1282-84)

The tears that drenched my sleeves ill accorded with the beginning of a new year. To mark the forty-ninth day after Ariake's death, I went to the temple of a holy man I trusted not to betray my confidence.

Because it was also the fifteenth day of the first month, and thus an assembly day,[30] I attracted no undue attention when I brought some of the gold Ariake had kindly left me and made an offering requesting services for his soul. On the paper in which I wrapped the offering I wrote a poem:

> Show him now the path to travel
> To that long-awaited dawn,
> Even though our bond be broken.

The holy man had an excellent reputation as a speaker, and his words were so appropriate to my condition that they brought me to tears. As I wept, I recalled some old poems about the dawn moon.

I was still in retreat on the fifteenth day of the second month, the anniversary of the Buddha's death. How many times had his death been commemorated before? Yet in my state of mind the service this year seemed especially sorrowful. I was soon comforted, however, when the *Lotus Sutra* was expounded and praised in the holy teacher's quarters during the fourteen days following the spring equinox. Each day I requested special prayers for the dead, but since I could not indicate whom they were for, I merely wrote "an unforgotten vow" on my petitions. It was most painful, however, and on the last day of the services I wrote this poem along with my usual request:

> The long-awaited moon
> Shall rise on that distant dawn,
> Now memories of the sun
> Just set bring grief.

Absolutely no word had arrived from His Maj-

esty since I had come to Higashiyama,[81] and knowing how things stood between us did nothing to
cheer me up. The night before I was to return to
the capital my spirits were at a low ebb. Since the
holy men were holding services all night, not sleeping until dawn, I spread out my lonely bed where I
could listen to them. Toward daybreak I fell asleep
and experienced an utterly lifelike vision of Ariake.
He said, "A dream in your sad world, this long road of
darkness." Then he embraced me.

I collapsed, becoming seriously ill and almost
losing consciousness. The holy man thought I
should remain, and be cared for there, but the carriage was ready, so I set out for the capital. Just as
we arrived at the western span of the Kiyomizu
Bridge, I saw the image from my dream actually
climb into the carriage with me, at which point I
fainted away. The attendant with me administered
what treatment she could until we reached my old
nurse's house, but even then I could hardly take a
sip of water.

I remained in critical condition until after the
middle of the third month, by which time it was evident that I was pregnant. There was no room for
any doubt about who the father was, for since the
dawn when Ariake and I parted finally I had not so
much as exchanged innocent glances with a man.[82]
I now longed for him, even though our relationship
had been a secret one full of sorrows, and I was
eager for the baby to be born so that I might see it
with my own eyes. My emotions overwhelmed me.

In the middle of the fourth month His Majesty
summoned me, saying it was a matter of importance. Unwilling to go in my present condition, I

sent word that I was still confined by illness. To this he replied:

> With nothing but a memory,
> How can your love persist?
> Departed from this sad world
> Is the dawn moon.

"Could it be something more than grief that summons forth such tears? What about your friend of old?"

When I read his letter I thought he was simply upset at my devotion to the memory of Ariake, but this was not the case at all. Nakayori, my nurse's son, had held the sixth rank when Kameyama was the reigning emperor, and upon that sovereign's abdication Nakayori was promoted to the fifth rank and made a lieutenant—all the while continuing to serve Kameyama. GoFukakusa apparently heard a rumor that Nakayori was serving as go-between for Kameyama and myself, and that Kameyama was using him to carry messages of love to me night and day in the hope that GoFukakusa and I would become estranged. At the time I knew nothing of this rumor.

Early in the fifth month, having regained my strength, I decided to return to the palace before my condition became obvious, yet upon arriving there I discovered to my chagrin that His Majesty had nothing to say to me. On the surface my life at the palace was unchanged, but I grew depressed as the days and nights passed monotonously. I continued to serve until the sixth month, when the death of a relative gave me an excuse to leave.

This time I wanted very much to conceal my pregnancy, so I secluded myself in the house of a relative near Higashiyama. There no one bothered to visit me, and I felt that my life had changed completely by the time my labor commenced on the twentieth day of the eighth month. The previous time I had also given birth secretly, but at least a few people called on me then. Now my period of waiting passed with only the cries of deer in the hills to console me. It was a safe delivery, and the child was a boy, but curiously enough, I had no feelings for him.

Ariake's dream of turning into a mandarin duck had proved to be accurate. I mourned my fate. As long as I could remember, I had regretted being separated from my own mother at age two, scarcely knowing her face; but this child was still in my womb when his father died. What did it portend?

Such thoughts were running through my mind when the baby was put down right beside me. I was told there was not even a wet nurse available. While one was being sought in vain, my poor baby fell asleep at my side. It was not long before he was soaking wet underneath. That would never do, I thought, and I quickly changed him. As he lay again sleeping beside me I began, for the first time, to understand the depths of a mother's love. For more than forty days I took care of him myself, begrudging every moment he was out of my hands. Then a suitable nurse was located in Yamazaki, and after she arrived the baby slept beside her.

Winter set in, but the thought of returning to life in the palace was as unpleasant as ever. At last His Majesty wrote inquiring about my reasons for staying away, and at the beginning of the tenth month I returned and was serving at the palace when the year ended.

Participation in the New Year's festivities only increased my sorrows, for although His Majesty never admitted anything was wrong, I sensed a growing estrangement and found life in his palace depressingly lonely. Only Akebono, now no more than a figure from my past, continued to inquire about me, verifying the words of that poem, "bitterness, unable to hold its own."[33]

The Buddhist lectures marking the equinox in the second month were held at the Saga Palace, and despite the fact that I was there with both retired emperors, I could not rid myself of the vision I had seen the previous year at this time. From my wretchedness I prayed to Buddha: "Thou who promised salvation to all, please guide him, lest he remain lost and wandering in delusion." I could think of nothing else.

> A hidden love and tears
> Enough to form a river—
> Were there a shoal of meeting
> I would drown this self of mine.

Thoughts in this vein only added to my wretchedness. Vexed at the ways of this world, I wanted to sink to the river bottom like a bit of debris, and I even began sorting through useless old papers. But then I thought of my two-year-old infant.[34] If I drowned myself, who would take pity on him? The same reasoning prevented me from entering holy orders. Suddenly he seemed very dear.

> With no one to visit the shore
> Where the seedling pine grows
> What kind of fate would it meet?

After Their Majesties had returned to the palace

I took a brief leave to visit my son and found that he was much bigger than I had imagined. Seeing him smile and babble and even laugh, I felt pangs of concern, and left wondering if my visit had been a good idea after all.

In early autumn I received a letter from my grandfather, Lord Takachika, which said: "Prepare to leave the palace permanently. I'll send for you tonight." Unable to comprehend this, I took it to His Majesty and asked him to explain, only to be turned away without a reply.

Next I went to Lady Genki (I think she was called Lady Sammi at that time) and told her of my bewilderment. "I can't understand what is happening. I received this letter and asked His Majesty about it, but he wouldn't answer me," I said. She replied that she did not know either.

It appeared I would have to leave. As I made ready for my departure, I recalled coming to the palace for the first time in the ninth month of the year I was four. Ever since that time I had felt a certain uneasiness about being away from the palace even briefly, so I could not accept the fact that today was really the end. I stared at even the trees and grasses in the garden until tears blurred my vision.

I was told that Akebono had arrived and asked where I was. Beside myself with anxiety, I went out to see him, my tear-spotted sleeves showing evidence of my weeping.

He wanted to know what the matter was, and for a silent moment I thought, "Even consolation brings pain." Then I handed him the letter I had received that morning. All I said was, "This is what makes me sad." I admitted him to my room and burst into tears. He too was at a loss to explain it, for it seemed no one could understand this business.

Several of the older court ladies came around to offer their sympathy, but being ignorant of the truth behind the situation I could only weep. That evening I was embarrassed to appear before His Majesty, knowing that it had to be his will that I leave; yet I had no idea what lay ahead, and I longed to see him once again, perhaps for the last time. I was trembling when I entered his quarters, where several nobles were chatting together. My costume was a red formal jacket worn over a raw silk gown with a design of vines and grasses embroidered on it in green thread.

GoFukakusa glanced at me. "Are you leaving this evening?" he asked. I stood there, unable to frame a reply, and he continued, "Perhaps I'll receive word of you through some mountain hermit. The green vines must be unhappy."[35] As he mumbled this he stood up and left, probably to go to Empress Higashi-Nijō's apartments.

Curiously, I felt no bitterness at his abrupt departure, yet I did not fully comprehend what had brought it about. Our relationship was of many years' standing, and he had frequently assured me that his personal feelings would never cause us to be separated. I felt an impulse to vanish from this world at once; but in vain, for a carriage awaited me. On the one hand I wanted nothing more than to run away and hide myself, but on the other, I was curious to learn what had happened. So I proceeded to Lord Takachika's mansion in the Second Ward.

Takachika greeted me himself.[36] He said, "Old age

has come upon me like an incurable disease, and lately my health has become so bad that I have little hope of surviving long. Yet still I have to worry about you. Your father is not alive and Takaaki is no longer here to care for you.[37] All the worry has fallen on my shoulders, and now because of this letter from Empress Higashi-Nijō, I have been forced to withdraw you from the palace."

He held out the letter for me to read: "I am displeased by her persistent involvement with His Majesty and her slights to me. You will recall her to your house at once and keep her there. Her mother is dead so you will have to make plans for her." The entire letter was written in the empress's own hand.

It would have been impossible for me to remain at the palace under such circumstances, and once I was completely away from it I experienced a sense of relief. Yet as I lay awake through the gradually lengthening nights listening to the sounds of wooden mallets beating silk, it seemed that they were echoing near my pillow to inquire after me. And sometimes I imagined that the wild geese winging through the cloudy sky had chosen the ivy around my worry-filled house to shed their tears on.

The days and nights passed slowly until the year drew to its close. Since I could play no part in any of the activities ushering the old year out and the new year in, I decided to fulfill my long-standing desire to make a one-thousand-day retreat at the Gion Shrine. Before, there had always been too many hindrances, but now, on the second day of the eleventh month (the first day of the hare), I set off, going first to the Hachiman Shrine to see

the *kagura* dances.[88] I remembered the poet who
had written "I never cease to give my heart to the
gods,"[89] and I composed this poem:

> Depend on the gods, I hang
> My hopes on them—a sash
> Of mulberry bark—in vain;
> I loathe my useless self.[40]

After a seven-day retreat at the Hachiman Shrine I
went on to Gion. With no further reason to remain
in the world, I now prayed to be led from this human realm through the gates of enlightenment.

This year marked the third anniversary of Ariake's
death. I attended a seven-day series of lectures on
the *Lotus Sutra* held at the temple of the holy man
from Higashiyama, going there each day and returning to Gion at night. The date of the final service coincided with the anniversary of Ariake's death,
and the tolling of the bells that day moved me to
tears.

> Echoes of ceremonial bells
> Joined by sounds of my sobbing.
> Does something in me linger yet
> In this world of sorrow?

Anxious to avoid gossip, I had our son raised in
secret, and from time to time I consoled myself by
visiting him. At the beginning of the new year[41] he
was toddling about a little and even talking some.
As yet, he had not the slightest knowledge of sorrow and suffering. I felt extremely sympathetic toward him.

During the previous autumn, that dreadful time,
my grandfather Takachika had died, but my grief had

not been excessive. Then the unexpectedly cruel turn of my own fate had so obsessed me that I had had no feelings left to mourn him; but now as the days lengthened and I was able to attend to religious services with fewer distractions, I began to think of him. He had been, after all, the last of my mother's relatives, and I felt the sorrow buried in my heart.

The cherry trees within the temple compound blossomed and came to full bloom. The sight of them recalled to my mind a poem said to have been composed by the god of the Gion Shrine in the Bun'ei era:[42]

> If within the sacred fence,
> A thousand cherry trees
> Burst into bloom,
> Those who planted them will flourish.

Believing this to be an oracle, many people planted trees in the Gion Shrine; and indeed the poem did seem to be a message from the gods.

I reasoned that if I too were capable of receiving the blessings of the gods, it would make little difference whether I planted a cutting or a seedling, and so I requested a branch cut from a cherry tree at the Amida Temple. (The intendant of the temple was High Priest Kin'yo of the Danna Temple, but my contact was the priest called Shingen, a son of Major Counselor Masaie.)

On the first day of the horse in the second month I gave En'yō, the priest in charge of business affairs at the Gion Shrine, an unlined plum red gown and a patterned thin silk gown as an offering for the dedicatory prayers made over my cutting. The dedicatory service was held in front of the eastern sutra hall. To the branch I tied a piece of fine, light blue paper on which I had written a poem:

> Rootless though you are
> Burst into bloom, O cherry tree!
> That the vows in my heart
> May be known to the gods.

My cutting lived, and when I later saw it blossom I was hopeful that my faith would not be unrewarded. Meanwhile I had begun to read one thousand sections of scripture, one for each day of my retreat. I felt awkward in my quarters, which were somewhat inconvenient, and so I decided to move to a hermitage behind the Hōdō Temple where there were two huts. I took the one to the east. There I continued my retreat and watched the year come to a close.

18 (1285)

At the end of the first month of the new year I received a letter from Empress Ōmiya that said, "We are busy planning a ninetieth birthday celebration this spring for Her Highness, Lady Kitayama, and although you have been absent from the palace for a long time, there is no reason you should not attend. You may join the court ladies serving Her Highness."

In reply I wrote that I would be most happy to do as she suggested, but that I was no longer in the palace because of His Majesty's displeasure. For this reason I wondered whether it would be proper to appear at such a joyous and formal occasion.

To this Her Majesty replied in a lengthy letter written in her own hand, saying: "There is no need to be hesitant. From the time you were a child Her Highness treated you, as she had your mother before you, as her own child. Hence there is every reason for you to attend her on this most important occasion. What is there to prevent you?"

Feeling it would not look right if I continued to refuse, I sent word accepting the invitation. Since I had already completed over four hundred days of my retreat, I found someone to substitute for me until my return.

Sanekane[43] sent a carriage for me. I was fearful that I had become too countrified to appear at such a grand ceremony, but I went, dressed in a light green gown lined in purple over a three-layered gown in shades of violet and scarlet.

It was, as I had anticipated, an elaborate affair. I learned that retired emperors GoFukakusa and Kameyama, Empress Higashi-Nijō, and Empress Yūgi (then still a princess) had already arrived.[44] Empress Shin'yōmei arrived secretly. The celebration was to begin on the last day of the second month, so the reigning emperor GoUda and the crown prince Fushimi came on the twenty-ninth. GoUda arrived first in a procession of three palanquins. His Majesty's palanquin was put down in front of the gate while shrine officials presented offerings, and court musicians provided music. After the imperial arrival was announced by Kinhira, an official in Empress Ōmiya's service, the palanquin was carried to the inner gate. From this point the imperial sword and jewel were borne by the middle commander Kanemoto. The crown prince arrived and straw matting was spread out under the gate. The reception hall was prepared under the direction of the master of ceremonies, Akiie, assisted by the regent Kanehira, the major commander Kanetada, and the middle commander of the third rank. Morotada, the minister of the left, accompanied the crown prince in his carriage.

By dawn on the day of the celebration the mansion was prepared. The main room, which faced south, had three sections. In the middle section a Buddhist altar had been set up near the bamboo blinds on the northern side, and a picture of the historic Buddha hung there. In front of the altar stood a table for incense and flowers, flanked on either side by candleholders. A raised mat for the priest reading the sutras was placed in front of that table, and behind it a mat for the priest conducting the service. On the veranda to the south was a table with two sutra boxes containing the *Long Life Sutra* and the *Lotus Sutra*. I was told that the prayers had been drafted by Mochinori, with the final copies written out by the regent Kanehira. Religious banners and filigreed ornaments hung on the pillars in the main room.

The emperor's seat, in the western section of the main room, consisted of embroidered cushions in the Chinese style surrounded by bamboo blinds. Beside this seat on the north, two tatami decorated with large crests were laid out for GoFukakusa, with similar tatami arranged for Kameyama's place. Empress Ōmiya's seat in the eastern section was surrounded by screens. Near the bamboo blinds to the south, curtains on T-shaped frames were set up for GoFukakusa's ladies. Looking at them as an outsider was painful.

Lady Kitayama's seat was in the outer section of the room on the west. Screens had been arranged around two decorated tatami, on which embroidered cushions were placed. Her Highness Lady Kitayama was the wife of the Saionji prime minister Lord Saneuji, the mother of Empresses Ōmiya and Higashi-Nijō, the grandmother of GoFukakusa and Kameyama, and the great-grandmother of Emperor GoUda and Crown Prince Fushimi. Thus it was only natural that everyone should unite to honor her. She was the granddaughter of the Washinoo major counselor Takafusa and the daughter of Lord Takahira, and hence closely related to my mother, being, in fact, her aunt. From early childhood my mother had been raised by Lady Kitayama, and my invitation to this celebration was due to the fact that I had received the same attention from Her Highness.

When I was invited I had asked if my clothes were appropriate. Empress Ōmiya first suggested I dress in purple and serve Lady Kitayama. Later, however, she reconsidered and decided that I should serve her. I had not expected this, and it made me feel awkward.

Empress Ōmiya's ladies all wore layered gowns in shades of plum red and violet, with darker undergowns and outer gowns of crimson. Their formal jackets were red. Saionji Sanekane provided me with an especially elaborate costume consisting of a deep maroon unlined gown beneath eight layers of gowns shaded from plum red to violet, over which I wore a painted crimson gown with an outer gown lined in yellow, and a green formal jacket.

The celebration began with the procession into the main room of GoFukakusa, Kameyama, and Crown Prince Fushimi; Empresses Ōmiya, Higashi-Nijō, and Imadegawa; Princess Yūgi; and the master of the crown prince's office, Sanekane.[45] The emperor wore a court robe with a train and raw silk pleated trousers. GoFukakusa's robe was worn with green laced trousers; Kameyama had on patterned trousers; and the crown prince wore embossed purple trousers. All Their Majesties sat within bamboo blinds.

The dancers and musicians performed a piece of court music called *Chōkōraku*. The group was directed by a drum player who had a Chinese-style drum,[46] and during the music two groups of dancers waved wooden halberds. Then they played a number in the *ichikotsuchō* mode. The dancers and musicians turned to face the assembled monks; then they divided into two groups and proceeded in. They entered the middle gate, passed the stage on either side, ascended the stairs, and went to their places. The lecturer, High Priest Kenjiki, the reader, High Priest Shūjō, and the high priest who served as chanter went to their seats; then an assisting priest struck a gong. The altar boys[47] were divided into two groups, and after the Sanskrit chanting they distributed baskets of petals. Then the musicians played a piece entitled *Shingachō*, and the priests circled around the altar once, scattering petals and chanting sutras. The Chinese drum player bowed before Their Majesties, and the child dancer Hisasuke was presented with gifts by

Tamekata, one of GoFukakusa's officials. Afterward a dance was performed with a royal staff.

A spring drizzle was falling, but no one seemed to mind. I looked over the crowds of people, feeling rather bored, and wondered how much longer this would go on.

The performers of the left danced several numbers, and then those of the right performed.[48] The second dancer, Ō no Hisatada, did a number called *Chokuroku no Te*. At this point Tadanori, the minister of the right, stood up and summoned Chikayasu from among the dancers of the left in order to reward him. He accepted the gifts, and by rights ought to have danced again to express his appreciation, but he was prevented by the immediate presentation of rewards to Hisasuke from the right group and to the musician Masaaki. Masaaki performed his obeisances with his reed pipes in his hand, an act everyone thought most fitting. Then the musicians played as the lecturer descended from his seat and gifts were presented to the priests.[49] Two more pieces[50] were played while the assembled priests filed out, followed by the musicians and dancers. Dinner trays were brought to Ōmiya, Higashi-Nijō, and Lady Kitayama. Imperial Adviser Shijō Takayasu served Lady Kitayama's meal, and Kinhira, chief of the left division of palace guards, carried her trays.

The following day was the first of the third month. The emperor, the crown prince, and both retired emperors were served a meal. The stage was removed, curtains were hung on all four sides of the main room, and folding screens were set up in the western corner. In the center section Chinese brocade cushions were laid on two decorated tatami for the emperor. Seats were prepared in the main room for the two retired emperors, and in the eastern section brocade cushions were laid on ornate tatami for the crown prince. The regent Kanehira attended the bamboo blinds for the emperor and retired emperors, and Lord Morotada was to perform this task for the crown prince, but he was late, and Sanekane had to do it for him. The emperor wore an ordinary court robe today with a wadded crimson gown showing beneath it, while GoFukakusa had on light purple laced trousers of a tightly woven material. Kameyama was dressed in laced trousers made to match an embossed court robe. His glossy silk undergown was also wadded and showing at the bottom. The crown prince, however, wore an unwadded undergown and elaborately embossed laced trousers.

Major Counselor Nagamasa served a meal to Emperor GoUda, and Imperial Advisers Takayasu and Kintsura removed his trays. GoFukakusa was served by Major Counselor Nobutsugu, Kameyama by Sanekane, and the crown prince by Kintsura. The crown prince's trays were removed by Takayoshi, who wore a white court robe lined in violet over a light purple gown with matching laced trousers and a crimson undergown. Today's festivities were splendid enough that he even wore a round quiver and an elaborate cap.

After the meal, musical entertainment commenced. Tadayo brought in a box containing the emperor's flute, which was named Katei.[51] The regent Kanehira took the box and placed it before His Majesty. The crown prince's *biwa*, called Genjō,

was brought in by Chikasada and presented by Sanekane. The nobles' flutes were in separate boxes.
Sadazane and Kinhira played the reed pipes; Kaneyuki, the *hichiriki*; Nobutsugu, the six-string *koto*;
Kanetada, the seven-string *koto*; Sanekane and Kinmori played *biwa*; and Kinnori and Saneyasu handled the wooden clappers. Munefuyu played a *koto*
and led the singing. They played selections from
various modes of court music, including adaptations
of folk songs.[52]

The musical entertainment was followed by a poetry writing party. Courtiers and officials of the
sixth rank set out the writing table and round straw
mats. All the poems, beginning with those of the
lowest-ranking people, were handed in. Tamemichi,
who wore a court robe, a sword with a leather
thong, and a round quiver, carried his bow with him
when he placed his poem on the table. Nobusuke
gathered the rest of the courtiers' poems and put
them on the table. Before Tamemichi went forward,
Akiie had placed a round straw cushion to the east
of the table for the crown prince to use during the
reading of the poems. Everyone agreed that this old
custom seemed very up-to-date.[53]

Among all the nobles dressed in regular court
robes, Michimoto's more formal costume stood out.
His patterned rust-colored gown lined in yellow
showed below his outer robe, and he was wearing his
sword and carrying his flat baton when he presented
his poem. The other nobles all had bows and arrows.
Major Counselor Nagamasa summoned Kin'atsu to
act as reader. The minister of the left, Morotada,
was requested to take charge of the poems, but he

was unable to do so, and the minister of the right,
Tadanori, did it for him. The minister of military
affairs, Yoshinori, and a Fujiwara middle counselor
assisted.

Lady Gonchūnagon wrote her poem on fine
crimson paper and passed it out under the bamboo
blinds.

Kameyama asked, "Why isn't there a poem by
Lord Masatada's daughter?"

"She doesn't feel up to writing one," Empress
Ōmiya replied.

"I don't see why she can't simply compose a
poem," Sanekane argued.

"Empress Higashi-Nijō told Lady Kitayama I was
not to compose any poems," I explained. I did compose this poem, but I kept it to myself:

> Admonished not to emerge
> Among the poets today,
> How unexpected this summons
> To the Bay of Poetry.

The poems by the emperor and Kameyama were
received by Kanehira. The crown prince still
ranked as a subject, so his poem was read by the
regular reader, but the emperor's and retired emperors' poems were conveyed by Kinhira to be read
by Kanehira. When the reading was over, the crown
prince was the first to retire, after which gifts were
given to the nobles.

Kanehira had written down the poem the emperor
had composed.[54] It read:

"A poem to celebrate the ninetieth year of Fujiwara no Ason Teishi of the junior first rank".[55]

This auspicious day of spring,
Beginning of the fertile month,
Promises still longer life to you.

Kameyama's poem was written down by Iemoto,
the minister of the center. His preface was identical
to the emperor's, except that it omitted the name
Teishi.

You have seen the advent
Of ninety springs already;
Now the warbler sings
Of one hundred years.

Kanetada recorded the crown prince's poem: "A
poem ordered by the emperor to celebrate the
ninetieth year of Fujiwara no Ason, junior first rank,
at the Kitayama Mansion on a spring day."[56]

May your years be limitless;
Ninety already passed,
Thousands yet to come:
This is but the spring.

Having recorded the other poems elsewhere, here
I will just quote Sanekane's:

May today's best wishes mean
Your years will be as numerous
As waves breaking on the shore—
More than man has known before.

Everyone agreed his poem was excellent, and they
compared it with two poems written on the occasion of Lord Saneuji's dedication of a full
canon of Buddhist sutras.[57] One was by GoSaga:

> All along the branch
> Petals unfold.
> The blossoms and my world
> Now in full bloom.

The other was by Saneuji:

> Row upon row of fragrant
> Cherry blossoms, fitting
> Decoration for our Lord's
> Long and flourishing reign.

Sanekane's poem was felt to be in no way inferior to these great poems.

After this there was a kickball game. The various colored gowns of the ladies hung out under the blinds. Each of the men, from the emperor, crown prince, Kameyama, Kanehira, and Iemoto on down, was dressed in a singularly beautiful costume. According to a precedent set by Emperor GoToba in the early thirteenth century, Kameyama kicked the ball first.

That evening after the kickball game the emperor returned to his own palace. He left reluctantly, under the pressure of an obligation to be back for the spring conferring of appointments.

The next day, because the emperor had gone, formality disappeared and everyone relaxed. Straw mats were laid down on the path from the northern hall to the Saionji main hall. Both retired emperors, dressed in ordinary court robes and tall hats, and the crown prince, also wearing a court robe with his trousers tied at his ankles, visited the various temples in the compound, on their way to the Myōon Temple. There was only a single cherry tree in bloom, and it appeared to have been awaiting this royal visit. I wondered if perhaps someone had taught it the poem, "After the others have fallen."[58]

There was much scurrying about in preparation for a concert in the temple, and a great many people mixed with the ladies, who of course covered their heads with gowns. Along with the others I also attended and watched both retired emperors and the crown prince arrive. In the outer part of the room sat Nagamasa playing the flute; Kinhira played the reed pipes; Kaneyuki, the *hichiriki*; the crown prince, the *biwa*; Sanekane, the *koto*; Tomoaki, the great drum; and Norifuji, the small drum. They performed several numbers,[59] then Kaneyuki sang the song, "Blossoms glow in the imperial garden."[60] It was beautifully sung and blended well with the orchestra. After he had sung that twice, Go-Fukakusa, joined by Kameyama and the crown prince, gave a beautiful rendition of the song "How hateful the weaver who made them."[61] After that Their Majesties returned to their apartments, although all the guests protested that they had not yet heard enough of their singing.

Seeing the splendors of society again pierced the depths of my heart and made me regret ever having come. The sound of GoFukakusa singing in the Myōon Temple echoed in my mind, so although I heard there was to be another kickball game, I decided not to attend and was still sitting in my room when Takayoshi came with a letter. "Surely there has been some mistake," I murmured, but he insisted on giving it to me. I opened it and read:

Separation might conquer
Feelings, or so I had hoped,
Attempting it these past months.
Does none of this cause resentment?

"I have tried to forget you only to discover that I cannot. Let's meet tonight and discuss the sorrows of these days."

My answer was simply:

All that I resent
Is continued existence
In this miserable state
As the years glide past.

Shortly after six o'clock, when the kickball game had ended, His Majesty suddenly entered the room where I was resting and said, "We're going boating, and you must come along."

Unwilling to be dragged into it so easily, I remained seated.

"You can go as you are," he said, bending down to tie the sash of my divided skirt.

I wondered why he thought we had suddenly returned to this footing again. How could he think this would erase the anguish of the past two years? Under the circumstances, however, I could hardly refuse; so I wiped away the tears I had shed and accompanied him. Dusk was falling as we boarded the boats at the fishing pavilion.

The crown prince had already boarded with three of his ladies, Dainagon, Uemon-no-kami, and Ko-no-naishi, all in formal dress. I was not in formal attire since I was wearing only a jacket over a thin gown with a three-layered undergarment.[62] I was conveyed to their boat with the two retired emperors. Musical instruments were put aboard, and small boats with nobles in them were secured to ours.

For the entertainment Nagamasa played the flute; Kinhira, the reed pipes; Kaneyuki, the *hichiriki*; Crown Prince Fushimi, the *biwa*; and Lady Emonno-kami, the *koto*. The large drum was handled by Tomoaki while Sanekane played the small drum. Everyone had such fond memories of this afternoon's concert in the Myōon Temple that they played in the same mode, and some tunes were repeated several times.[63] Kaneyuki sang, "Mountains beyond mountains,"[64] and then GoFukakusa and Kameyama performed together. Even the creatures under the water must have been surprised by the beauty of their singing.

We had rowed out from the fishing pavilion to where the sight of tangled, gnarled branches of ancient pines covered with lichen made it hard to believe that we were in a garden pond. It seemed as though we had come upon some distant land. "Have we perhaps come over two thousand *li* and more?" mused Kameyama.[65] He began to compose a linked verse:[66]

> Gliding through
> Waves of clouds,
> Waves of mist;

Kameyama turned to me and said, "You refused to play in the concert because of your vow, but you can certainly continue this."

It annoyed me to be singled out, but I complied, adding this verse:

> Into the endless glory,
> Of my lord's reign,

Sanekane:

> Which far surpasses
> Even reigns of old
> In tribute paid.

Tomoaki:

> Cloudless radiance
> Reflects the gods.

The crown prince:

> After ninety years,
> Still wave upon wave
> Of prosperous age.

Kameyama:

> Movement grows painful—
> The ways of this world.

I added:

> Suppressing sorrow
> Deep in my lonely heart.

"How well I understand the feeling she expresses," GoFukakusa added sympathetically. He then continued the verse:

> Ceaseless tears,
> The dawn moon.

"The significance of the dawn moon is rather vague," Kameyama commented.

After dark the servants from the bureau of house-

keeping who were in attendance on the crown
prince lit torches and placed them here and there.
It was most unusual and amusing to watch them
attempting to hasten the imperial return. Soon we
were back at the fishing pavilion, and as Their
Majesties disembarked, I wondered if they had at
last had their fill of parties. My own emotions must
have been comprehensible to the others, yet I felt
terribly alone, as though I was being cruelly tossed
about on the bobbing raft of life with no one to
reassure me.

To go back a bit, something happened this noon
concerning Kiyokage, one of the crown prince's
bodyguards, who was wearing a matched top and
trousers of a shiny, reddish-blue color, with wisteria
embroidered over a pine tree design. He is known
as being punctilious in matters of deportment and
fastidious in his dress—even down to the ornaments
on his hat, which must be perfect. Today he was
sent to the emperor's palace with a message. At the
same time—as we later learned—the minister of
finance, Tadayo, had been sent here with a message
from the emperor, but they took different routes
and missed each other.

I heard about some of the gifts presented on this
occasion: The emperor received a *biwa* and the
crown prince a six-string *koto*. Imperial favors were
also given. GoFukakusa promoted Toshisada to the
senior fourth rank lower grade, and the crown prince
granted Koresuke the senior fifth rank lower grade.
Sanekane turned his *biwa* prize over to Tamemichi,
who was promoted to junior fourth rank upper
grade. I learned of many such appointments, but
there is no need to record the details here.

After the crown prince had also departed everyone seemed hushed and filled with regrets. There
were plans for the retired emperors to visit the
Saionji main hall, and I received several invitations
to accompany them, which I declined, knowing it
would simply add to my sorrow.

Book Four

19 (1289)

Toward the end of the second month I set out from the capital at moonrise.[1] I had given up my home completely, yet my thoughts quite naturally lingered on the possibility of return, and I felt that the moon reflected in my fallen tears was also weeping. How weak-willed I was! These thoughts occupied my mind all the way to Ōsaka Pass, the place where the poet Semimaru once lived and composed the poem that ends, "One cannot live forever in a palace or a hut."[2] No trace of his home remained. I gazed at my reflection in the famous clear spring at the pass and saw a pathetic image of myself attired down to the tips of my walking shoes in this unfamiliar traveling nun's habit. As I paused to rest, my glance was caught by a cherry tree so heavy with blossoms that I could hardly take my eyes from it. Nearby four or five well-dressed local people on horseback were also resting. Did they share my feelings?

> Its blossoms detaining travelers
> The cherry tree guards the pass
> On Ōsaka Mountain.

I composed this poem as I continued on to the way station known as Mirror Lodge, where at dusk I

saw prostitutes seeking companions for the night
and realized that this too formed part of life. Next
morning, awakened by a bell at dawn, I set out once
more.

> I pause to view Mirror Mountain,
> But it does not reflect
> The image hidden in my heart.

After several days I arrived at Red Hill Lodge in
Mino province, where I stopped for the night, weary
and lonely from the days I had spent in unaccus-
tomed travel. At the inn worked two young sisters
whose skill as entertainers, especially their sensitive
playing of the *koto* and the *biwa*, reminded me of
the past. When I ordered some *sake* and asked them
to play for me, I noticed that the elder sister appeared troubled. She attended closely to her *biwa*
playing, yet I could tell that she was on the verge
of tears, and I guessed that we were very much alike.
She must have wondered too about the tears that
stained my dark sleeves, so out of keeping for a
nun, for she composed this poem and passed it to
me on a little *sake* cup stand:

> I wonder what emotion
> Caused you to resolve upon
> The life of a wandering
> Wisp of smoke from Fuji.

I was moved by her unexpected sympathy to write
in reply:

> Smoldering flames of love
> Sent forth the smoke
> From Fuji's Peak
> In the Suruga Range.

I was reluctant to leave even this kind of a friend, but of course I could not remain indefinitely, and so once again I set forth.

At the place known as Eight Bridges, finding that the bridges were gone and the rivers dried up,³ I felt as though I had lost a friend.

> The web of my troubles still
> Streams out in all directions,
> Yet not a trace remains
> Of the Eight Bridges.

I continued on to the Atsuta Shrine in Owari province and worshiped there. Because the shrine was in the domain of my father, during its annual festival in the fifth month he had regularly sent it a horse as an offering and requested that prayers be said for his well-being. In the year of his final illness Father added some raw silk to his usual offering, but at Reed Harbor Lodge, en route to the shrine, the horse had died suddenly, and startled local officials had to substitute another in its stead. When we learned of this event we took it as a sign that the gods had not accepted Father's prayers. I spent the night in the shrine, touched by these memories, which aroused feelings of loneliness, grief, and despair.

I had left the capital late in the second month intending to push myself hard on my journeys, yet I was so unused to traveling that my progress was slow. Now the third month had already begun. A bright moon rose early, flooding the night sky just as it did in the capital, and once again His Majesty's image floated through my mind. Within the sacred precincts of the Atsuta Shrine cherry trees bloomed in rich profusion. For whom were they putting on this brilliant display?

> Blossoms glow against spring sky
> Near Narumi Lagoon,
> How long now before
> Petals scatter among pines.

I wrote this on a slip of paper and tied it to the branch of a cryptomeria tree in front of the shrine.

For a week I remained in prayer at the shrine before resuming my travels. As I approached the Narumi tidelands I glanced back at the shrine and saw patches of the scarlet fence that surrounded it gleaming through the mist. I struggled to suppress the tears that welled up.

> Have pity on me, O gods
> Enshrined by braided strands
> My fate has twisted now to grief.

Following the moon across the Kiyomi Barrier, my mind was filled with troubles from the past and fears about the future as numerous as the grains of white sand on the vast beach that stretched before my eyes. Next I reached the Ukishima Plain at the base of Mount Fuji, which someone once compared in the fifth month to a dappled fawn. Now the metaphor seemed apt,[4] judging from the apparent depth of the snow on that high peak, as deep, it seemed, as the layers of worry covering this transient self of mine. No smoke arose from Mount Fuji now, and I wondered what the poet Saigyō had seen yielding to the wind.[5] I crossed the famous Mount Utsu without being aware of it, for I saw no ivy

vines or maple trees.[6] In fact, only later upon inquiring of someone did I realize I had passed it.

> The ivy that flourishes
> In leaves of verse
> Appeared not even in a dream.
> I crossed Mount Utsu unaware.

The Mishima Shrine in Izu province held an offeratory service identical to the one at Kumano,
even down to the awesome dragon. It was here that
the late General Yoritomo had stayed a while, and
where some high-ranking court ladies had donned
traveling clothes and performed the "ten thousand
prayers," as they are called.[7] I realized how they
must have suffered, yet could they have been as burdened with troubles as I? It was toward the end of
the month when the moon rose late, and the
brevity of the moonlit night added to my feelings
of loneliness. Fortunately I was able to enjoy the
shrine maidens' nighttime performance of sacred
kagura dances. Four girls wearing special costumes
wove back and forth in the dance called *Harena*. I
was so intrigued that I spent the whole night at
the shrine, leaving only when the singing of birds at
dawn summoned me away.

Late that month I arrived at the island of E no
Shima, a fascinating place that is not easy to describe. It is separated from the mainland by a stretch
of sea, and has many grottoes, in one of which I
found shelter with a pious mountain ascetic who
had been practicing austerities for many years.
Senju Grotto, as it was called, was a humble yet
charming dwelling, with fog for a fence and
bamboo trees for screens. The ascetic made me feel

welcome and presented me with some shells of the area, whereupon I opened the basket my companion[8] carried, took out a fan from the capital, and offered it to him.

"Living here as I do, I never hear news from the capital," he said. "Certainly things like this aren't brought to me by the wind. Tonight I feel as though I've met a friend from the distant past." My own feelings quite agreed.

It was quiet with no one around and no special event taking place, yet I could not sleep a wink that night. I lay upon my mattress of moss brooding on the great distance I had traveled and the cloak of worries that covered me, and I wept quietly into my sleeve. Then I decided to go outside and look around. The horizon was lost in a haze that might have been clouds, waves, or mist; but the night sky high above was clear, and the brilliant moon hung motionless. I felt as though I had actually journeyed two thousand *li*. From the hills behind the grotto I heard the heart-rending cries of monkeys and felt an anguish so intense it seemed new. I had undertaken this solitary journey with only my thoughts and my grief in hopes that it would dry my tears. How distressing to have come so far and yet to have the worries of the world still cling to me.

> A roof of cedar branches,
> Pine pillars, bamboo blinds,
> If only these could screen me
> From this world of sorrow.

The next day I entered Kamakura and visited Gokuraku Temple. The behavior of the priests reminded me so much of Kyoto priests that I felt a touch of homesickness. Then I climbed Kehaizaka Mountain and found a spot that afforded a prospect of the city. How different from the view of Kyoto from the eastern hills! Houses hugged the mountain slope in terraced rows, huddled together like things stuffed into a pouch. I found this an altogether unattractive sight.

I visited the beach at Yui, with its great *torii*.[9] From there I glimpsed Tsurugaoka Hachiman Shrine in the distance and reflected upon the bond from a former life that had caused me to be born into the Minamoto clan, which the god Hachiman has promised to protect above all others. What retribution has overtaken me, I wondered. Then I recalled praying for Father's future reincarnations[10] and receiving the answer: "In exchange for your own good fortune in this life." I do not mean to imply that I begrudge him this, for I would not complain even if I had to hold out my sleeves and beg. Did not the poetess Ono no Komachi, who was in the line of Princess Sotoori, end her life with a bamboo basket over her arm and a straw coat on her back? Yet could she have been as miserable as I was? Arriving at the Tsurugaoka Hachiman Shrine, I was impressed by the distant seascape which made the prospect more striking than the view from Mount Otoko,[11] but I was struck by many incon-

gruities. The *daimyō*,[12] for example, did not wear
the white garb of pilgrims, but came to the shrine
in everyday dress of various colors.

I continued to visit various shrines and temples—
Egara, Nikaidō, and Ōmidō—on my way to Ōkura
Valley, where Lady Komachi, a relative of Tsuchimikado no Sadazane, was in the service of the
shogun. I had written to her, and she had expressed
her surprise that I was nearby. She had invited me
to visit her, but I was hesitant about imposing, and
stayed instead at a nearby inn, where she continued
to inquire after me. At the end of the fourth month
I had recovered from the rigors of my journey, but
the priest whom I was depending on to serve as
guide on a trip to Zenkō Temple became so ill that
he lost consciousness. We had almost given up hope
for him when he began to show a slight improvement. It was then that I too was taken ill.

With two of us sick, people began to worry, but
the doctor gave assurances that my illness was not
anything serious. It was simply the result of the un-
accustomed hardships of my trip, he said. Still, I
felt as though death was imminent, and I was unbearably lonesome. Always before when I was sick
for two or three days with even the slightest thing—
a cold, a runny nose, or any other minor disposition
—numerous diviners and doctors would be summoned, a family heirloom or prized horse would be
offered to a god or Buddha renowned for miracles,
and people would fuss over me and feed me rare
Nanrei oranges or Kempo pears. Now, however, although I had been sick in bed for many days, no
one offered prayers to the gods or called upon
Buddha in my behalf; and there was no one to worry

about what I ate or if I took my medicine. Just lying
in bed day after day made me acutely aware of how
my life had changed. But the span of our life is fore-
ordained, and sometime in the sixth month I began
to feel better. I was not quite up to continuing my
pilgrimage, so I spent the days in idleness until the
eighth month.

On the morning of the fifteenth I received a letter from Lady Komachi: "Today is the day of the
Hōjōe festival[13] at the Iwashimizu Hachiman Shrine
in Kyoto. What memories does it bring to mind?"

I replied with a poem:

> Useless memories!
> Though of Iwashimizu lineage
> No water from its stream
> Flows through to me now.[14]

She responded:

> Yet have faith, for the gods
> Weave their compassion
> Round those who draw near.

The Hōjōe festival was also celebrated at the
Tsurugaoka Hachiman Shrine in Kamakura, and I
was curious enough about it to go and have a look.
Considering the location, the shogunal procession
was quite impressive. The costumes were striking:
The *daimyō* all wore formal robes, while others
had on ordinary gowns with swords. When the
shogun descended from his carriage at the Red
Bridge, however, I was startled by the disgraceful
appearance of the nobles and courtiers who attended
him. They looked positively shabby. Taira
Yoritsuna's[15] son Iinuma, the vice minister of the

shogun's board of retainers, had the deportment of a regent. He was most impressive. I did not find the horseback archery and other festival events of any particular interest, so I returned home.

A rumor had been circulating that something was about to happen in Kamakura, and while we were speculating on who was involved we learned that the shogun was leaving his palace immediately to return to the capital.[16] Wanting to see his departure, I went to the palace and saw a shabby palanquin—and an informal one at that—drawn up to the veranda. A lieutenant from Tango was in charge until the arrival of the regent's representative, Iinuma, who ordered that the palanquin be carried backward,[17] claiming there was precedent for such an order. Even before the shogun had boarded the palanquin, some coarse-looking servants walked into his living quarters without removing their straw sandals and began tearing down the bamboo blinds. It was an unbearable sight.

After the shogun had departed, several of his ladies-in-waiting came out, but there were no palanquins for them, and they had nothing to cover their faces with. They stood sobbing, asking where the shogun had been taken. Those who had found patrons among the *daimyō* were escorted by young retainers waiting for dusk to see them off. The sight of the ladies ready to go their separate paths was indescribably painful for me.

The shogun went first to Sasuke Valley, where he was to remain for five days before proceeding to the capital. In order to witness his final departure, I went to a nearby temple, which enshrined the famous god Oshide no Shōten. Upon my arrival I made some inquiries and learned that the departure was set for 2 A.M. That evening it started to rain, and as the appointed hour approached, the rain became torrential, and high winds arose. The storm was bad enough to make me wonder if evil spirits were abroad, but I was told that the departure time would not be changed, and I went out. The palanquin, wrapped with straw matting to protect it from the rain, was so unsightly that I averted my eyes from it. The shogun was already in the palanquin, but there had been a delay, and it still stood in the courtyard. After a while the shogun blew his nose. He did it quietly, but from time to time I could hear him. I pictured him weeping.

Although Prince Koreyasu held the title of shogun, this did not mean that he had engaged in great military exploits.[18] His father, Prince Munetaka, was known as the second son of Emperor GoSaga, but I understand that Munetaka was actually born a few months or a year before GoFukakusa, which would have made him the eldest son. If Munetaka had become emperor, Koreyasu would probably have succeeded him; but the lowly position of Munetaka's mother prevented this. And although Munetaka went to Kamakura to become shogun, he remained a member of the imperial family, being known as the prince of the general affairs ministry. Hence Munetaka's son Koreyasu was a nobleman beyond all cavil, and rumors of his illegitimacy were unfounded: His mother was a Fujiwara of the highest standing. Recalling the purity of Koreyasu's lineage on both sides, I could only weep.

The sacred river at Ise, the very stream!
If they have not forgotten,
How sad this must be for the gods to see.

I could well imagine the misery of the shogun's journey back to Kyoto, yet I was disappointed that he did not compose a single poem about it; especially since his father, the former shogun, had under similar circumstances written "Dawn Snow at Kitano."[19]

Soon word was out that GoFukakusa's son Prince Hisaakira was to come to Kamakura as the next shogun. The palace was repaired and refurbished, and seven *daimyō* were appointed to serve as his retinue. One of these was Yoritsuna's son Iinuma, who already called himself Shinsaemon, although that title had not yet been officially conferred on him. He insisted on traveling to Kyoto via the Ashigara Pass so as not to follow the path of the banished ex-shogun. Everyone agreed that this was going to extremes.

As the day of the new shogun's arrival approached, there was a flurry of activity. Early one morning, two or three days before he was due, I received a letter from Lady Komachi. Wondering what she had to say, I opened the letter and was surprised to learn that my advice was wanted. Empress Higashi-Nijō had sent Yoritsuna's wife, Onkata, a five-layered gown that was cut out but not sewn together, and they wanted to consult with me about it. Lady Komachi added: "It doesn't matter that you have entered holy orders, and besides no one knows who you are. I simply said you were a friend from the capital." Her urgent request was

hard to decline, for she persisted even after I had
refused several times, finally even including a letter
from the regent. I felt that this had the force of an
order, and since the request itself was a simple one
not worth such a fuss, I agreed to go.

Within the regent's estate was a building known
as the Sumidono, which was decorated much more
lavishly than a palace. Inlays of gold, silver, and
precious stones glistened like jeweled mirrors. It was
not quite paradise, but everyone wore gowns of the
finest silks and embroidered brocades, and the curtains and hangings were so dazzling in their beauty
that the whole place seemed to glow.

Lady Onkata appeared wearing a white formal
train over a two-layered gown of Chinese brocade,
which had a large scarlet maple tree woven on a
light green background. She was a tall woman, imposing in both appearance and manner, and I
thought her very impressive. Then Yoritsuna,
dressed in a small-sleeved white informal robe, entered from the far side of the room and joined her
without ceremony. His appearance was disappointing.

They brought out the costume the empress had
sent, and I recognized a five-layered gown that was
supposed to be worn with successively darker shades
of scarlet toward the inner gown, which in this case
was of unlined green material. There was also a pale
pink outer gown that should have had purple and
green designs on opposite sides, but it had been
sewn together wrong. The layered gowns had been
assembled with the lightest layer properly on the
outside, but immediately under it was the darkest
one, so that the layers became successively lighter

rather than darker toward the inside. It was quite incongruous. When I asked how this had happened, I was told that because none of the shogun's wardrobe ladies had had time to do it, the ladies of Yoritsuna's household had sewn it together without any notion of how it should look. While I was instructing them how to correct this amusing mistake, a messenger from the regent arrived.

"We have received advice about the exterior of the shogun's palace from some members of the Hiki family. Have the lady from the capital look over the furnishings of the living quarters." The summons was annoying, but under the circumstances it would have been rude not to have complied with it. The shogun's quarters, furnished in the customary formal style, were not unpleasing, and there was nothing that required drastic rearrangement. I left after making a suggestion or two about the placement of a chest of drawers and the proper way to hang robes.

On the day of the shogun's arrival Wakamiya Avenue was lined with spectators. Many people had gone to the pass to welcome the shogun, and the first of these had already returned. After a number of horsemen had passed in stately procession—perhaps there were as many as forty or fifty—there was a cry of "Here he is!" and twenty or so servants dressed in the garb of imperial attendants passed by. Then came a procession of smartly dressed *daimyō* in a line that stretched four or five blocks, and immediately behind them, in a palanquin with the bamboo blinds rolled up, was the new shogun, dressed in an embossed robe of green and yellow. Iinuma attended him, wearing a green and white robe. At the palace all the proper people, including the regent Hōjō Sadatoki and Ashikaga Sadauji, wore unpatterned robes. There was a splendid ceremonial viewing of horses. Three days later the new shogun visited the regent's mountain estate, where I understand he was entertained in great splendor. These events saddened me with memories of distant days at court.

21 (1289-90)

During this period[20] Iinuma, who was known for his love of poetry, occasionally sent Wakabayashi no Jirōsaemon to invite me to poetry gatherings. At the first of these I discovered Iinuma to be a much more likable man than I had anticipated. I attended several of his gatherings, taking great pleasure in the composition of poems and linked verse.

In the twelfth month I decided to go to Kawaguchi in Musashino province to visit a nun who was the widow of the lay priest of Kawagoe. From there I would continue on to Zenkō Temple after the first of the year. Content with these plans I left Kamakura only to encounter a blinding snowstorm which made the two-day journey very difficult.

The nun's residence had a remote, rustic air about it. The Iruma River flowed in front, and on the far bank stood the Iwabuchi Lodge, where a group of entertainers lived. There were no mountains at all in this province. Far into the distance in every direction stretched the famous Musashino Plain, its fields of reeds drooping under the bite of winter frost. I felt the loneliness of life in these desolate plains so far from the capital. Grief and self-pity weighed upon me as the year came to its close.

I persisted in dwelling on the past. I could not recall my mother's face, for she had died when I was only two. When I turned four I was taken, toward the end of the ninth month, to the palace of Retired Emperor GoFukakusa. His Majesty graciously bestowed his favors on me from the time my name was entered on the roll of his attendants, and I experienced the feel of worldly success. During the years that I was well received at the palace I cherished the secret dream of becoming the pride and joy of my clan. Such expectations did not seem unreasonable, yet I decided to give up everything and enter the path of renunciation. This seemed in accordance with my fate. The sutras say, "Neither family, nor wealth, nor rank can accompany you in death." I thought I had renounced all such worldly attachments, but I still found myself longing for the palace of my youth and recalling His Majesty's great kindness. Reminded of these things, my only solace was to weep until tears darkened my sleeves.

To add to my gloom, at this time a heavy snow-storm darkened the sky and drifting snow blocked all roads to the outside. As I sat dejectedly gazing out at the storm, the nun sent a note asking how I felt at being snowbound. I replied:

> Have pity on one burdened by sorrow
> And soon to vanish like the snow
> Burying the garden, blocking the paths.

Others would probably find it strange that her solicitude caused me to weep all the more.

In a mood of quiet endurance I waited to see the

new year in. The song of a warbler flitting about in the branches of the plum tree near the eaves startled me into an awareness that spring had come. It was still difficult to face the hard truth that life never flows backward in time, and so I wept for the past even as the new year began.

Toward the middle of the second month, I decided to set out for Zenkō Temple. The Usui Pass and the Maroki Bridge on the Kiso plank road were dangerous even to set foot on.[21] I had hoped to pause along the way and visit famous places, but I fell in with a group of travelers and allowed myself to be swept along without stopping. Later, when the other travelers were ready to leave Zenkō Temple, I explained that I was bound by a pledge and would remain there in retreat for a time. They were concerned about my staying on alone, but I was firm: "Who can accompany me on that final journey through the afterworld? I entered this life alone; I shall leave it alone. People who meet must part; things that are born must die. No matter how beautiful the plum blossoms, in the end they return to the ground. No matter how many tints the autumn leaves reveal, once the wind rises they do not last long." I remained there alone.

The temple was not in a scenic area, but it was noted for its famous image of Amida Buddha, whose power I had such faith in that I devoted much of my time to reciting invocations to it.[22] In the area there lived a man from Takaoka known as the Iwami lay priest, who was said to be a most hospitable person. Some ascetics and nuns I had become acquainted with told me about the poetry and music parties at his house, and invited me to attend one with them. I went and discovered an impressive house superior to anything else in this countrified place. It was comforting to have people to talk with, and I remained there until autumn.

Early in the eighth month I decided I had lingered long enough. I wanted to go back to Musashino to view the autumn scenery, and so I headed for the temple of Asakusa, which intrigued me because of its eleven-faced Kannon renowned for its miraculous efficacy. To get there I had to pass through vast fields so densely covered with bush clover, *ominaeshi*, reeds, and pampas grass that no other plants were able to grow in them. The height of the grasses was such that a man on horseback could pass through unseen. For three days I pressed on through the fields without reaching my destination. Traveling accommodations could be found on small side roads, but otherwise there was only the plain stretching far into the distance behind and before me.

The hall that housed the statue of Kannon stood on a small hill in the middle of the treeless plain, where the moon really did arise "from fields of grass."[23] I remembered with a pang of nostalgia that tonight was the fifteenth, the night on which moon-viewing parties were held at the palace. GoFukakusa had once presented me with a gown as a keepsake, but because I had offered it to the god Hachiman when I dedicated my copy of a sutra, I could not claim it was "here with me now." Yet I was unable to forget the palace, and my feelings, as "I prepare offerings of incense," were certainly as deep as Michizane's.[24] The moon, having risen from the fields of grass, climbed higher as the night deepened, and the dew on the tips of the grasses sparkled like jewels.

> Once I viewed it from the palace,
> The moon which on this night
> Forces memories to return.

My eyes filled with tears.

> Gazing at the brilliant moon
> As it sails through cloudless skies
> Could I forget his face?

It was reckless to remain in the open fields, so at daybreak I returned to my lodgings.

Later, when as nearly as I could tell I was in the vicinity of the Sumida River, I came to a large bridge similar to those at Kiyomizu and Gion in the capital. Crossing the bridge, I met two well-dressed men and inquired of them, "Where is the Sumida River? Isn't it in this area?"

"This is the Sumida River," they replied, "and you are on the Suda Bridge. Once there was no bridge here, but crossing by ferry became such a nuisance that this bridge was built. The proper name for the river is Sumida, though in the local dialect this is called the Suda River Bridge. A long time ago on the far side of the river there was a village named Miyoshino (which means good plain), where the rice harvest was always barren. The governor of the province believed the name of the village was responsible. After the name was changed to Yoshida (good rice paddies), the harvests were large and fruitful."

I recalled how Narihira had put a question to a

capital bird here, but I did not see any birds at all.[25]

> In vain have I come to inquire.
> Not a sign of any bird
> Living at Sumida River.

River fog closed in so thick I could not see behind or before me, but my own tears blinded me even more. From high above the clouds the cry of a wild goose came as an echo of my feelings.

> Tears darken the sky;
> The doleful cry of a goose
> Questions the weeping traveler.

At the site of the famous Horikane Well the only remaining trace was a single withered tree. From this point I had meant to travel inland, but I felt that I had never in my lifetime been permitted past the barrier at the end of love's road,[26] and as these wanderings did nothing to help me forget that, I decided instead to return to the capital by way of Kamakura.[27]

I remained in Kamakura until the middle of the ninth month, when I decided to return to the capital. Just before I left, the friends I had made all paid me farewell visits, and on the eve of my departure Iinuma came to spend one last night writing poetry with me. He had made elaborate preparations, and I found his kindness extraordinary. We spent the entire night composing poems. Once earlier I had asked Iinuma if he knew the whereabouts of the legendary river of tears, but he had denied knowledge of it. Now, after we had whiled away most of the night, he asked if I really had to leave at dawn.

When I replied that I must, since life's journey leaves no time to linger, he composed a poem, put it on his *sake* cup stand, and departed.

> The river of tears
> Flows over my sleeves,
> I cannot bid it stop
> Nor you stay, such is our bond.

I was still wondering whether to reply or not when he sent me a traveling outfit with another poem:

> Frail though our tie may be,
> Wrap this gown around you,
> Don't ever part with it.

During my stay in Kamakura we had often met casually, and I was aware that some people viewed our relationship with suspicion. With this in mind I replied:

> Our parting now will dampen
> Rumors we have not denied.
> This gown will rot away
> From tears of intense longing.

I was in no particular hurry to get back to the capital, but neither was there any reason to remain in Kamakura, so I departed that morning at sunrise. My friends supplied me with a palanquin to transport me from way station to way station, and in no time at all I had reached Mount Saya no Naka, where Saigyō had once composed the poem, "Yet here I am alive."[28] Recalling it, I wrote:

> How painful to cross over
> In the dead of night

Mount Saya no Naka;
Even should I live
Will I come again?

I arrived at Atsuta Shrine, where during an all-night service, I met some ascetics who said they had come from Ise Shrine. I asked if it was far and was told that there was a boat from Tsushima. The prospect of visiting Ise excited me, but first I wanted to carry out more of my vow of copying sutras, hoping to stay at Atsuta Shrine long enough to finish the remaining thirty scrolls of the *Kegon Sutra*.[29]
As payment for my expenses I offered the traveling clothes and other gifts I had received from my Kamakura friends, but the priest in charge of religious affairs at the shrine began to be difficult, and I was prevented from starting. While trying to work out a satisfactory arrangement I was taken ill again and suffered so much that I was unable to accomplish anything. I returned to the capital.
Life in Kyoto was scarcely more pleasant for me, so late in the tenth month I went to nearby Nara, still fatigued from my long travels. Not being of Fujiwara birth,[30] I had never been here before and knew no one. All alone, I went immediately to visit Kasuga, with its imposing two-story gate and four tiled-roof shrines. I wondered if the storms that often blew down from the mountains were strong enough to startle one out of the sleep of illusion, and if the running water gurgling through the foothills could wash away the stains of worldly life. Such thoughts occupied my mind as I entered the Wakamiya Shrine. There the rays of the evening sun were glistening on the shrine roof and gleaming

through the treetops on the hillside, as two of the young shrine maidens danced before the gods. They both appeared to be of good family.

An all-night service was conducted in an area of the Wakamiya Shrine. The night was spent in song and dance, for the Buddha, who joins us in this corrupt world out of his deep compassion, uses songs and stories to guide us to paradise. This well-known fact is illustrated vividly by one of the stories I heard. There was a high priest named Shinki who was a disciple of the high priest Rinkai, resident monk of the Kita Cloister in Kōfuku Temple. Shinki felt that the sound of drums and bells hindered his meditation. Consequently he made a vow: "If I ever become a head official of one of the six sects, the sound of drums and the clanging of bells will be prohibited." When, shortly thereafter, his ambition was realized and he was put in charge of Kōfuku Temple, he immediately carried out his wish, and for a long while no music accompanied the worship at Kasuga. Lonely silence filled the crimson gates around the shrine, while the dancers grieved with ever-deepening sorrow. Yet they steadfastly trusted in the will of the gods. Shinki declared, "No desires remain to me in this life. My only wish now is to devote myself wholly to the way." Accordingly he entered religious seclusion, confidently offering to the gods the joy his religious understanding had brought him. The god of Kasuga Shrine appeared to him in a dream and declared: "At the same time I forsook the Pure Realm and came to this defiled world of life and death determined to help ignorant mankind achieve enlightenment, you ordered the cessation of music and dance, making it more difficult than ever for men to achieve salvation. I resent your interference in my work. I will not accept your offering." As a result of this dream, music was never again prohibited, no matter how troubled the times. This tale strengthened my faith and filled me with awe.

The next morning, on a visit to Hōke Temple, I went to the cloister, where I met the nun Jakuenbō, daughter of Lord Fuyutada. She talked to me about the relentless cycle of life and death, causing me to consider remaining in the cloister for a while. But realizing that it was not in my nature to quietly devote myself to scholarly pursuits, and aware of the unending confusion that still dwelled in my heart, I decided to leave.

On the way back to Kōfuku Temple I passed the house of Sukeie, the head administrator of the Kasuga Shrine, although at the time I did not know whose house it was, or even that it was a house. The impressive roofed gate led me to believe that it was a temple building, and I walked in. I immediately discovered my mistake and saw it was not a temple at all but the private residence of an important person. The chrysanthemums in the garden, elegantly planted to form a hedge and already nipped by the frost, were as fine as any I had seen at the palace. Two young men came out of the house and inquired where I was from. When I responded that I was from the capital, one of them said, "We're embarrassed to have you see our miserable chrysanthemums." The man who made this graceful remark was Sukeie's son Sukenaga, the assistant head of Kasuga and the elder brother of Suketoshi, the honorary governor of Mino province.

       Outside court life now
       This far-wandering self
       Fading, frost-bitten chrysanthemums
       Recall the distant capital.

I wrote this on a slip of paper, attached it to a chrysanthemum, and left. I presume they read it, for a messenger came running after me urging me to return, which I did. They entertained me lavishly, and I accepted their invitation to remain for a while.

Later I went to visit the Chūgū Temple, curious to learn more about its connection with Prince Shōtoku and his consort.[31] The head of the cloister there was a nun called Shinnyobō, whom I had seen once at the palace. She was older than I, and my acquaintance with her scarcely went beyond knowing her name, so I was not sure how she would react to my visit. But she greeted me kindly, and I remained there for a time.

Later I went to Hōryū Temple and then to Taima Temple, where the daughter of Lord Yokohagi had dedicated herself to the worship of Buddha. Once a strange nun came to her and said, "Bring me ten bundles of lotus stems, and I will weave you a mandala depicting paradise." The nun took strands from the lotus stems and dyed them various colors, simply by dipping them in water from Dyeing Well. When the fibers were ready for weaving a court lady appeared, requested some oil for her lamp, and wove from ten that night until four the next morning. As the two strangers were about to leave, Yokohagi's daughter asked, "Will we ever meet again?"

She was told, "Long ago Kashō preached the

Buddhist law; then, reincarnated as Hōki Bodhi-sattva, he came here to the Taima Temple and inaugurated Buddhist services. We have come be-cause you sincerely believed in the Western Para-dise. If you trust in this mandala, you will not suffer." Then the two women disappeared into the western sky. I found inspiration in this tale, which has been transmitted in written form.

I noted with appreciation how at Prince Shōtoku's tomb the rocks were so skillfully arranged that I really felt an imperial presence. Joyful at the thought of the merit I had accumulated by recently finish-ing my copy of the Lotus Sutra, I offered a small-sleeved gown at the tomb before I left.

22 (1291)

In the second month of the following year I visited the Iwashimizu Hachiman Shrine on my way back to the capital. It was a long journey from Nara to Iwashimizu, and the sun was setting when I arrived and began to climb the Inohana trail leading to the inner garden. Among the pilgrims on the road was a dwarf from Iwami province. Talk centered on his deformity; no one could imagine what kind of karma might have caused it. I noticed in passing that the residence facing the riding ground was open. That was where members of the imperial family stayed when visiting the shrine, but it was also open when the supervising priest was in residence. No one along the road had mentioned an imperial visit, and that was the farthest thing from my mind as we passed by. I was climbing up to the shrine itself

when a man who seemed to be an imperial messenger approached and told me to go to the residence facing the riding ground. I asked him, "Who
is staying there? Do you really know who I am? Certainly the message cannot be meant for me. Are
you sure it is not for that dwarf?"

"No, I'm quite certain there's been no mistake.
The summons is for you. Retired Emperor Go-
Fukakusa has been here since yesterday."

I was dumfounded. In all these months I had
never forgotten him, but when I committed myself
to a new way of life and took my leave from Lady
Kyōgoku's apartments, I thought I would never see
him again in this world. Besides, I had no idea anyone could recognize me now, dressed in these
humble clothes that had been through frost and
snow and hail. Indeed, I wondered who had
spotted me. It was unlikely to have been His
Majesty, but perhaps one of the ladies thought she
recognized me and was even now wondering if she
had made a mistake. I stood there in bewilderment
until a junior imperial guardsman came to hurry
me along. There was no opportunity to flee as they
led me to an entrance on the north side of the
building.

"Come inside where you won't be so conspicuous.
Come on." It was His Majesty's voice, unchanged,
speaking directly from the past. I did not know what
he wanted, and my heart was so agitated that I was
unable to move at all. "Hurry up, hurry up!" he
urged. Hesitantly, I entered.

"I recognized you easily," he said. "You must
realize that even though many months have passed,
I have never forgotten you." He began talking of

events past and present and of his weariness with this constantly changing world. We stayed up the entire night, until all too soon the sky began to brighten. "I must complete the religious retreat I have begun," he said. "We can have a more leisurely meeting another time." Before leaving he took off the three small-sleeved gowns he was wearing next to his skin and presented them to me. "Don't let anyone know of these keepsakes, yet keep them with you always." At that I forgot completely the past, the future, and the darkness of worlds yet to come. My heart filled with an inexpressible agony as the dawn brightened inexorably. His Majesty murmured goodbye, and I gazed fondly after him as he retired to an inner room. His presence lingered in the fragrance of his scent still clinging to my black robes. The gowns he had given me were so conspicuous they would certainly attract attention. I would have to wear them under my own dark robes, awkward though that was.

> To wear your gowns—
> Love tokens from the distant past,
> Now tears stain dark sleeves.

It seemed a dream within a dream as I departed with his image futilely contained in the tears on my sleeves. We had at least met this once, but I doubted that the opportunity for another quiet tryst would ever come. My wretched appearance must have shocked His Majesty; perhaps he even regretted having called me. To remain here brazenly as though awaiting another summons would have been much too indelicate. And so I prepared to set out for the capital, suppressing my emotions by lecturing my heart.

Before actually leaving, however, I wanted to observe for one last time—now as an outsider—His Majesty make the rounds of the shrine. Fearing that I might attract his attention in my nun's habit, I decided to put on the gowns he had given me over my own robes. Then I mingled with a group of court ladies to watch. Garbed now in priestly robes, His Majesty looked utterly different from how he had appeared in the past, and the change affected me deeply. When he began to ascend the steps to the shrine, Middle Counselor Suketaka, who was at that time still only an imperial adviser and chamberlain, took His Majesty's arm and helped him up. Last night His Majesty had remarked that our similar attire made him feel nostalgic, and he had recalled events going back as far as my childhood. His words still echoed in my ears, and his image shimmered in my tears as I descended the holy mountain. Even after I had turned north toward the capital, I felt as though part of me had remained behind on the mountain.

Aware that I could not remain in the capital for long, I returned to the Atsuta Shrine and attempted to fulfill the vow I had made last year to copy some more of the Buddhist sutras there. I was working late one night when a fire broke out in one of the shrine buildings. You can imagine the consternation of the shrine officials. Unenlightened man seemed unable to contain this sacred fire, and within minutes the building had gone up in smoke. By daybreak nothing remained but ashes. Carpenters arrived, and the head priest and the master of ritual prayer came around to inspect the ruins. The building had been known as the Unopened Shrine and was said to have been constructed in the distant past by a god who then dwelt there. Now amid the still-smoldering remains of offerings on the foundation, there appeared a lacquered box about a foot wide and four feet long. Everyone gathered around to look at it in astonishment. The master of ritual prayer, a man said to be especially close to the gods, opened one side of the box a crack and peered inside. "I see a red brocade bag with something in it. It must be the sacred sword,"[82] he reported. The box was consecrated and deposited in the Yatsurugi part of the shrine complex.

Shrine documents that survived the fire related the miraculous history of this sword: "The god of this shrine, Prince Yamato-takeru, who had been born in the tenth year of the reign of his father, Emperor Keikō,[83] received an imperial command to go and subdue the eastern barbarians. On his way to battle he stopped to take leave of the gods at Ise Shrine, where he was given a sword and a brocade bag and told: 'In a former incarnation, when you were known as Susanoo no Mikoto,[84] you took this sword from the tail of an enormous dragon in Izumo and presented it to me. Here is a brocade bag also. When your life is endangered by the enemy, open it and look inside.'

"Later, in the plain of Mikarino in Suruga province, when the prince's life was threatened by a fire, the sword that he was wearing unsheathed itself and began cutting down the grass around him. The prince then used the flint he found in the brocade bag to start a fire, which immediately spread toward his enemies, blinding and then destroying them. Consequently the area was known as Yakitsuno, which means burning field, and the sword was named Kusanagi no Tsurugi, grass-mowing sword." This legend was particularly awe-inspiring because it confirmed a vision I had once had.

All this excitement, however, left me in no mood to concentrate on copying sutras, so I went to Tsushima and took a ferry to Ise. It was early in the fourth month, and the tips of the branches of the trees had all turned to delicate shades of green. I went first to the outer shrine at Yamada no Hara, where the grove of Japanese cedar was indeed the very place one would choose to await the first song of the cuckoo.[35] There were several priests in attendance at the shrine office, and I was aware that since I was wearing a Buddhist habit, I would need to be circumspect in my actions at this Shinto shrine, so I inquired where and how I might carry out my pilgrimage. They told me I could go through the second gate as far as the garden.

The place was awe-inspiring. I lingered near the office until several men who appeared to be shrine officials came out and inquired where I was from. "I've come here from the capital on a pilgrimage," I replied.

"We are usually reluctant about allowing people in Buddhist orders to visit the shrine," one of them said, "but you look so tired I am sure the gods would understand." They invited me in and treated me hospitably, even to the extent of offering to show me around. "You're not permitted inside the shrine itself, but you can look in from the outside," they explained. Then one of them guided me to the edge

of a pond overhung with the branches of an
enormous cedar, where a priest solemnly purified
us and prepared some *nusa* offerings.[36] I wondered
how that kind of purification could cleanse the taint
buried deep within my heart.

I had arranged for lodging in a small house
nearby, and as I prepared to return there I asked
the names of the men who had been so kind to me.
"I am Yukitada, and I'm the third assistant head
priest," one replied. "I am in charge of the shrine
office. The man who showed you around is
Tsuneyoshi, the second son of the first assistant
head priest." Their kindness would be hard to
forget.

The gods descend to earth for all mankind:
What kindness you who serve the gods
Have shown toward a moss-cloaked nun.

I wrote this on a scrap of prayer paper, attached it
to a branch of sacred *sakaki*, and sent it to the
priests, who replied:

Know that we who dwell
Deep in the shade of holy cedars
Share the blessings of the gods with all.

I remained here for a week praying for greater
understanding of the nature of life and death. The
shrine officials helped time to pass pleasantly by
sending me poems and inviting me to join them in
composing linked verse. There was, of course, no
reading of Buddhist sutras within the shrine precincts, but less than a half mile away was the
Hōrakusha, where Buddhist services were continually performed. One evening at dusk, as I was walk-

ing over toward Hōrakusha, I stopped at the Kannon Hall, where some nuns were worshiping, and
asked for lodging. "Impossible!" was the sharp reply.
So cruelly turned away, I composed this poem:

> Weary of the world like you,
> I wear the same black robes.
> What means this hue if you reject me so?

I wrote this on a prayer slip, attached it to a branch
from the nandin evergreen growing before the gate,
and sent it inside. They didn't answer my poem,
but they did let me stay, and we soon became acquainted.

A week later, when I decided to go to the inner
shrine, my former guide Tsuneyoshi sent me this
poem:

> Now the wanderer rolls on like
> A wave on the Bay of Poetry
> Where our friendship arose;
> Regrettable our parting.

I replied:

> And were I not a wanderer
> How would it matter?
> Can one remain forever in this world?

There were some people of refinement at the
inner shrine who had heard of my visit to the outer
shrine and were anticipating my arrival. The knowledge of their expectations made me uneasy, but not
to the point of preventing me from going. I stayed
at a place in Okuda that was right next to the home
of a lady of some importance. Soon after I arrived

a young serving girl delivered a letter from the lady with this poem:

> To hear of the capital
> Fills me with yearning,
> Involuntary tears
> Glisten on my sleeves.

"I would very much like to meet you," she added, and I learned that she was the widow of Nobunari, the second assistant head priest of the inner shrine. I replied:

> Questioned about the past
> I cannot forget,
> Grief quells
> All words of response.

Early one night when the moon was to rise late, I set out to visit the shrine. Since the Buddhist garb I wore limited my freedom of movement, I worshiped from the upper bank of the Mimosuso River. The shrine was surrounded by dense rows of *sakaki* trees as well as by a series of sacred fences, so that I felt distant from it; yet when I remembered that the crossed beams on top of the roof were cut horizontally in order to insure the protection of the imperial line,[87] a heartfelt prayer for the emperor flowed effortlessly from my lips.

> Deeply dyed in love
> My heart's hue unchanging
> Like my prayer remains
> Long life for my lord.

A chilling breeze swept through the sacred precincts, and the waters of the Mimosuso River flowed

quietly on. The light of the moon, rising now from
Mount Kamiji, was so brilliant that I felt sure it
shone far beyond our land.

Leaving the sacred precincts after a quiet period of
worship, I passed before the building that served
as the office and living quarters of the first assistant
head priest, Hisayoshi. With its entrances all closed
up, the building stood out conspicuously in the
brilliant moonlight. It struck me that the outer
shrine was known as the Moon Shrine, and so I
composed this poem:[88]

> Your element is sunlight,
> But why shut out
> The bright rays of the moon?

I wrote this on a prayer slip, attached it to a *sakaki*
branch, and placed it on the veranda of the office.
The priest must have found it at dawn, for soon
afterward this poem arrived, also attached to some
sakaki:

> Why shut out the moon?
> My doors are kept unopened
> That an old man might sleep.

After spending a week in quiet retreat at the inner shrine, I inquired about the possibilities of a
trip to Futami Beach, wanting to visit that place
that had so attracted the goddess.[89] A priest named
Munenobu offered to be my guide, and we set off
together. We viewed the beach where pilgrims
purify themselves, the strand of pine behind it, and
a rock said to have been split in two by lightning,
and then proceeded down the beach to the Sabi no
Myōjin Shrine, where we boarded a boat for a tour

of the islands of Tateshi, Gozen, and Tōru. Gozen Island got its name, which means "offering," from the great clusters of edible *miru* seaweed growing near the island. The priests from Ise Shrine gather this seaweed and offer it to the gods. *Tōru* means "to pass through," for this island is a gigantic rock, a portion of which has been worn away by the sea, leaving an opening for boats to pass under what now looks like a huge roof beam. There were many other beautiful sights in the vast seascape.

A sacred mirror made by a god to reflect the image of the sun goddess was enshrined at Koasakuma. It is said that it was once stolen and dropped into deep water. When it was recovered and presented at the shrine, the goddess spoke through an oracle: "I have vowed to save all living things—even the fishes in the boundless sea." Then, by its own power, the mirror vanished from the shrine and reappeared on the top of a rock, beside which grew a lone cherry tree. At high tide the mirror lodged in the top of the tree; at low tide it remained on the rock. This illustration of the vow of universal salvation filled me with great hope and made me decide to remain quietly in this vicinity for several more days. I obtained a room in the Shioai district at the residence of the chief administrative official of Ise Shrine, where everyone's kindness made me feel very much at home.

Several days after arriving I went with some of the ladies one night to view the moon at Futami Beach, reputed to be a lovely sight. I was profoundly moved by the beauty of the scene. All through the night we engaged in pleasant pastimes at the beach, returning home as dawn broke.

Could I ever forget?
Clear moon shining
On sparkling beach,
Its image lingers in dawn's sky.

Somehow word of my visit to the shore reached
GoFukakusa's palace, most likely through a serving girl named Terutsuki, who was related to someone at the shrine headquarters. When an unexpected letter came, I presumed it was from a lady
I knew at the palace, yet I felt a strange sensation
upon opening it. "Now that you are making friends
with the moon at Futami, I suppose you've forgotten
me completely. I'd like to talk with you again, as we
did so unexpectedly that night." The letter transmitted His Majesty's sentiments at some length. Unable to trust my own feelings, I sent this poem in
reply:

Though I live elsewhere,
Could I ever forget
The clear moon shining down
On that familiar palace?

There was no purpose in my staying longer, so I
returned to the outer shrine for a brief visit before
heading back to Atsuta to finish my sutra copying.
Surely the disturbance caused by the fire had
quieted down enough now to permit this. I realized,
however, that I was not at all eager to leave Ise. I
wrote this poem of parting and offered it at the
shrine:

O god of Ise, guide me
Through the span of life

> Allotted to me still
> In this world of grief.

I was prepared to set out the next day at dawn when a letter arrived from Hisayoshi, the first assistant head priest of the inner shrine. "Your parting fills me with great regret," he wrote. "Be sure to return for the festival in the ninth month." How kind he was! I responded with this poem:

> Long life and prosperity
> To my Lord and you!
> In the ninth month I shall return.

About midnight I received an answer, which said: "Others might not understand your heartfelt blessing. What can I reply to a poem that blesses our Lord and me?" With this came two bolts of famous Ise silk and this poem:

> As long as pines are
> Evergreen at the sacred fence,
> Endless years I would wait
> For that joyous autumn day.

While it was still night I went to Ōminato Harbor in order to catch the boat that left with the dawn tide. As I rested beside the salt kiln of some humble shore dweller, I recalled the words of an old song: "Among the rocks where cormorants live, or on a beach frequented only by whale, it matters not, if one has a lover."[40] What was my own fate to be? Were I to wait forever, there would be no one to comfort me; were I to cross distant mountains, there would be no place of rendezvous.

We were to depart at daybreak. While it was still

dark a letter came from Priest Tsuneyoshi of the outer shrine: "I had intended to send this to you at the inner shrine, but I forgot, so I am sending it now."

> You go with the tide I heard
> And wept, though a stranger.
> Those waves lap strange and distant shores
> Whose very names sound sad.

I replied:

> Our bond is that of strangers
> Yet now that I depart
> To return to distant shores
> Receding waves dampen my sleeves.

At Atsuta Shrine there was still the hubbub and confusion of reconstruction, but I was unwilling to postpone the completion of my pledge any longer, and I managed to arrange for a place to finish copying out the remaining thirty scrolls of the *Kegon Sutra*, which I then dedicated at the shrine. The ceremony of dedication was in the hands of an insignificant country priest who did not seem to understand what he was doing, but I made sure that various services were performed, including some music to please the guardian gods of the sutra. Then I returned to the capital.

23   (1292 or 1293)

I knew I would remember until my death that unexpected meeting with His Majesty at the Iwashimizu Shrine. Afterward from time to time he would send one of his relatives to my old home with a message, but he refrained from importuning me to make decisions, and I was grateful for his continued sympathy as I passed the days and months in idleness until the ninth month of the following year. At that time His Majesty sent several letters urging me to visit him at the detached palace in Fushimi, where he was staying. "This is a quiet, relaxing place," he wrote, "and there is little chance of gossip spreading."

My love-filled, guilt-ridden heart acquiesced, and I went secretly to the lower palace at Fushimi. The oddness of the situation fully dawned on me when someone came to show me in. While waiting for His Majesty to appear, I went out on the veranda of the Kutai Hall and gazed at the Uji River and its lonely scene until the ever-flowing ripples of the river found their way to my cheeks, bringing to mind the old poem: "Where wind-rippled waves are all there is to see."[41]

I lingered in reverie until His Majesty appeared late in the evening. The moon was bright, yet at the sight of him so changed from his past appearance, tears clouded my eyes. Once again we had a long talk ranging from that time in the distant past when I had played at his knees as a young child to the day I fled his palace certain that all was over. Yet these events, all from my own past, somehow failed to touch any deep feelings in me.

"Why have you let so much time pass without ever expressing your feelings about things?" he asked. "As long as we are living in this world of sorrow we are beset with grief." Indeed, what grievance did I have besides that of having to live as I did? Often I had thought of how it would feel to be able to disclose my sufferings and thoughts to someone and be comforted, but now I could find no words to express this wish. As His Majesty continued talking, I could hear the mournful cries of the deer on Mount Otowa and the sound of the dawn bell at Sokujōin warning us that day was breaking.

> The cries of deer
> Joined by the bell's sound
> Inquire about my tears
> As the sky brightens with dawn.

I kept this poem to myself.

Daybreak approached, and I prepared to leave, tears streaming down my face. His image lay deep within my heart. GoFukakusa said, "I hope that we can meet again on another moonlit night in this lifetime, but you persist in placing your hopes for our meeting only after the far distant dawn of salvation. What kind of vows are you cherishing? A man is more or less free to travel eastward or even to China, but there are so many hindrances for a traveling woman that I understand it to be impossible. Who have you pledged yourself to as a companion in your renunciation of this world? I still cannot believe it is possible for you to travel alone. What about Iinuma, from whom, as you wrote, you parted over a 'river of tears,' or the man at Kasuga and his hedge of chrysanthemums, or Tsunayoshi and that 'joyous autumn day'? These were surely more than frivolous exchanges. You must have made some deep and lasting pledges. And there must certainly have been others too with whom you have traveled." His Majesty kept at me with questions and remarks of this sort.

At last I replied, "Ever since I left the mist-shrouded palace to wander perplexed in frost-covered places, I have understood the scriptural passage: 'The restless world of unenlightened men is like a burning house,' for I have known no rest even for a single night. The sutras also say, 'Examine your present state to discover your past karma.' I am well aware of the wretchedness of my condition. Bonds that are once severed cannot be retied. I have certainly not met good fortune in this life, even though my Minamoto lineage puts me under the protection of the god Hachiman. When I traveled east for the first time, I went directly to the Tsurugaoka Shrine just to worship him. In this life I think constantly of salvation, petitioning the gods to dissolve my sins that I may be reborn in paradise.

"The vow of the gods to reward honesty has marvelous efficacy. I swear to you that though I traveled eastward as far as the Sumida River in Musashino, I did not so much as make a single night's pledge to any man. If I did, may I be excluded from the promise of Amida to save all mankind and may I sink to the deepest hell for all eternity. And if any bond of love attracted me when I visited the pure waters of the sacred river at Ise, may I incur the punishment of the great god Dainichi,[42] who is said to rule both the diamond and the womb realms. My poem on the autumn chrysanthemums at Kasuga was simply a means of dispelling my nostalgia. If there is a man from the slopes of Nara southward to whom I have pledged my troth, may the four great gods whom I worshiped at the

Kasuga Shrine withdraw their protection, leaving
me to suffer the eight tortures of hell.

"I grieve over the fact that I have never known
the face of my mother, who died when I was two,
and I shed tears of longing when I recall the care
my father gave me until he too passed away when I
was only fifteen. I was yet a child when you kindly
blessed me with your concern and generously bestowed on me your deep compassion. Under your
tutelage, the sorrow of being orphaned gradually
disappeared, and I grew up and received your favor.
Why did I not value it fully? What an inept, stupid
ass I was—although even an ass understands the
four debts of gratitude.[48] How then, as a human
being, could I have possibly forgotten your love?
Your kindness shone on me when I was young like
the light of the sun and moon combined, and as I
grew, you lavished more affection on me than a pair
of doting parents. Many years have drifted past since
we parted so unexpectedly, yet I shed tears for the
past whenever I meet you on one of your excursions,
and I am never unaffected when official positions
and ranks are conferred and I learn of another family's prosperity or of the rise of an old acquaintance.
When I try to still the feeling prompted by these
occasions I find I am unable to hold back my tears,
so I journey far and wide in an attempt to overcome
my emotions. Sometimes I stay at cloisters; other
times I mix with common men. When I find a place
where people are sympathetic and compose poetry,
I stay for several days, and of course there is no
dearth of people who enjoy starting rumors, whether
in the capital or in the countryside. I have heard
that sometimes, against her better judgment, a nun

will get involved with an ascetic or mendicant she happens to meet, but I have never fallen into such a relationship. I spend my idle nights in solitude. If only I had such a relationship even in the capital. If only I had someone to share my bed, it might help ward off the mountain winds on cold and frosty nights. But there is no such person; no one awaits me, and I pass idle days under the blossoms. In the autumn, when leaves turn, the insect voices, weakening as the frost deepens, reflect my own unhappy fate as I spend night after night in travelers' lodgings."

His Majesty continued to press me: "On pilgrimages to holy places I'm sure you keep your vows in purity, but here in the capital, where you have no vows to keep, what is to prevent you from renewing an old friendship?"

"I have not even reached the age of forty yet, and I have no idea what the future holds—though I doubt that I shall have a very long life—but now, as of this very moment, I assure you I have no such relationships, either old or new. If I am lying, may all the works in which I've placed my hope for salvation—the two thousand days of reading the *Lotus Sutra*, the considerable time I have spent copying sutras in my own hand—may all these become but burdens in hell; may all my hopes come to naught; may I never live to see the dawn of Miroku's salvation, but instead remain forever damned to hell."

I could not tell the effect of what I had said, for he remained quiet for a time before replying. Then he said, "The feelings of a person in love are never logical. It is true that after you lost your mother and then your father, I willingly accepted the responsibility of raising you, but things did not go as I had intended, and I felt that our relationship was, after all, only a shallow one. All this time has passed without my realizing how much you cared for me. The Bodhisattva Hachiman first made this known to me when we met on his sacred mountain."[44] As His Majesty spoke, the setting moon slipped behind the ridge of the mountains to the west, and the rays of the rising sun lit up the eastern sky.

I left quickly, feeling the need to be discreet in my nun's garb. As I returned to my lodgings, I wondered if His Majesty's parting words, "We must meet again soon," might not be a promise I would carry with me beyond death.

After His Majesty had returned to the capital I was somewhat surprised by the person he chose to bear a message of such genuine concern that I felt pleased and honored. I would have been content with even the slightest expression of affection, so the extent of the love revealed by his message left me overjoyed—even though I could share its words with no one. Since the end of our relationship long ago, his treatment of me had been beyond reproach, and I no longer had vivid memories of our love. Yet now that I knew more clearly some of the feelings His Majesty had hitherto concealed, those events of long ago would not recede from my memory.

Several years went by after this until I decided to go back to Futami Shore. If the gods themselves had visited there twice, I thought my return was in order, particularly since I wanted to pray for enlightenment. From Nara I took the Iga Road, visiting the Kasaoki Temple en route.[45]

Book Five

24 (1302-3)

The prospect of a sea voyage so intrigued me that I decided to retrace the travels of Emperor Takakura, who had once visited the Itsukushima Shrine in Aki province.[1] At Toba I boarded a boat that took me to the mouth of the Yodo River, where I transferred to an oceangoing vessel. But it proved to be lonely at sea, and when I learned we were passing Suma Bay, I thought of the courtier Yukihira, and wanted to ask the breeze "blowing through the mountain pass" the location of the house where Yukihira had "lived alone with tears and dripping seaweed."[2]

The ship anchored near shore each night. It was early in the ninth month, and the weakening cries of insects from clumps of grasses already withered by the frost were barely audible, but the "voices of a thousand—no, ten thousand mallets"[3] carried through the cold night the news that villagers were beating cloth. I listened to the waves lapping beneath my pillow and felt the full force of autumn's melancholy. Acutely aware that my destination really made very little difference, I saw myself as "the boat vanishing behind an island in morning mist."[4] I understood Genji's feelings when he begged his roan to carry him back to the capital.[5]

Our journey continued until we arrived at a place in Bingo province called Tomo. On the small island of Taika, not far offshore from the bustling mainland port of Tomo, there was a row of small huts belonging to women who had fled from lives in prostitution. Born into households whose business meant they were fated to be constantly reborn into the six realms, they had been mired deep in the toils of illusion. They would perfume their gowns in hopes of alluring men, and comb their dark hair, wondering on whose pillows it would become disheveled. When night fell they would await lovers, and when day broke, grieve over the separation. I admired them for having renounced that way of life and come here to live in seclusion.

When I inquired about the religious practices they observed and the reasons behind their conversions, one of the nuns spoke up, "I am the leader of the women on this island. Formerly I made my livelihood by assembling girls and selling their charms. We would attempt to lure travelers, rejoicing if they stopped, disconsolate if they rowed on by. We would vow eternal love to complete strangers and encourage drunkenness beneath the blossoms. I was over fifty when some karmic effect suddenly enabled me to shake off the sleep of illusion, give up my old life, and come to this island, where each morning I climb the mountain and gather flowers to offer to the Buddhas of the past, present, and future." Her words filled me with longing.

In a couple of days, when the ship was ready to embark again, the former prostitutes bade me farewell and asked how long before I would be return-

ing to the capital. At their question, it suddenly occurred to me that I might never return there.

> How many days and nights?
> One cannot determine life
> From this dawn to the next.

We reached Itsukushima, where in the distance
a *torii* gate towered above a broad expanse of waves,
and a great number of boats were moored to the
pilings of some seven hundred feet of boardwalk,
which stretched out over the water. The shrine
women, here called *naishi*, were busy with preparations for a major festival, and a dance rehearsal was
held on the twelfth day of the ninth month on a
stage connected to the shrine and built, like the corridors, out over the water. Eight *naishi* in small-
sleeved gowns with white overskirts danced to the
usual kinds of music. The sight of the dance called
"Rainbow Skirt and Feathered Gown," once performed by Yang Kuei-fei for the T'ang emperor
Ming Huang, summoned forth my own nostalgic
memories.

On the day of the festival, the dancers in their
colorful brocade costumes looked exactly like Bodhisattvas. The dancers of the left wore red, those
on the right, green. Another dancer, wearing an elaborate crown and ornamental hairpins, resembled
Yang Kuei-fei. As evening approached, the intensity
of the music increased. I was particularly impressed
by the "Autumn Wind Song." At sunset most of the
assembled crowd left to return to their lodgings;
only a few of us remained behind to spend the night
in prayer in the deserted shrine.

From the mountains behind the shrine the bright

thirteenth-night moon arose as if in homage to the gods, and its reflection gleamed from the depths of the waters rising with the tide beneath the shrine buildings. In a prayer expressing my trust in the god who came here, as a manifestation of Amida, to dwell amid the winds of ignorance that blow across the great sea of undefiled reality, I said, "Thy divine light shines into the farthest corners of the myriad worlds, and all those who call upon thy holy name are saved. May I too be led to salvation." Discontent gnawed at me when I thought about my present state and how wonderful it would be if I were pure at heart.

After remaining at Itsukushima for a short time, we were on our way once again. On board ship I met a well-born lady who told me she came from Wachi, in the province of Bingo. "I came to Itsukushima to fulfill a vow," she said. "Why don't you come to visit me at my home?"

"I want very much to go to Ashizuri no Misaki in Tosa now,"[6] I replied, "but I will try to visit you on my return."

The main image in the temple at Ashizuri no Misaki was a figure of Kannon. The temple grounds were not fenced in, there was no head priest, and travelling monks and ascetics could gather there without regard to class or position. When I asked how this had come about I was told the following story: "Long ago a monk came here with a young disciple to act as his servant. The disciple put compassion above all else. One day another young monk arrived—no one knew where he had come from— and joined them for their meals. The disciple always shared his portion with the newcomer, but his master admonished him, 'Once or twice is enough. You must not continue sharing your meals so freely.' When the young monk came at mealtime the next day, his friend said to him, 'I would like to share with you, but my master has scolded me, so this must be the last time. Please don't come again.' Then he shared his meal with the newly arrived monk, who said, 'Such kindness as you have shown me is unforgettable. Please come and see where I live.' The disciple accepted the invitation, and they went off together. The older monk grew suspicious and secretly followed them to the cape, where the two young men got into a small boat, took up the oars, and headed south. The old monk cried, 'Where are you going without me?' The young monk replied, 'We're going to the realm of Kannon.'[7] As the older monk watched they stood up in the boat and turned into Bodhisattvas. In grief and anguish the monk wept and stamped his foot, giving the place its name, Ashizuri no Misaki, the Cape of Foot Stamping. Leaving his footprints in the rocks, the old monk turned away emptyhanded. He met this sad fate because he had considered himself superior, so ever since then, people living here have avoided making distinctions." Hearing this tale, I was filled with hope; wasn't this perhaps one of the thirty-three forms Kannon had vowed to appear in to save mankind?

In Aki I spent a night of quiet worship at the Satō Shrine, which is dedicated to the god Gozu Tennō.[8] I was filled with nostalgia, for this god is also worshiped at the Gion Shrine in the capital.

I went by ship to Sanuki province in order to visit the tomb of Emperor Sutoku at Shiramine in Mat-

suyama[9] and to call on some of my relatives who
lived nearby. Upon learning that Buddhist services
were held in the Lotus Sutra Hall of the Imperial
Mausoleum in Matsuyama, I felt renewed hope for
Emperor Sutoku's salvation, even if he had fallen
into great suffering. When Saigyō visited here he
wrote a poem about the emperor that ends with the
question: "What will become of you?" Thinking of
that poem, I was reminded of another one: "Were
we born to suffer so?"[10] These expressions of past
emotions moved me to write this:

> If you remember grief
> Borne in this lifetime,
> Then from your mossy grave
> Look upon me with compassion.

Because much still remained of the five Mahayana sutras I had vowed to copy, I made preparations to work on them while I stayed in Matsuyama.
Not far from the mausoleum I found a small hut
where I set up a place to work and began a series of
sutra readings and services of repentance.

It was the end of the ninth month, and even the
cries of the insects had died away; yet I felt no need
for companionship. Three times each day I read the
sutras and recited the confessions of the sins of the
five senses and the mind. Still, the words His Majesty
had spoken to me lay unforgotten in the recesses of
my mind. Nor was it possible to forget him while I
retained a bone plectrum he had given me years ago
when I was very young and he was teaching me to
play the biwa. Though I had given up that instrument long since, I still retained the plectrum. Now

I decided to offer it to the Buddha, and I wrote this poem:

> This keepsake was held once
> In the hands of his past self:
> Gazing upon it now
> I weep into my sleeves.

I copied twenty of the forty scrolls of the *Great Collection Sutra,* depending for my support on local acquaintances. In order to dedicate the sutra at Matsuyama, I decided to use the second of the three undergowns His Majesty had given me some years before. I had offered the first one to the Atsuta Shrine for ceremonies there. Now I presented this one to the temple here in payment for the service of dedication. I wrote:

> O that our pledge had been:
> "Till the dawn of salvation's moon,
> This token of remembrance."

Toward the end of the eleventh month I was happy to learn of a ship bound for the capital, but no sooner had we embarked than a heavy sea with high winds, snow, and hail made progress difficult, and I was in a state of terror. When we put ashore I inquired about Bingo province, and upon being told it was nearby, I disembarked at once and set out for the home of the lady I had met earlier on board the ship to Itsukushima, following her written directions to Wachi. The first several days I spent there passed pleasantly enough for me, except that there were four or five cruelly overworked men and women whom the master abused almost every day. It was more than I could stand to watch. What

kind of place was this? I also learned that the men
used falconry to kill large numbers of birds, and
that they hunted down wild animals as well, so
heavy was their evil karma.

The lay priest Hirosawa Yosō, who was closely
connected with the Kamakura government,[11] sent
word that he would visit here on his way to Kumano
Shrine, whereupon the household, and indeed the
entire district, went into a flurry of preparations.
The master of the house where I was staying wanted
a picture painted on a screen he had had covered
with silk, and without really considering it, I said
that if I had the proper materials I would be glad to
paint the screen. Everything I needed was available
in Tomo, I was assured, and a servant was sent to
fetch it. I began to regret my offer, but seeing no
way out of it, when the materials arrived I did the
painting. The master expressed his delight and
added, "You must settle down here," which seemed
even at the time to be a strange remark.

During his elaborate welcome, the lay priest noticed my painting. "Such skill is not usually found
in the countryside. Who is the artist?" he asked.

"Someone staying here," was the reply.

"I suppose she can also write poetry. It would be a
pleasure for me to meet such an accomplished
person."

Uneasy at the thought of meeting him, I suggested we could have a more leisurely visit on his return from Kumano, and I fled in confusion.

A few ladies had come to Wachi especially for the
lay priest's visit, among whom were daughters of
the master's elder brother, who had an estate in

Eta. "Why don't you come and visit us?" they asked.
"Eta is beautiful."

I was beginning to feel acutely uncomfortable in
this house, and yet the snow made it impossible
for me to head back toward the capital, so I decided
to accept their invitation and remain with them until the end of the year. My departure was quite cas-
ual, but afterward the master of Wachi became
inexplicably angry and threatening. "A servant I had
had for many years escaped. Then I found this one
at Itsukushima, and now she has been spirited off
to Eta. I'll murder somebody for this," he ranted.

I could not comprehend his outburst. "He's out of
his mind to say such things," I was told. "Just ignore
him."

At Eta there were many congenial young ladies
around, and though I was not particularly fond of
the place, it was certainly more pleasant than where
I had been staying. I was still fretting over what had
happened when the lay priest stopped again at
Wachi on his return from Kumano. The master there
complained to him of the "outrageous thing" that
had happened. "My elder brother stole one of my
servants," he claimed.

The lay priest was not only the steward of the
region but the uncle of the brothers as well, and he
intervened: "What is all this? Are you actually
quarreling over some unknown servant? Who is she,
anyway? It is quite natural for people to travel about
on pilgrimages, and you have no idea what her status
might be in the capital. The crudeness you are dis-
playing is embarrassing to all of us."

The lay priest then came to Eta, where we had
made preparations to receive him. The master here

explained how matters stood, concluding with the remark, "My brother and I have ended up quarreling over a traveler we don't even know."

"This is most unusual," the lay priest agreed. "Have someone accompany her to Bitchū province and see her off." I rejoiced at his suggestion.

When I met the lay priest in person he said, "Talent can be the source of difficulties. I understand that the master at Wachi wanted to keep you because you are so accomplished."

As we entertained ourselves composing verses, I was able to get a closer look at the lay priest and realized that we had both attended a linked-verse party at Lord Iinuma's house in Kamakura. We spoke of the many things that had happened since then. When he left to return to his home in nearby Ita it was snowing hard, and the landscape with its bamboo picket fences was unfamiliar to me.

> I have renounced this world and yet
> My sorrows still are numerous
> As bamboo pickets in these fences.
> How doleful winter is!

With the arrival of the new year I wanted to set out immediately on my return trip to the capital, but everyone discouraged me. "It's still much too cold. And what about a ship?" My resolve wavered until the end of the second month. When he heard of my definite plans to leave now, the lay priest Hirosawa came over from Ita, and we again composed poems together. He also presented me with many going-away gifts. Hirosawa was the guardian of Prince Munetaka's daughter, who was then living with my friend Lady Komachi, and I suspected that he had considered these connections in giving me the presents.

The cherry blossoms were in full bloom when I arrived at Ebara in Bitchū province. I broke off a branch and asked the man who had accompanied me on this stage of my journey to deliver it to Hirosawa with this poem:

> Though rising mist divides us,
> O cherry blossoms,
> May the tidings of the wind
> Carry thoughts of me.

Two days down the road a special messenger came with this reply:

> Is it only blossoms
> I cannot forget?
> My heart goes with you
> But cannot speak.

Kibitsumiya Shrine lay on the way to the capital, so I dropped in for a visit. The buildings were furnished in a style quite different from that of most shrines, with portable curtains and other accouterments typical of a nobleman's mansion, making it altogether a fascinating place. I did not linger, however, for the day was still young, and the weather was fine. Before long I reached the capital, where I pondered the strange experience I had had. What awful fate might have befallen me had not the lay priest arrived? That man at Wachi was certainly not my master, but who would have defended me? What could I have done? I realized how dangerous pilgrimages can be.

25 (1304)

I settled down for a time at a residence on the out-skirts of Kyoto, where news from the court reached me occasionally, and it was there that I learned of Empress Higashi-Nijō's illness at the beginning of the new year. Since there was no one I could ask about her condition, I fretted and worried in igno-rance. I heard that there was little hope for her re-covery and that she was being removed from the palace.[12] Impermanence is life's only rule, and yet how terrible it must be for Her Majesty to be taken from the palace where she had lived for so long. She had shared this virtuous reign with His Majesty, had helped him with business each morning, and had accompanied him to bed each night. Now that the end was near, why should things be different? Why must she be moved away? How dreadful for her. Then word came that Her Majesty had breathed her last.

At this point I decided to visit the palace to see for myself what was happening. When I arrived I surmised that Empress Yūgi was about to depart, for some imperial guards were in attendance by her carriage. The minister of the left, Lord Kinhira, was also present. Apparently Empress Yūgi's departure was imminent, for the carriage was drawn up near the entrance; but then she gave orders that they were to wait a while longer, and she disappeared again inside the building. This was repeated two or three times, so overwhelming was her grief and her reluctance to leave the mother she would never see

again. By this time a number of people had gathered near her carriage. "Just when I think she is
finally in the carriage, suddenly she goes inside the
palace again," someone murmured. When she finally
did board the carriage, Empress Yūgi was in such
a terrible state of agitation that the bystanders could
not restrain sobs of sympathy. Everyone, whether
naturally kind-hearted or not, shed tears for her.

Empress Higashi-Nijō had had several children,
but since all of them, with the exception of Empress Yūgi, had died young, I could well imagine the
depth of feeling that must have existed between
mother and daughter. Empress Yūgi's appearance
confirmed my opinion. Such grief had formed a part
of my own experience, and I wondered how I would
be reacting now if I were still in the position I had
held so long ago.

> My worthless body
> Still alive to see this death—
> A woeful dream.

The funeral service, as I was told afterward, was
held at Fushimi Palace, with both Cloistered Emperor GoFukakusa and Empress Yūgi present. I
had a vivid picture of their grief.

In the sixth month of the same year I heard that
His Majesty GoFukakusa had been taken ill. Upon
learning that he had malaria, I experienced extreme
anxiety. Word came that he had improved, followed
at once by the news that his condition had worsened
and that services to the god Emma Ten were being
held on his behalf. I had to know how he was, and
so I went to the palace, only to find that there was

no one I could question. I returned home empty-handed and composed this poem:

> Without a dream
> How will he know about
> These lonely tears
> I hide behind my sleeves?

I learned that he was having daily attacks, then that his life was in danger, and the dreadful possibility that I might never see him alive again drove me to despair. It was more than I could bear. On the first day of the seventh month I secluded myself in Iwashimizu Hachiman Shrine and began a series of a thousand prayers to the god Takeuchi,[13] beseeching him to spare His Majesty this time. But on the fifth I dreamed of a solar eclipse from which the sun did not re-emerge . . .[14]

. . . still wondering about His Majesty's illness, I went to Saionji Sanekane's mansion, where I made a formal request: "As one who used to be in the service of His Majesty, I would welcome an opportunity to speak with Lord Sanekane briefly." But no one was willing to transmit it; perhaps because they were put off by my nun's habit. I then wrote a letter and attempted to persuade a member of the household to take it to him—again to no avail. Later that night a servant willing to convey my letter finally appeared. Lord Sanekane's reply said, "How many years have passed! I'm not even sure I remember you. Come back the day after tomorrow."

I felt an excitement akin to happiness when, on the night of the tenth, I returned to the mansion only to be told that His Majesty had taken a turn for the worse and Lord Sanekane had gone to the palace. Now his time has come, I thought, and tears welled up in my eyes. I set out along the route the imperial horsemen use, stopping at the Kitano and Hirano shrines to pray. "Take my life instead of His Majesty's," I pleaded. Then I realized that if my supplication were to be granted and I disappeared like the dew, I would have died for His Majesty without him even knowing of it. That too made me sad.

> Should I die for my Lord
> May the white frost on my grave
> Appear to him in a dream.

From dawn to dusk each day my thought dwelled on His Majesty; each night till daybreak I grieved for him. On the evening of the fourteenth I again went to the Saionji mansion in Kitayama; this time I met Sanekane. We talked for a while about the past, and then he told me with a calmness I found unsettling that he held little hope for His Majesty's recovery. I had come for the purpose of asking if I might see His Majesty for one last time, and I was still casting about for a way of phrasing my request when Lord Sanekane said, "His Majesty spoke of you. Go and visit him." I left the house quickly, unwilling to let anyone see the tears that welled up in my eyes.

On the way home I passed through Uchino, where I met crowds of people on their way to visit Toribeno Cemetery.[15] I too would be there someday, I realized.

> Visitors now to dew-soaked
> Grassy graves at Adashi—
> How long will they feel pity?

On the night of the fifteenth, thanks to Sanekane's help, I entered GoFukakusa's palace from Second Avenue, and caught a dreamlike glimpse of His Majesty. Around noon on the sixteenth His Majesty's passing was announced, and although I had tried to prepare myself for this event, when it actually happened I could not suppress my sorrow nor assuage my loneliness and grief. I returned to the palace and saw attendants dismantling the altars where prayers for his recovery had been offered. Others seemed to be milling aimlessly about, yet it was deathly still, and all the lights in the palace had been extinguished. Before dusk the crown prince retired to the palace on Second Avenue, and gradually other people also disappeared. Early that evening the two Rokuhara deputies came to pay their final respects. Together they arranged for a most impressive tribute: The deputy of the north ordered that torches be placed in front of the houses facing Tomi Street, and the deputy of the south had two lines of retainers sit on stools in front of watch fires along Kyōgoku Street.

Even when it grew late I could not bring myself to return home, and lingered alone in the empty courtyard, summoning up memories of the now distant past. As images of His Majesty floated before my eyes I felt pangs of grief impossible for words to describe. Before my eyes the bright moon slowly ascended the clear night sky.

> Tonight even the bright moon
> Seems a cruel mockery!
> How happy I would be
> If it dimmed and clouded over.

When the Buddha died long ago the light of both the sun and moon was dimmed, and birds and beasts, though mindless, mourned for him. Now surely the moon shining so intensely in the sky seemed cruel indeed, as if it refused to comprehend the depth of my sorrow.

At dawn I returned home nervous and restless. I learned that a relative of the Taira middle counselor was to be in charge of the funeral arrangements, and I called on a court lady of my acquaintance who was related to him. "Please help me see His Majesty once more, even if it is only a distant view of the casket," I begged. She replied that my request was impossible.

There seemed no other recourse, yet I was determined to find an opportunity to approach the casket. I put a court lady's gown over my head and loitered around the palace all day to no avail until finally, when it was time for the large outside shutters to be let down for the night, I was able to slip quietly around some bamboo blinds and approach the room where I thought the casket lay. A light was burning. The thought that the casket was there made me feel dazed and giddy. Then an announcement was made that it was time for the funeral to begin, and a carriage was drawn up for the casket to be borne onto it, whereupon it was wheeled to the door of Retired Emperor Fushimi's quarters. When it was pulled away again, the sleeves of Emperor Fushimi's robes, which had obviously been used to wipe away his tears, attested to the extent of his grief.

I left the palace and went out onto Kyōgoku Street to follow after the procession. All day long I had been inside, and when the carriage had ar-

rived for the casket I was in such a state of confusion that I could not remember where I had left
my shoes. Now I found myself running behind the
carriage barefoot. At the corner of Kyōgoku Street
and Fifth Avenue, where the procession turned west,
the carriage brushed against the side of a bamboo
tree growing along the avenue, and a screen was
knocked loose. During the pause, while one of the
attendants was replacing it and I was able to collect
myself enough to become aware of my surroundings
in the dark, I saw the lay priest Sukeyuki.[16] He
was standing beside the cart, the sleeves of his black
gown soaked with tears of a grief I also shared.

I kept thinking I should stop, but at the same
time I was unwilling to go home. As I drove myself
on, my bare feet ached so that with each step I fell
further behind the procession. At Fuji no Mori I
saw a man and asked him if the procession had continued straight ahead. "The casket cannot pass in
front of the Inari Shrine,"[17] he replied, "but I'm not
sure which way it turned. There is no one along this
road, and it is almost four in the morning. If you
do not know where you are going, you may get
lost. Shall I accompany you home?" The thought of
turning back now was unbearable, so I left him and
walked on alone, weeping as I went. It was almost
dawn when I arrived at the crematory. The service
was over; a few wisps of smoke were trailing off into
the sky. I wondered what had caused me to live to
see this sight.

From there I went to the nearby Fushimi Palace.
Last spring, when Empress Higashi-Nijō died, Empress Yūgi had someone to share her grief with, but

now GoFukakusa's death left her all alone with feelings I could only try to imagine.

> The dew has vanished.
> Grief of the final journey
> Forces my thoughts back—
> Alas, my sleeves.

I wanted to inquire after her—an idle wish, for all doors were barred to me, and it did no good to wander hopelessly about. That evening I returned home.

When I heard that Empress Yūgi was wearing deepest mourning, I could not help wondering if my own gowns would be darkly dyed were I still a court lady. On the occasion of Emperor GoSaga's death, when I was serving Emperor GoFukakusa, my father had claimed that I was close enough to the deceased emperor to wear deep mourning; but Emperor GoFukakusa had disagreed. "She's still a child. Her customary clothing in subdued colors will do," he had said. Yet in the eighth month of that very year I had to put on mourning for my father. Such memories flooded my mind.

> My dark black sleeves
> Will dye no deeper shade;
> My grief at one with hers.

Hoping to assuage my grief, I went to Shitennō Temple, a place that attracted me because it was said to be one of the sites where the Buddha had preached. There I planned to spend some time quietly reading the sutras, undistracted by other things. Yet thoughts of GoFukakusa continued to plague me, and I remained curious about how Empress Yūgi was feeling.

> The mist of spring wet
> Sleeves now stained dark
> By autumn's soaking fog
> And deepening pain.

I returned to the capital in time for the forty-ninth-day ceremonies, arriving at Fushimi Palace just as the service was commencing. Of one thing I was certain: None of the many participants there felt as much pain and grief as I did. After the service, as numerous offerings were being made, I had to face the realization that today marked the end of official mourning observances.

It was early in the ninth month, and my gloomy imagination pictured how autumn frost and tears vied with each other in the empress's quarters. Retired Emperor Fushimi, I understood, was now residing in GoFukakusa's palace, and I remembered how, when Fushimi had been made crown prince long ago, I had watched him move into the corner apartments of that very palace. My grief and pain mounted; why should autumn be so sad? My father and His Majesty had both died in autumn, yet I, who had tried to offer my humble life in exchange for His Majesty's, continued to live on in this sad world. That I should have been here for this forty-ninth-day service was too cruel.

There is a tale told about the god Fudō of the Jōjō Hall in Mii Temple. When the priest Chikō was at death's door, his disciple Shokū prayed: "My debt to my master is heavy. Please take my humble life instead of his." When Shokū offered his life for his teacher's, Fudō intervened: "Since you would give your life for your teacher's, I will give mine for yours." Chikō recovered from his illness, and Shokū also lived a long life.

The debt I owed His Majesty was far greater than the debt Shokū owed his teacher. Why then had my offer been fruitless? I understand that the god at Iwashimizu Shrine was given the title Hachiman Bodhisattva, the Eighty-thousand Bodhisattva, because he gave his life for so many people. It should not have mattered that I was so insignificant, and His Majesty had certainly not neglected Hachiman. Perhaps there is some karma that just cannot be changed.

These thoughts ran through my mind on my way home. Once there, I found I could not sleep, and composed this:

> I hear insects voicing
> My grief, sharing with me
> The wakefulness of the aged
> In the ninth month.

Tears of yearning for the past fell upon the garments I had spread out for my solitary bed. When my father left this world, he vanished with autumn's dew, and now the mist of this autumn has blended with the briar's smoke. The clouds blanket us in grief. Is his spirit in the rains, or is it in the clouds?[18] How difficult that journey must be.

> Yearning to know
> The cloud road you have taken,
> I wonder why this world
> Is so without magic.[19]

Twenty scrolls of the *Great Collection Sutra* remained for me to copy, and I hoped to finish them within the hundred days following GoFukakusa's death, but since I had no gowns except my nun's habit, I could not even offer the clothes off my back as payment for my expenses. I barely had enough to live on, so what could I use? It was a rueful predicament.

I did, however, have a memento from each of my parents. Before my mother passed away she asked that I be given a flat lacquered cosmetics case with a round mandarin duck pattern. The hair accessories and mirror inside were decorated with the same design. From my father I had a writing set. The cover of the writing box had a design of cranes within a diamond-shaped pattern in raised lacquer against a gold-flecked lacquer background. On the inside, in my father's hand, the words "days of good fortune, auspicious months" were inscribed in gold.

I had planned never to part with these keepsakes, and to have them with me even on my funeral pyre. When I set out on my pilgrimages, I always left them in the care of friends, feeling as anxious about them as I would have about a beloved child. Each time upon retrieving them immediately after my return, I felt as though I were reunited with my parents. Having had the cosmetics case for forty-six years and the writing set for thirty-three, I was naturally reluctant to part with them. For days I turned the matter over in my mind, asking myself: What good are treasures too fine for one's position in life? Wouldn't it be better to give them up for His Majesty's sake? I didn't have any children to whom I could bequeath worldly treasures,[20] and if I were successfully to complete my vow of copying the sutras, these mementos would have to become someone else's treasures.

When I finally decided it would be best to offer them to Buddha with prayers for His Majesty's enlightenment and my parents' salvation, I found that the decision, though far from easy, was not as painful as I had feared. Soon I heard that someone who was going off to be married in the east was looking for a cosmetics case. Perhaps because the gods took pity on me I was offered much more than I expected, and I sold it with the delightful sense that my plans were coming to fruition after all. When I handed over the case I included this poem:

> Mementos of two parents:
> Today I part with one,
> Wistfully letting go
> The jeweled comb case.

On the fifteenth of the ninth month a service of confession began at the Sōrin Temple in Higashiyama. When I had previously copied twenty scrolls of this sutra, I had recalled GoFukakusa often, cherishing the past and yearning for him in the present, but now I was obsessed by thoughts of him. Day and night I prayed that his spirit might attain perfect enlightenment. I was deeply aware of the depth of our karmic relationship.

In the midst of my sadness, the cries of the deer on Mount Kiyomizu struck a sympathetic chord in me, and the voices of the insects in the hedges soothed my tears. I stayed up for the late-night services and watched as the moon, which I had seen rising from the east, sank slowly into the west. In

the quiet after the services, I listened with awe to
the chanting of a lone sage on Mount Sōrinji.

> If I were to visit
> Death's own mountain paths,
> Would I see his shade
> Lingering there?

I requested this sage to go to Yogawa to get some
writing paper and holy water for me and accompanied him as far as East Sakamoto, proceeding
from there to Hiyoshi to see an old woman who was
especially devoted to the god enshrined there. She
often took me with her. . . .[21]

I wanted to present an offering at Emperor Go-
Fukakusa's grave, but I was afraid of what people
would think. Remembering the extent of his veneration for the Kasuga Shrine, I made my offering at
the main shrine there. The cries of the deer on the
slopes reflected my mood.

> Mountain deer, meadow insects,
> I hear their many cries
> Befriending my tears.

26 (1304–5)

This year marked the thirty-third anniversary of Father's death. With my request to the holy man describing the kind of services I wanted, I included
this poem:

> How cruel the wheel of fate—
> Three tens plus three times around
> Since that day we parted.

I visited Kaguraoka, where Father had been cremated. The moss was deep in dew, and as I made
my way under branches along the overgrown paths,
I looked at the stone grave markers, lingering reminders of the dead. I was also saddened by the
knowledge that none of my father's poems had been
included in the most recent imperial anthology.[22]
Had I still been serving at court, perhaps I might
have been able to appeal, for one of his poems had
appeared in every anthology since the *Shokukokinshū*.[23] The thought that my heritage—a poetic tradition upheld by our family for eight generations—
had come to such a hollow end upset me. My father's last words resounded in my ears.[24]

> Lamenting our ancient name
> I have set myself adrift,
> A fishing boat forsaken
> On the Bay of Poetry.

This was my state of mind when I returned home
that night and had a dream. I saw my father just as
he had been long ago, and as we faced each other I
was filled with emotions from the past. I poured
out my discontent and he responded, "Our family
contains many generations of poets. Your paternal
grandfather, the prime minister Michimitsu, composed the poem 'dew brightens fallen leaves,' and I
wrote 'could I but believe that spring has passed.'
On the occasion of an imperial visit to Washinoo
your maternal grandfather, Lord Takachika, wrote
this: 'Today's visit adds luster to the blossoms.'[25]
No one on either side of our family has ever forsaken poetry. We are an old family, descended from
Prince Tomohira, and the waves of our influence

have always been felt in the Bay of Poetry." As he
stood to leave, Father gazed upon me and recited:

> Sow all the words you can
> For in a better age
> Men shall judge the harvest
> By its intrinsic worth.

I awoke with a start. His shadow lingered in the
tears on my sleeves; his words echoed near my
pillow.

After that dream my commitment to poetry deep-
ened. I took advantage of an opportunity to go to
Hitomaro's grave, and I spent seven days there.[26]
The last night I spent in prayer.

> Born in a grove
> Of luxuriant bamboo,
> Am I fated to be
> But an empty stalk?

The old poet Hitomaro appeared to me in a
dream. I sketched his likeness and recorded his
words in "A Eulogy for Hitomaro." If it was within
Hitomaro's power, he would grant my wish; and if
my wish were fulfilled, I would offer a service to
Hitomaro, reading my eulogy before the sketch.
With these intentions I put the document away in
the bottom of a chest, but the months passed to no
avail. On the eighth day of the third month of the
following year I took out these things anyway, and
held a service in Hitomaro's memory.

The fifth month arrived, and with it the realization that it would soon be the first anniversary of
GoFukakusa's death. I had pledged to copy five Mahayana sutras: Three were already complete; two

now remained to be done. In this life we ought not put things off till tomorrow. I had already given up the memento from my mother; I still retained my father's. What should I do now? No matter how long I kept it, I could not really take it with me on my journey beyond death. After pondering a while I finally decided to give it up. But rather than selling it to just anyone, wouldn't it be preferable to give it to someone I knew? Yet when I considered this carefully, I realized that no one knew of my pledge, and an acquaintance would assume I was forced to sell the memento merely to make ends meet, abandoning it to the rushing river of life. This would not do either.

I heard that a certain official was visiting the capital on a journey from Kamakura to Kyushu. He offered to buy my writing set, and I realized with a pang of sadness that the memento from my mother had been taken to the east, and the one from my father was now to be carried across the western sea.

> Flowing ink and tears streaming
> Into a sea of grief
> To meet at last—such is my faith—
> On a distant shoal.

This expressed my feelings at parting with the writing set.

I decided to start copying the remaining sutras in the middle of the fifth month; and since I had to make a brief trip to a place in Kawachi province near the grave of Prince Shōtoku, I remained there and completed twenty scrolls of the *Wisdom Sutra*, dedicating them at the tomb of the prince before returning to the capital early in the seventh month.

On the anniversary of His Majesty's death I went first to his tomb and then to Fushimi Palace, where services were already under way. Retired Emperor Fushimi was the chief mourner at the ceremony, which was conducted by High Priest Shakusen. The sutras the priest was reading had been copied by Emperor Fushimi on the back of some of GoFukakusa's letters, a fact that made me realize that Emperor Fushimi and I shared the same feelings of reverence and sadness.

Empress Yūgi also sponsored a service, this one conducted by the younger brother of High Priest Kenki. It was an impressive ceremony, and once more the sutras had been written on the back of GoFukakusa's letters.

On this day I felt that my grief was to end. The brilliant rays of sunlight did not bother me at all as I stood alone in the courtyard watching the dignitaries depart one by one after the services, and for once I felt no need to express my sorrow to someone.

> A long span of time,
> My sleeves never dry:
> Today, I understand, tears cease.

I caught a glimpse of Retired Emperors Fushimi and GoFushimi as they proceeded to the lecture hall. Emperor Fushimi's mourning robes were very dark, but today was the last day he would wear them.[27] Then Retired Emperor GoUda arrived and entered the same lecture hall. I was exhilarated by these sights, for even though His Majesty GoFukakusa was gone, his glory lived on in his descendants. Shortly after this I heard that Cloistered Emperor

Kameyama had been taken ill. It was difficult to believe that misfortune could continue. The illness was his chronic one, but there was no reason to suspect the end was near until I suddenly heard that the case was considered hopeless and that Kameyama had already been removed to Saga Palace. Could more happen after the grief of the past two years? This time the sorrow did not affect me directly, but nonetheless I was saddened by it.

I had vowed to complete the remaining twenty scrolls of the *Wisdom Sutra* by the end of the year and wanted to do this at Kumano, so on the tenth of the ninth month I headed there, hoping to arrive before it turned bitter cold. Though Kameyama's condition remained unchanged, I wondered uneasily how long he could last; yet I was strangely unaffected by any sense of loss, and felt none of the grief I had known last year at GoFukakusa's death.

I copied the sutra in the mountains near the Nachi waterfall, where it was convenient to get water for my regular morning and evening ablutions. Late in the ninth month a fierce storm blew down from the peaks, rousing my emotions to such a pitch that my sobs seemed to match the roar of the falls.

> Tears of anxiety
> Stain my sleeves darker and darker:
> If only someone—even a stranger—
> Would inquire why I cry!

Then something happened that suggested that the god of Kumano had accepted the sacrifice of my parents' mementos and my dedicated efforts at sutra copying. Only a few more days' work remained on the sutra, and I was reluctant to think that the time to leave this mountain was approaching. I spent one entire night in worship. Just before dawn I dozed off and dreamed that I was beside my father, who informed me that His Majesty GoFukakusa was visiting the shrine. I looked for GoFukakusa and found him standing with his body bent to the right, dressed in a persimmon-colored gown with a design of long-tailed birds. I approached him through some bamboo blinds on his left. Then he proceeded to the Shōjōden part of the shrine, raised the blinds a little, and smiled. He appeared to be in very good spirits.

Still in my dream, I heard that Empress Yūgi was also paying a visit to the shrine, and I went off to look for her. She was dressed in white trousers and a small-sleeved robe and was in the building known as the Nishi no Gozen with the blinds rolled halfway up. As I watched she took two white gowns from different places and said to me, "It must be difficult to bear the knowledge that the mementos from your parents have been carried away in different directions. I am putting these two gowns together to give to you." Accepting the gowns, I returned to the main building and spoke with Father. "GoFukakusa had acquired all the virtue necessary to be born an emperor. What karma has caused him to become so deformed?" I asked.

"His deformity is caused by a tumor on his hip," Father explained. "That in turn is caused by the many ignorant people like ourselves who cling to His Majesty and whom he pities and protects. It is through no fault of his own at all."

I went to see His Majesty again. His face was still

cheerful as he beckoned me come closer. I approached and fell to my knees as he picked up two small branches about the size of chopsticks, each of which was whittled down to a pure white point at one end and had two *nagi* leaves at the other.[28] I thought he was presenting them to me when I suddenly awoke. The confessional service had already begun in the Nyōirin Hall. I looked about in confusion and discovered a white fan with cypress wood ribs right beside me. The fact that it was not summer made this a strange and auspicious event indeed. I picked up the fan and entered the meditation hall, where I related what had just happened. One of the Mount Nachi monks, a Buddhist official from Bingo named Kakutō, said, "The fan, which is symbolic of the thousand-armed Kannon, is clearly an auspicious sign."

Images from that dream remained vividly in my mind while I finished copying the sutra. As I made an offering of the last of the gowns given me by His Majesty, I began to weep, for it was the one I had thought I would keep forever.

> Year after year this keepsake,
> His small-sleeved gown,
> Has been with me, until today—
> Stricken by the loss of it.

I dedicated the sutra at Mount Nachi and began the journey home.

> Startled from dream, dawn's moon
> Lingering at my pillow
> The voice of the falls
> Accompanies my tears.

It gave me some comfort to have as a keepsake the
fan that had appeared with my dream.

Upon returning to the capital I learned that Emperor Kameyama had died. This relentless procession of grievous events made me even more acutely
aware of the cruel and transient nature of life. Like
a drifting wisp of smoke I lingered on alone as the
year changed.

27 (1306)

In the beginning of the third month I went to
Iwashimizu Hachiman Shrine, as was my custom
early each year. Since the new year I had been living
in Nara, hearing little but the cries of the deer, and
so I had no inkling of an imperial visitor to the
shrine. As usual I took the Inohana path, and when
I saw that the residence facing the riding ground
was open, I recalled that long-ago meeting.[29] At the
main part of the shrine I noticed trappings indicat-
ing an imperial visit and inquired who was making
the pilgrimage. Upon being told that Empress Yūgi
was here I was deeply moved, for in the light of the
dream I had had last year it seemed a fateful event.
I spent the entire night in prayer. At dawn I saw a
shy, low-ranking court lady busy making preparations and approached her to ask who she was. She
told me her name was Otoranu. With some emotion
I inquired about life at the palace, only to discover
that all the court ladies who had served in my day
were gone. Now there were only young people.

Wanting somehow to reveal my identity, I decided to look on from afar as Empress Yūgi made

the rounds of the shrine. I waited for her without even returning to my lodging for breakfast. When I heard her arrival announced, I hid in a corner and watched as her imposing palanquin was carried up before the shrine. The man charged with presenting the *nusa* offering was Saionji Sanekane's son Kanesue, who bore such a striking resemblance to his father in the days when I had known him as a young captain of the guard that I was deeply moved.

Because today was the eighth, the ladies set out to visit the Toganoo Shrine. They rode in an informal procession in two plain wicker palanquins, and since no one recognized me, I was able to trail along and observe Her Majesty by going on foot in the company of two young court ladies. When we had arrived at the shrine and Empress Yūgi was worshiping, I stood staring at her back, weeping openly without any thought of hiding or fleeing.

After she had finished her devotions and turned around, the empress saw me. "Where are you from?" she inquired. Though I longed to speak of the past, I simply said, "I'm from Nara." "From the Hokke nunnery?" she asked, and must have thought it strange that my only response was a flood of tears. I felt I should leave with these few words, but I was so benumbed with grief that I stood as if fixed to the spot, loath to part from Her Majesty even though it was already time for her to return. We were standing at the top of some high, steep steps, and she was obviously uncertain about going down. I drew closer and said, "Lean on my shoulder as you descend." She gave me a puzzled look. "I used to attend you when you were very young," I explained.

"Don't you recognize me?" And I burst out weeping again.

Empress Yūgi kindly inquired about me. "Now you must come and see me often," she said. I recalled my dream and my accidental meeting with Emperor GoFukakusa at this very shrine, and I rejoiced that my secret faith had not been in vain.

One of the court ladies I had been walking with had told me in our conversations that her name was Hyōe no Suke. Around dusk that evening I broke off a branch of cherry blossoms and sent it to Hyōe no Suke's quarters with this promise: "I'll come to call on you at the palace before these blossoms have scattered." Empress Yūgi was to return to the capital the next day, so *kagura* dances and other religious entertainments were performed that night.

I had originally planned to leave early the next morning before Her Majesty's departure, but my feelings of deep gratitude toward Hachiman Bodhisattva for causing our meeting prompted me to remain at the shrine for three more days. When I arrived in the capital I sent a note to my friend at the palace inquiring about the blossoms:

> Have the blossoms now
> Been swept by the summoning wind?
> My promise must seem emptier
> With each passing day.

This was her reply:

> Why should the blossoms
> Yield to the gusts of wind,
> Though the day you promised
> Is now long past?

From then on, the frequent letters I received from Empress Yūgi's palace warded off my loneliness and even revived feelings I had known in the past.

Early in the seventh month Empress Yūgi went to Fushimi Palace for the commemoration of the third anniversary of GoFukakusa's death. I also wanted to participate in the services on this somber occasion, but I was distressed to realize that this year, with no more keepsakes remaining to me, I would not even be able to complete the one sutra left to copy. At least I could go to Fushimi and participate in the observances as an outsider, and so at dawn on the fifteenth I visited GoFukakusa's tomb in Fukakusa and worshiped before a newly painted portrait of His Majesty that hung in the Lotus Hall. How trivial this life must seem to one beyond the grave. I was unable to contain my tears, and the nearby worshipers and priests participating in the services recognized that my grief was unusual and invited me to come up closer. I went forward and worshiped with a sense of relief mingled with wonderment at the tears I still had.

> You disappeared like dew—
> Now your image here
> Causes dew to fall afresh
> Once more on these sleeves.

By the light of the clear moon of the fifteenth night, I went to Hyōe no Suke's quarters, where we talked for a long while of our lives in the past and present. Feeling restless when I left, I lingered for a while near the Myōshōin until I heard someone call, "They're bringing it now." What was happening, I learned, was that the portrait of His Majesty

I had viewed this morning at Fukakusa was being brought here by four men, apparently underservants, who carried it in and placed it on a special stand. The two men in charge wore dark robes and seemed to be priestly artists. A custodian and a pair of imperial guards also stood by as the paper-wrapped portrait was brought in. I watched this as if I were in a dream. Though I had no memories of GoFukakusa's reign as emperor, when he had commanded ten thousand troops and directed a hundred governmental bureaus, I could remember serving him when he held the title of Retired Sovereign. In those days, even on the most informal excursions, high nobles had always awaited his carriage, and courtiers had constantly attended him. At the thought of him now, wandering unattended on the unknown roads of death, a pang of grief seized me as if for the first time.

At dawn I received a letter from the Madenokōji senior counselor Moroshige,[30] who wrote: "I am given to understand that you are nearby. How did you feel last night?" I responded with this poem:

> Shrilling insects and the moon,
> Parts of a lingering sadness—
> His visage in the cloudless night.

On the sixteenth, at a service in praise of the *Lotus Sutra*, statues of the Buddhas Shakamune and Tahō were placed on a single lotus dais. Other elaborate services were also conducted. The arrival of Cloistered Emperor Fushimi meant that strangers like myself were strictly prohibited in the courtyards and buildings. I was annoyed to be kept at a distance, and frowned on because of my dark robes, but I was bent on hearing the services, even though —as it turned out—I had to stand by a dripstone under the rain gutter. I thought enviously of my old position, longing for the past I had renounced, until after the reading of prayer strips and the confessional service I could no longer contain my tears. A priest of some rank standing beside me asked, "Whom do you mourn so?" Though GoFukakusa was long dead, I felt constrained and said only, "I have lost someone as close to me as a parent. The service marking the end of this period of mourning affects me deeply." Whereupon I left hastily.

That evening, after Their Majesties' return to the capital left the palace quiet and nearly empty, I began to feel forlorn in spite of myself. It did not seem time to go home yet, so I lingered for a while near the palace.

At this time I was still maintaining a correspondence with a close relative, the former Koga minister.[31] In response to one of my letters he had written:

> Here in the capital
> Autumn's mood is upon me.
> Will you linger many nights
> To see Fushimi's moon at dawn?

His solicitude did not make my grief easier to bear.

> Memories of the past—
> Three autumns gone,
> Three nights at Fushimi,
> Dawn moon tinged with grief.

He replied:

> Indeed, the past
> Must seem the present
> In Fushimi now
> With autumn's melancholy.

On the fifteenth I had given a fan to Empress Yūgi, thinking she might want to offer it to the priests. On the face of the fan I had written:

> My lord has been gone three years!
> How strange that I am yet alive,
> Autumn's dew once more
> Staining sleeves that never dried.

After GoFukakusa's death I had felt as though there were no one with whom I could share my feelings. Then last year on the eighth day of the third month I held a service in memory of Hitomaro, and on the exact same day of this year I met Empress Yūgi. Amazingly, the jewellike image I had seen in my dream became real.[32] Now I am anxious about the outcome of my long-cherished desire, and I worry lest the faith I have kept these many years prove fruitless. When I attempted to live in lonely seclusion, I felt dissatisfied and set out on pilgrimages modeled after those of Saigyō, whom I have always admired and wanted to emulate. That all my dreams might not prove empty, I have been writing this useless account—though I doubt it will long survive me.[33]

Notes

1. In 1271 GoFukakusa was a twenty-nine-year-old retired emperor, and Lady Nijō, fourteen years old, was one of his ladies-in-waiting. According to the lunar calendar used in premodern Japan, the first day of the new year came in late January or February and marked the official beginning of spring.

2. On the first three mornings of the new year various kinds of spiced *sake*, specially prepared by the Bureau of Medicine and tasted by young maidens, were formally served to the emperors and to certain of their officials. This ceremony, known as the medicinal offering (*onkusuri*), was performed to ward off illness in the coming year.

3. The retired emperor is suggesting that Lady Nijō become his concubine by alluding to Section 10 of *Tales of Ise*, a tenth-century collection of lyrical episodes, where a mother requests the hero to marry her daughter. In the poems they exchange a wild goose is used as a metaphor for the girl.

4. This seems to be from Akebono, whose relationship to Lady Nijō at this point is unclear. They later become declared lovers. Lady Nijō's reaction to his gift suggests that their affair is still in its early stages.

5. Court ladies took turns sleeping outside the room of their master or mistress at night.

6. Kawasaki was an area on the northeast edge of the capital, just west of the Kamo River.

7. To satisfy complex taboos that had to do with the avoidance of unlucky directions, people were often forced to spend a night away from their permanent residences. This was especially common on the eve of the spring seasonal change,

a date determined by a solar calendar rather than the official lunar one.

8. A girl wore shoulder-length hair parted in the middle until her coming-of-age ceremony, when a piece of it was tied up on top of her head.

9. This poem is from Akebono. It alludes to Section 112 of *Tales of Ise:* "After many earnest declarations of devotion to a certain man, a lady fell in love with someone else. The first man composed this poem: Captured by the gale, the smoke from the salt-fires of the fisherfolk at Suma has drifted off in an unforeseen direction." Translated by Helen Craig McCullough (Stanford University Press, 1968), p. 144.

10. By Fujiwara Masatsune. Poem 1094 in the *Shinkokinshū*, an imperial anthology completed in 1206.

11. An allusion to Poem 712 in the *Kokinshū*, the first imperial anthology, compiled around 905: "If this were a world without lies, how happy your words would make me."

12. An allusion to *The Tale of Genji.* This line is from the poem Prince Genji composed in exile at Suma when he shed tears of bitterness and affection as he thought about the emperor who had banished him.

13. Another allusion to *The Tale of Genji.* This line is from the poem of foreboding that Yūgao composed when Genji, without revealing his identity, took her to a deserted mansion where she later died: "Unaware of the shape of the mountain peak the moon courses through the sky. Will its light be blotted out?"

14. This was one of the buildings on the grounds of Go-Fukakusa's Tomi Street Palace.

15. *Shinkokinshū* Poem 1843 by Fujiwara Kiyosuke: "Will I live to cherish memories of these days too? What once was sad now seems dear."

16. These deities are all part of the enormous pantheon revered by esoteric Buddhist sects. The Koga family, which Nijō's father Masatada headed, had considerable property in Owari province, and a member of the family or one of their retainers usually served as governor.

17. Fudō is the most important of the great guardian kings (*myōō*), deities who represent the fierce aspect of Buddha and who are believed to quell all kinds of evil spirits. Fudō

is a well-known figure in Japanese popular religion as well as in esoteric Buddhism. The legend of Shōkū's petition to Fudō is related by Lady Nijō in Chapter 25 below. The line chanted here is from the *Fudō Sutra*.

18. The Shinto shrines that received propitiatory offerings from the imperial court whenever an important event occurred.

19. According to historical records, Empress Higashi-Nijō gave birth to a girl, the future Empress Yūgi, in 1270, not in 1271. Lady Nijō probably changed the date to give her tale better structural unity.

20. Unfortunately the translation of this description is mostly guesswork, for the Japanese original is basically unintelligible.

21. A mountain in eastern China (south of Peking) where souls of the dead were believed to go. The god of Mount Tai (Taizan buku) was believed to control the span of human life and was often appealed to by masters of divination and Buddhist priests.

22. Moxa cautery was a common form of treatment for various illnesses. A small amount of dried *yomogi* leaf was placed on the patient's skin and burned.

23. The Kamakura Bakufu, the military government controlling the country, had two Kyoto deputies who resided in the Rokuhara district on the southeast edge of Kyoto. These deputies, who had full authority in Kyoto except in matters of the highest national importance, were chosen from the Hōjō family and often became Kamakura regents. In 1272 the Rokuhara deputies were Tokisuke and Yoshimune. Tokisuke, the elder but illegitimate brother of the Hōjō regent Tokimune, was plotting a rebellion. The regent discovered the plot, killed or captured the conspirators in Kamakura, and ordered Yoshimune to kill Tokisuke.

24. An allusion to *Kokinshū* Poem 832 by Munetsuke Mineo: "Cherries of Fukakusa, if you have a heart, this year at least blossom in black."

25. The color of mourning was determined by one's relationship to the deceased; the closer the relationship, the deeper the shade.

26. Masatada's father, Prime Minister Michimitsu, died in 1248, and there seems to have been a family quarrel over the

inheritance. Masatada's real mother was already dead, and as a result of this disagreement with his stepmother, he appears to have been disowned.

27. Intensive mourning lasted for forty-nine days after a death. During this period the dead person's spirit was believed to be wandering in a void between incarnations. Therefore the bereaved family remained together and held Buddhist services every seven days.

28. This refers to the succession dispute between GoFukakusa and Kameyama that is described in the Introduction.

29. Emperor GoToba was banished to the Oki Islands in the Sea of Japan, north of Izumo, in 1221 for his part in the Jōkyū disturbances.

30. The dawn of salvation, a time in the immensely distant future when Miroku Buddha is to descend to earth to teach salvation.

31. This congratulatory ceremony expressed the father's recognition of the yet-unborn child.

32. These phrases are from the Chinese poet Po Chü-i's poem, "A Song of Unending Sorrow." One of the most popular Chinese poems in Japan, it describes the love of the emperor for his concubine Yang Kuei-fei.

33. The eldest son and heir of Nakatsuna, Masatada's faithful steward.

34. From the lines recited at the ceremony of initiation into Buddhist orders: "Caught in the vicissitudes of the three realms of unenlightened men one cannot break the bonds of affection. To throw away affection and enter the eternal way is to truly repay obligations."

35. Mototomo (1232–97) was Lady Nijō's second cousin. He seems to have been in competition with Masatada for rank and position, but no specific reason for this reference is known. Mototomo held the position of prime minister briefly in 1289, and his granddaughter was GoUda's empress and Emperor GoNijō's mother.

36. For Emperor GoSaga. The visitor, who remains nameless, was probably Akebono.

37. Mandarin ducks are considered love birds because they remain with a single mate. Po Chü-i refers to one-winged birds in "A Song of Unending Sorrow": "May we fly through the heavens as one-winged birds united."

38. From Akebono.

39. Throughout this scene there are allusions to Section 5 of *Tales of Ise*, where the hero visits a girl by stealing over a dilapidated wall.

40. This bird (*kuina*), which winters in the Kyoto area, has a metallic cry that is thought to sound like the clanging of a bell.

41. A character in the twelfth century tale *Sagoromo monogatari*, who is humorously portrayed as a vulgar, ignorant woman.

42. The Dogo spa near Matsuyama in Shikoku, formerly Iyo province, was famous for the many boards laid around its hot springs. This was a common metaphor for a large number.

43. In *The Tale of Genji* the hero is sorely distressed by the uncouth sounds he hears when he spends the night at Yūgao's humble home.

44. Another reference to *The Tale of Genji*. Kumoi's nurse discovers Yūgiri visiting her charge and complains that he is only of the sixth rank and therefore in too humble a position to court Kumoi.

45. It was inappropriate to visit the shrine because she was in mourning for her father. There is no extant record of this dream, but recording dreams was a common practice. The face she saw was probably that of her dead father.

46. At this point in the succession dispute, Kameyama had the upper hand.

47. A woman usually gave birth in an upright position.

48. It was customary for an emperor to present a sword to a newborn son, and after the tenth century to a daughter as well.

49. Here I have omitted three lines of very garbled text.

50. This palace, which was originally built in 1184, had been inherited by GoFukakusa in 1272. At least part of it burned down in 1273 and was not rebuilt until 1275.

51. When Lady Nijō's pregnancy was in its fifth month, the time maternity sashes were usually presented.

52. A line from *Shinkokinshū* Poem 470 by Emperor Go-Toba.

53. This passage suggests a scene in *The Tale of Genji* after Lady Aoi had given birth to Yūgiri and immediately before she died.

54. The customary period of defilement after childbirth.

55. This description has intrigued art historians because neither of the extant scrolls of Saigyō's pilgrimages contains the poem or the scene depicted here.

56. According to the Confucian code a woman is subject first to her father, then to her husband, and finally to her son.

57. In establishing a retired emperor's office Kameyama, GoFukakusa's younger brother, was preparing to take over as chief retired emperor, the position GoFukakusa felt entitled to.

58. Ōmiya, mother of both GoFukakusa and Kameyama, favored her younger son Kameyama.

59. Sanekane was the lover Lady Nijō called Akebono. This and what follows suggest that Takaaki and GoFukakusa knew of the liaison.

60. A short woodwind with two reeds and the sound of a high-pitched oboe. The *koto* is a Japanese zither with six, seven, or thirteen strings, and the *biwa* is a kind of lute.

61. She puns on the word *sakana*, which may mean either tidbits to eat with *sake* or entertainment, and alludes to this folk song: "The pretty· jar of *sake* is set among the guests. 'Hey there, our host, look for some food. Bring us some food.' 'To the shore of Koyurugi I will go to gather seaweed.'"

62. An *imayō* or popular song of the period; it is unknown except for this reference. The song is based on a poem by Po Chü-i called "The Charcoal Seller."

63. Both the crane and the tortoise are traditional auspicious symbols for longevity.

64. Types of clothing and carriages were strictly regulated according to the rank of the owner. Only women of high standing were permitted to wear three-layered gowns.

65. Both boys and girls put on their first pleated trousers (*hakama*) in a ceremony called *chakugo* when they were between three and seven years old. Usually the most distinguished of the child's relatives performed the honorary task of tying the sash of the trousers.

66. Rather than at the gate, as lower-ranking people had to do.

67. Nijō means Second Avenue. Court ladies were often given the names of streets, which were ranked according to

their prestige. Nijō was one of the higher-ranking names. Her father's attitude toward this name is not at all clear.

68. Nijō's father was the eighth generation from Prince Tomohira.

69. This refers to the Corner Mansion, which was turned into a residence for GoFukakusa's son, the future Emperor Fushimi, when he was made crown prince. The Great Willow Hall must have been named for a tree in its garden.

BOOK TWO

1. The commonest contest with men opposing women was the *ensho awase*, an informal love poetry contest. Whatever the contest was, it is not described.

2. This ceremony took place on the fifteenth day of the first month. Sticks made to stir a special rice gruel were afterward used to strike women on the loins in the hope that they would conceive male children.

3. The years thought to be inauspicious for men were generally their twenty-fifth and forty-second, while women could expect bad luck when they were nineteen and thirty-three.

4. Carving up the live fish would violate the Buddhist precept against killing. Ryūben belonged to the Shijō family, famous for its culinary skills.

5. The paternal grandmother was Michimitsu's wife, the Koga nun, who was only Nijō's step-grandmother. The identity of the aunt is unclear.

6. In the Japanese text it is not clear who made these reparations, Sanekane or his grandmother, Lady Kitayama.

7. The Chōkō Temple was important because its endowments constituted the major portion of the imperial revenues.

8. The abbot of the Ninna Temple, although Lady Nijō does not identify him. She later calls him Ariake.

9. The fourth son of Masatada's steward, Nakatsuna; he was a private secretary to Kameyama.

10. It was customary to remain in the house and not change clothes for three days after a move.

11. It was believed that when an article of clothing or a paper doll was rubbed against an ailing body, the ailment would be transferred to the article itself, which was then presented to a priest or diviner, who prayed over it and ceremoniously disposed of it.

12. "Paths of darkness" is a familiar metaphor for love—the passion and attachment of which kept one chained to this world. This line is taken from *The Tale of Genji*.

13. A well-known line from a poem in *The Tale of Genji*: "Not even to fishers that on the shore of Suma their faggots burn must we reveal the smouldering ashes of our love." Translated by Arthur Waley (The Modern Library, 1960), p. 243.

14. The last part of *Shinkokinshū* Poem 400. The poem begins, "Don't forget the sky of Naniwa on autumn nights."

15. This village was conventionally linked in poetry with a white shrub commonly known as the "flower of sadness."

16. She seems to have removed the gown with the large crimson fans she wore earlier. The Japanese text further specifies that the two-layered gown was white with green lining, had small sleeves, and was made of glossy raw silk.

17. This line is from a poem in *The Tale of Genji*: "Where snow-drifts were deepest, where the ice gave under my feet, unerring I found my way; it was only about you that I was lost" (Waley, p. 1019).

18. Full-fledged nuns were actually supposed to keep 348 precepts (monks were only bound by 250).

19. An area on the northeast edge of the capital, it was named after a temple that had once been there.

20. *Kokinshū* Poem 1023: "From my pillow and from the foot of my bed love comes pursuing. What am I to do? I'll stay in the middle of the bed!" Translated by Donald Keene, *Japanese Literature* (New York, Grove Press, 1955), p. 56.

21. According to Buddhist thought the human spirit can be reborn into six realms: the realms of hell, hungry ghosts, beasts, *asuras*, men, or heaven. The first three are the lower realms.

22. In *The Tale of Genji*. To show off her spring garden, Murasaki no Ue held an elaborate party for Empress Akikon-omu's ladies.

23. A kickball field had a different kind of tree in each of its four corners: a willow in the southeast, a cherry in the northeast, a pine in the northwest, and a maple in the southwest. The trees were often potted in tubs so they could be moved. The object was gracefully to keep the ball from falling to the ground. It was normally played by men.

24. Another allusion to *The Tale of Genji*: "Startled from my dream by a wandering gust of the mountain gale, I heard the waterfall, and at the beauty of its music wept" (Waley, p. 90).

25. The *gosechi* dances were normally performed in the eleventh month; here Kameyama is entertaining his guests by imitating that occasion.

26. Murasaki no Ue was Genji's favorite, but not his official wife. Onna Sannomiya (called Nyosan by Waley) was the daughter of ex-Emperor Suzaku and became Genji's official wife late in his life.

27. Nyogo no Kimi was Akashi no Ue's daughter (Waley calls her Princess Akashi).

28. This probably refers to the move to the new Sixth Street Palace (described in Chapter 8) when Nijō rode in the first carriage on the left, the position reserved for the highest-ranking court lady.

29. A line from *Shinkokinshū* Poem 330: "I cannot pass by without plucking bush clover even though my dyed gowns are dampened by the dew."

30. Emperor GoUda, Kameyama's son, was eleven; Crown Prince Fushimi, son of GoFukakusa, was thirteen.

31. The poem he wrote the first night they made love (Chapter 8).

32. The name of Amida Buddha is invoked ten times with the phrase *Namu Amida Butsu*. Amida and his two Bodhisattva companions, Kannon and Seishi, are believed to descend to welcome the faithful to paradise.

33. The hero of the old tale *Sumiyoshi monogatari* discovered his sweetheart hiding with some nuns at Sumiyoshi by means of a vision.

34. The area near Fushimi Palace where she had gone after fleeing the party.

35. Sugawara Kiyonaga was a high-ranking man in the service of GoFukakusa. He also had close connections with the Koga family.

36. A person's true feelings, even if they were subconscious, were thought to exert an influence on someone else's health. The jealous spirit of Lady Rokujō in *The Tale of Genji* killed several of Genji's lovers unknown to Lady Rokujō herself.

37. A line from Poem 332 in the *Shikashū*, the sixth anthology, completed about 1154. Izumi Shikibu claimed she wrote this poem "when I was bitter toward a man": "I did not consider the mountain peak evil, yet even there seeds of human sorrow flourish."

38. The text does not make it clear where they spent the night.

39. This is the end of the fourth month. No further reference is ever made to this pregnancy or to the birth or abortion of the child.

40. Babies' heads were shaved. The child was not quite three years old by Western count.

41. Historical sources reveal that Sanekane had several daughters, three of whom became empresses, but there is no way of knowing if any of these daughters was actually Lady Nijō's child. Because the *Masukagami* suggests that Lady Nijō rode in Empress Eifuku's wedding procession, scholars have speculated that Lady Nijō might have been her mother. Eifuku became Emperor Fushimi's consort.

42. In 1277 Takatsukasa Kanehira, then fifty years old, was both regent to the boy emperor and prime minister.

43. The island paradise to the east described in Chinese cosmology. GoFukakusa is alluding to Po Chü-i's poem, "A Song of Unending Sorrow," in which the emperor sends a diviner to find his dead sweetheart Yang Kuei-fei, who is at Mount Hōrai.

44. To be in the service of two families was normally forbidden. In this case, moreover, the two families were technically not of the same rank, for Kanetsune was a regent. Hence his offer indicates the high status of the Koga family.

45. The poem she wrote when leaving the palace after her quarrel with Takachika (Chapter 11).

46. *Imayō*. These songs were in effect the popular music of the court.

47. This term was used both for a type of song and dance and for the female entertainers who performed it.

48. Japanese commentators suggest she has a tryst with Akebono, and the description of her return bears out this interpretation.

49. This was a common folk belief. It is also referred to in *The Tale of Genji* (Waley, p. 68).

50. Presumably it was Kanehira, although Lady Nijō never identifies him directly.

51. Based on one of the many legends about Priest Sōō, this *imayō* refers to an episode in which the priest's prayers split the image of Fudō when he was attempting to cure Empress Somedono of a possession. She was possessed by the spirit of High Priest Kakinomoto no Ki, who was in love with her when he died. Lady Nijō and Takaaki are reminded of her relationship with the priest Ariake.

52. Trained cormorants tethered by the neck are put into the water to catch fish. This art is still practiced today as a tourist attraction.

BOOK THREE

1. Empress Kyōgoku, consort of Emperor Uda (reigned 887–97), according to one version of the legend.

2. Fuyutada, a high-ranking member of the Ōmikado family, courted Sukedai before she married Masatada, Nijō's father. Both men were twenty years older than GoFukakusa.

3. When they met at Takaaki's, and Lady Nijō vowed never to see him again (Chapter 10).

4. This line is from *Kokinshū* Poem 1042: "Vowing to love no more I purified myself in holy waters. And yet the gods did not accept my ablutions." A variant of this poem appears in *Tales of Ise*, Section 65.

5. An implement used in Buddhist services. It is a small rod with five prongs on each end to represent five kinds of wisdom.

6. GoFukakusa and Ariake were both sons of Emperor GoSaga, but by different mothers.

7. A recondite allusion to an episode in *The Tale of Genji* in which Genji hints to his wife, Onna Sannomiya, that he knows Kaoru is not really his child but is willing to accept him as such.

8. The fifth day of the fifth month was the date of the Iris Festival (*ayame no sekku*).

9. When Kanehira accosted her (Chapter 13).

10. This poem centers on a common pun on the Japanese word for root (*ne*), which also means the sound of sobbing. His sleeves are wet from the water in which the iris grow and

the tears he sheds. This is actually a variation of Poem 1042 of the *Shinkokinshū*.

11. An allusion to his coming through the broken wall of her nurse's house (Chapter 5). It suggests she is there again.

12. Lady Nijō also puns on *ne*, but she uses it to mean root and sleep, hinting of her affairs with other men.

13. Jōzō (891–964) was a famous ascetic about whom there are many legends. Somedono and the blue ghost appear in various tales, and the story of the lovesick woman is found in several works beginning with the *Manyōshū*.

14. Probably a reference to GoFukakusa's fourth son, who had entered the Ninna Temple in 1278. His vows were administered by Ariake.

15. This poem contains a pun on the nickname of her lover. Ariake no Tsuki means "dawn moon."

16. An elaborate ceremony that occurred in 1270 at the Saga Palace.

17. From *Tales of Ise*, Section 7: "How poignant now my longing for what lies behind—enviable indeed the returning waves" (McCullough, p. 74).

18. The language here is so confusing that what I have described as a set of gongs might be a mirror or a small shrine.

19. This line is from Poem 620 of the *Wakan rōei shū*, a collection of Chinese and Japanese poems compiled about 1013: "I can faintly see the color of the tiles on the tower gate of headquarters. I can barely hear the tolling of the bell at the temple of Kannon." The poem was written by Sugawara Michizane (845–903) while he was in exile at a governmental outpost in Kyushu. GoFukakusa's audience appreciated his skill at matching a classical poem with their own situation—a palace outside the capital, the sound of bells.

20. A felicitous poem (774) in the *Wakan rōei shū*: "Days of good fortune, auspicious months, our joy is boundless. A thousand autumns, ten thousand years, happiness without end."

21. According to contemporary beliefs, the third and most degenerate period of the world (*mappō*) began in 1052. In this ten-thousand-year period only the doctrine of Buddhism would survive, enlightenment and practice having disappeared in earlier epochs. This belief did not preclude hopes of entering paradise, however.

22. Kameyama is stretching the point. In *The Tale of Genji* Suzaku and Genji are half brothers, but Onna Sannomiya is Suzaku's daughter, not his concubine. The section describing the events of this night is vague and confusing, perhaps because Lady Nijō meant it to be. The interpretation upon which this translation is based is only one of several possibilities.

23. GoFukakusa had a short-lived affair with the former high priestess (Chapter 6).

24. A line from a poem Genji recited while in exile at Suma. Waley gives an expanded translation: "The Gods at least, the myriad Gods look kindly on my fate, knowing that sinful though I be, no penalty have I deserved such as I suffer in this desolate place" (pp. 253–54).

25. GoFukakusa's consort and Empress Ōmiya's younger sister, Higashi-Nijō, was fifty, Lady Nijō was twenty-four, and GoFukakusa was thirty-nine.

26. An example of the amalgam of Buddhist and Shinto practices in Japanese religion. Buddhist monks from the Kōfuku Temple in Nara frequently carried the tree that represented the Shinto god body (*shintai*) of the Kasuga Shrine into the capital to frighten the court into compliance with their demands.

27. Ariake is unwilling to dedicate the sutras directly to Buddha lest he be reborn in paradise. He would rather be reborn in this world, be united with Lady Nijō, and then dedicate the sutras so that they might attain paradise together. The dragon king is a popular figure in Buddhist lore, but the reference here is obscure.

28. An allusion to *Kokinshū* Poem 80, which was written by an ill poet: "Behind my curtain, unaware of the passing of spring—even the blossoms that waited have faded and fallen."

29. From a poem Genji wrote following the death of Murasaki no Ue: "Whilst I in heedless grief have let the days go by, together now the year and my own life are ebbing to their close" (Waley, p. 743).

30. *Fusatsu*: a semimonthly assembly where monks heard Buddhist doctrine expounded and confessed their sins.

31. Higashiyama is a large area with many temples in the

eastern hills of Kyoto. This is the most explicit statement Lady Nijō makes about her whereabouts during this period.

32. There are chronological problems here. Lady Nijō claims that the last time she saw Ariake was eight days after she had given birth to their first child, an unlikely time for her to have become pregnant. However, Lady Nijō's date for Ariake's death does not coincide with any of the varying dates given in historical records.

33. Poem 883 from the Senzaishū, the seventh imperial anthology, completed about 1188: "Love is overwhelming—bitterness, unable to hold its own, returns to the road of love."

34. He was only six months old by Western count.

35. The green vines refer to Lady Nijō because of the design on her gown.

36. The most plausible date for this section is 1283, but according to other sources Takachika died in 1279. Later Lady Nijō refers to Takachika's death in the autumn of 1283.

37. This statement suggests that Takaaki has died, but his death date is not recorded in official sources, and Lady Nijō is surprisingly quiet on the subject.

38. An alternate Japanese system of enumerating events is based on a cycle that utilizes a series of twelve animal names (e.g., the hare, the horse). Kagura is a term for Shinto music and dances. Kagura is traditionally performed at Iwashimizu Hachiman Shrine to the south of Kyoto on the first day of the hare in both the spring and the fall. However, Lady Nijō has made a mistake in dating here, for the first day of the hare did not coincide with the second day of the eleventh month in any year between 1278 and 1287.

39. High Priest Jōsei (1129-99), who was intendant of the Hachiman Shrine, went to see kagura and wrote this poem (Shinkokinshū Poem 1887): "I never cease to give my heart to the gods—in vain I tie my paper poems to sacred trees."

40. This poem and the one she has just alluded to contain puns on objects used in Shinto worship: yu, "mulberry bark," and yudasuki, "mulberry bark sash."

41. At the beginning of 1284 the child was seventeen months old.

42. The Bun'ei era was 1264-74. This poem (with one different line) appears as Poem 2732 of the Gyokuyōshū, the

fourteenth imperial anthology, completed around 1313. It is attributed to the Gion god, with a note explaining that the god revealed it to a man in a dream.

43. Empress Ōmiya's nephew as well as Lady Nijō's former lover Akebono.

44. The festivities were held at the Saionji family's Kitayama mansion on the northwest outskirts of the capital, where Lady Kitayama resided.

45. I have omitted from this paragraph the following two sections, which list some of the other participants by their long titles. I have abbreviated these titles and added personal names: "I could hear the solemn tolling of the bell accompanying the chanting of the sutras. To the east of the sutra table sat the regent Kanehira; the ministers of the left and right, Morotada and Tadanori; the major counselors Nagamasa, Sadazane, Michiyori, Nobutsugu, Michimoto, Sanekane and Kanetada; and the middle counselors Saneshige, Ienori, and Kinhira. To the west of the stairs were the major counselors Takayuki, Tomomori, and Kinmori, and the imperial advisers Takayasu and Motoaki. . . . Kanetada and Michimoto, the major captains of the left and right, and Motoaki, chief of the right division of the palace guards, carried bows and wore quivers of arrows on their backs."

46. *Keirōko*, a small drum with two leather heads imported from China. It was hung around the neck and played with sticks held in both hands. A drummer is the usual conductor of court music (*gagaku*).

47. Lady Nijō lists their names: "Shigetsune, Akinori, Nakakane, Akiyo, Kanenaka, and Chikauji."

48. The two major divisions of court music are labeled left and right. Music of the left is of Indian and Chinese origins, while music of the right came from Korea. The pieces performed are named in the text: "the left danced *Manzairaku, Kakubyōshi, Kaden,* and *Ryō-ō;* while the right performed *Chikyū, Engiraku,* and *Nasori.*"

49. Here I have omitted the following sentences: "The middle commanders Kin'atsu and Tamekane and a minor commander wore the formal robes of military officials, with flat ceremonial quivers on their backs. Other officials wore civilian robes and carried swords with leather thongs or, more often, narrow swords."

50. Pieces entitled *Kaikotsu* and *Chōkeishi*.

51. It was a common practice to give names to valuable objects such as musical instruments and swords.

52. The text lists the following: "In the *ryō* scale, *Anatoto* and *Mushiroda*, two sections of a *gaku* called *Tori*, a piece in the *ritsu* scale called *Aoyanagi*, *Manzairaku*, and a section of *Sandai*."

53. Again Lady Nijō includes a long list of the participants: "The regent Kanehira; the ministers Morotada, Tadanori, and Mototomo; the major counselors Yoshinori, Tameuji, Nagamasa, Michimoto, Sadazane, Sanekane, Nobutsugu, and Kinnori; the middle counselors Kin'yasu, Saneshige, Ienori, and Kinhira; the imperial advisers Takayasu and Tameyo; and Takahiro, a chamberlain of the third rank."

54. Here the text contains two glosses added by early copyists to help identify the emperor: "That emperor is known as Zenjō Sen'in." "He is now the cloistered emperor of the junior line."

55. Lady Kitayama. Teishi was her personal name.

56. The text adds: "He seemed to be following an old precedent when he added the character for 'to present.'"

57. An elaborate service held in 1259 at the Kitayama mansion. Empress Ōmiya, Saneuji's daughter and GoSaga's consort, had requested the ceremony, which is described in the *Masukagami*.

58. *Kokinshū* Poem 68: "Mountain village blossoms. No one will see you there. If only you could bloom after the others have fallen." The implication is that then people would come especially to view them.

59. The text gives these names: "*Saishōrō*, three sections from *Sogō*, *Hakuchū*, and *Senshūraku*." These pieces are all in the *banshikichō* mode.

60. Based on *Wakan rōei shū* Poem 113 by Chang Fu: "Blossoms glow in the imperial garden; swift carts raise dust on main streets. Deep in the mountains monkeys shriek; the moon sparkles on roads through rock."

61. *Wakan rōei shū* Poem 466 by Sugawara no Michizane: "Dancer dressed in layers of fine silk; how hateful the weaver who made them; the piece they play is exceeding long, how cruel the musicians unwilling to stop."

62. Formal dress was more elaborate and included a train.

63. The tunes given here are also in the *banshikichō* mode: "Five sections of *Sogō, Rindai, Seikaiha, Chikurinraku, Etenraku.*"

64. *Wakan rōei shū* Poem 596 by Ōe no Aki: "Mountains beyond mountains; whose skill carved those blue-black peaks? River follows river; what artist dyed those jade-green streams?"

65. Kameyama is alluding to a poem by Po Chü-i. A *li* is approximately a third of a mile.

66. Poetry composed by two or more people contributing alternate verses of seventeen and fourteen syllables.

BOOK FOUR

1. Because the Japanese used the lunar calendar, the moon always rose late toward the end of each month. Lady Nijō probably set out just before dawn, a rather common departure time.

2. *Shinkokinshū* Poem 1851. It begins: "This kind of life or that, it all comes out the same."

3. Lady Nijō enhances the description of her travels by allusions to earlier literature and the use of natural metaphors to suggest her feelings. This technique, which employs many word plays, later became formalized in the travel songs (*michiyuki*) of classical drama. Here the allusion is to Section 9 of *Tales of Ise*, where the hero traveling east from the capital has "arrived at a place called Yatsuhashi in Mikawa Province. It was a spot where the waters of a river branched into eight channels, each with a bridge, and thus it had come to be called Yatsuhashi—'Eight Bridges'" (McCullough, p. 74).

4. Another allusion to Section 9 of *Tales of Ise*: "At Mount Fuji a pure white snow had fallen, even though it was the end of the fifth month. 'Fuji is a mountain that knows no season. What time does it take this for, that it should be dappled with fallen snow?'" (McCullough, p. 76).

5. Poem 1613 of the *Shinkokinshū*: "The wisps of smoke from Fuji yield to the wind and lose themselves in sky, in emptiness—where go the aimless passions too that through my life burned deep inside." Translated by William LaFleur. Saigyō was the poet-priest Lady Nijō had long admired.

6. Another reference to Section 9 of *Tales of Ise*: "At Mount Utsu the road they were to follow was dark, narrow, and overgrown with ivy and maples" (McCullough, p. 75).

7. The references to the dragon and to the "ten thousand prayers," literally "ten thousand beaches" (*hama no ichiman*), are unclear. Minamoto no Yoritomo (1147-99) was the founder of the Kamakura Bakufu.

8. This is the only reference Lady Nijō makes to a servant, though it is highly unlikely that she would travel without at least one.

9. One of several *torii* (gates to Shinto shrines) associated with the Tsurugaoka Hachiman Shrine. The shrine had originally been built on the beach, but was moved to a hill inside Kamakura by Yoritomo in 1180.

10. In Chapter 4 Lady Nijō described a visit to the Iwashimizu Shrine in 1273 to pray for her father's soul. She mentioned a vision but did not explain it.

11. The location of the Iwashimizu Hachiman Shrine south of Kyoto.

12. In the Kamakura period *daimyō* were the lords of large estates who, in theory at least, owed their allegiance to the Kamakura government, whose titular head was the shogun.

13. A ceremony of freeing captive birds and fish, which is held at many Hachiman shrines on September 15 (the fifteenth of the eighth month in Lady Nijō's time). The ceremony reflects the Buddhist prohibition against taking life.

14. Hachiman, the god worshiped at both Tsurugaoka and Iwashimizu, was the patron god of the Minamoto clan, of which Lady Nijō was a member. Here she is complaining that this relationship has been of no use to her.

15. The most powerful man in the Kamakura government at this time.

16. The shogun, the imperial prince Koreyasu, was deposed by the government because of a political disturbance in Kamakura in 1289.

17. Banished criminals and traitors were traditionally condemned to ride this way if they were of high enough rank to be entitled to ride at all.

18. Shogun is an abbreviation of the title Sei-i Taishōgun, which means "barbarian-subduing generalissimo."

19. The poem was on one level a description of Kitano Shrine in the snow, while on another level it requested the gods to clear the shogun's name of the unjust accusations that had been made against him. Prince Munetaka (1242[?]–

74) was deposed in 1266 when he attempted to assert some independence.

20. I have omitted an incomplete sentence and a copyist's note from the beginning of this chapter: "As the end of the year approached, I realized with some disappointment that I had not been able to carry out my plans to visit Zenkō Temple, yet Lady Komachi's . . . (Here a section has been cut out. It is unfortunate. I wonder what it said.) . . . which I felt was most unusual."

21. The Kiso plank road was on the route from Kyoto to Zenkō Temple, not between Musashino and Zenkō Temple. This geographical error may indicate that Lady Nijō never went to Zenkō Temple. On the other hand, Kiso was a place with many poetic associations, which Lady Nijō may have mentioned for purely literary purposes.

22. This statue of Amida is believed to have been made of gold by the Buddha himself. It was received as a gift from the King of Korea in 552, and many attempts to destroy it were made until 602, when it was taken to Nagano, where Zenkō Temple was later built to house it.

23. "At the end of the road the sky joins Musashino plain; from fields of grass the moon arises." *Shinkokinshū* Poem 422 by Yoshitsune.

24. In this passage Lady Nijō is alluding to several things. Saigyō described the moon over the Musashino plain on the fifteenth of the eighth month. On that same occasion some years before, Genji, in exile at Suma, had gazed at the moon and recalled the words of the exiled poet Sugawara no Michizane that Lady Nijō quotes here: "This night last year I was at the palace; now broken-hearted I compose autumn poems alone. This gown from His Majesty is here with me now; each day I prepare offerings of incense."

25. When the hero of *Tales of Ise* arrived at the Sumida River (in Section 9), he saw a bird named "capital bird" and recited this poem to it: "If you are what your name implies, let me ask you, capital bird, does all go well with my beloved?" (McCullough, p. 76).

26. Lady Nijō is alluding to Poem 758 of the *Shinshokusenshū*, the ninth imperial anthology, completed about 1234: "Whatever I do, at the end of love's road stands a barrier. How far it is to Meeting Mountain."

27. On one level this section is a recapitulation of Lady Nijō's life and current position. When, at the beginning of this work, GoFukakusa asked her father for her hand, he alluded to Section 10 of *Tales of Ise*, using a goose of the fields of Miyoshino as a metaphor for Lady Nijō. Here Nijō learns that Miyoshino's name has been changed; a wild goose sympathizes with her; and all that remains of a famous poetic landmark, the Horikane Well, is a single withered tree. Painfully aware of her changed status in life, Lady Nijō recognizes that not even her travels can really comfort her, and she heads back toward home.

28. *Shinkokinshū* Poem 987: "Aware of advancing age I wondered once if I should ever cross it again, yet here I am alive at Mount Saya no Naka." *Saya no naka* means "in the middle of the night."

29. As becomes apparent later, Lady Nijō had made a vow to copy out in her own hand five of the numerous Mahayana sutras: the *Kegon, Lotus, Wisdom, Nirvana,* and *Great Collection Sutras*. Each of these is made up of a large number of scrolls.

30. The Kasuga Shrine and Kōfuku Temple in Nara were the tutelary houses of worship for the Fujiwara clan.

31. Prince Shōtoku (572–621) is known both for his political reforms and his propagation of Buddhism. He was a popular figure of veneration in Lady Nijō's time, considered by some to be an incarnation of Kannon. The Chūgū Temple was originally constructed as a residence for Prince Shōtoku's mother, and his consort is supposed to have ordered a mandala, fragments of which still exist.

32. This sword, a mirror kept at Ise Shrine, and a jewel at the imperial palace are the three regalia of the Japanese emperor. Because it houses this sword, Atsuta Shrine is considered the second most sacred shrine in Japan; Ise, which is the major shrine to the sun goddess from whom the imperial family was believed to descend, ranks first.

33. Keikō was a prehistoric emperor believed to have reigned from A.D. 71 to 130.

34. Susanoo was the brother of the sun goddess, Amaterasu, whose adventures and mischievous pranks are described in early legends and myths.

35. An allusion to *Shinkokinshū* Poem 217 by Saigyō: "Though I cannot hear them now, this is certainly the place for cuckoo—this grove of cedar at Yamada no Hara." The cuckoo, usually admired for its beautiful voice, was also considered the messenger between this world and the next.

36. *Nusa* are folded strips of paper hung from a vertical stick and used in Shinto purification rites.

37. A chief feature of shrine architecture is the crossed beams (*chigi*), which stick up at each end of the roof. The tips of the *chigi* are cut either horizontally to indicate that a goddess is enshrined within, or vertically for a male god.

38. It was a common though mistaken belief of Lady Nijō's time that since the inner shrine was dedicated to the sun goddess, the outer shrine was dedicated to a moon god.

39. The name Futami means "two looks." According to a Japanese myth recorded in the *Kojiki*, when the goddess Yamatohime was searching for a place to deposit the sacred mirror, this piece of shore so attracted her that she came back for a second look.

40. These lines are taken from an *enkyoku* piece entitled "Sleeve Harbor" (*sode no minato*). *Enkyoku* were songs commonly performed at banquets in the Heian period.

41. Taira no Tadamori's poem, No. 229 in the *Kinyōshū*, the fifth imperial anthology, completed around 1127: "Dawn's moon dims on Akashi Bay where wind-rippled waves are all there is to see."

42. The cosmic figure of esoteric Buddhism; all other Buddhas are thought to be aspects of him. He is sometimes identified with the Shinto sun goddess, Amaterasu.

43. According to Confucian thought, one owed debts of gratitude to heaven, the sovereign, one's parents, and mankind.

44. When GoFukakusa and Lady Nijō met at Iwashimizu Hachiman Shrine on Mount Otoko, as described in Chapter 22.

45. There is no copyist's note here, but the text seems incomplete enough to suggest that something is missing. Book Five begins abruptly nine years later.

BOOK FIVE

1. After Takakura visited Itsukushima in 1180, Lady Nijō's grandfather Koga Michichika wrote an account of the journey. Itsukushima is a Shinto shrine built out over the water on the Inland Sea west of modern Hiroshima. It dates from the early ninth century.

2. Lady Nijō alludes to two poems by Yukihira, who was once exiled to Suma Bay. Poem 876 in the *Shokukokinshū*, the eleventh imperial anthology, completed in 1251: "A sea breeze from Suma Bay blowing through the mountain pass cools and refreshes the traveler's sleeves." *Kokinshū* Poem 962: "Should by chance someone inquire, say I live alone on Suma Shore with tears and dripping seaweed."

3. The sound of beating cloth is normally associated with sorrow in both Chinese and Japanese literature. This line is from a couplet by Po Chü-i.

4. Poem 409 from the *Kokinshū*: "Dimly seen through morning mist on Akashi Bay, the boat vanishes behind an island; my longing follows it."

5. When Genji was in exile at Suma he listened to the waves lapping by his pillow, and when he moved to Akashi he begged his horse to carry him home.

6. Ashizuri no Misaki is located on the southern tip of the island of Shikoku. Some scholars question whether Lady Nijō actually went there, for she does not describe her journey, and the internal chronology of this section is improbable.

7. Fudaraku, a mountain on the southern coast of India where Kannon was believed to have lived. In Buddhist sutras Fudaraku is often located on the ocean to the south.

8. The location of this shrine is not clear. If Lady Nijō actually went to southern Shikoku, this may refer to a shrine on the southeastern coast of that island. Another possibility is a shrine near Itsukushima.

9. Emperor Sutoku, the eighty-fourth emperor of Japan (reigned 1123-41), tried to rebel against the reigning emperor in 1156 and was consequently exiled to Sanuki province in Shikoku, where he died in 1164.

10. Saigyō visited Emperor Sutoku's grave in 1168, and finding it unattended, he wrote this poem: "Once my Lord, you

occupied the jeweled throne, but now that it has come to this, what can you do?" (*Sankashū* Poem 835). The second poem alluded to here is by Emperor Tsuchimikado (reigned 1198–1210), the eighty-third emperor of Japan and the grandfather of GoFukakusa. After the Jōkyū disturbances of 1221 he was banished to the southern part of Shikoku, and on his way there he composed this poem: "Were we born to suffer so in this sad world? My tears do not comprehend such logic" (*Shokukokinshū* Poem 1854).

11. Hirosawa Yukisane (Yosō was his Buddhist name) held the post of government steward of Bingo province. At this time he was about sixty years old.

12. According to ancient Shinto beliefs, death polluted a building; hence dangerously ill people were usually removed from a palace. Here the sequence of events is not quite clear. It appears that the empress actually did die in the palace, and then her body was removed.

13. A Shinto deity worshiped at a subsidiary shrine within the Iwashimizu complex. Takeuchi no Sukune is said to have been a minister of state who served six emperors a total of 210 years between the first and the fourth centuries. Consequently he is worshiped as a god of longevity.

14. There is a double gloss here. One copyist is recording the words of an earlier copyist, who had found the basic text damaged: "The text says: 'The paper is cut off here. It is unclear. I will begin copying the section after the cut.'"

15. The Festival of the Dead (*Urabon*) is held from the thirteenth to the sixteenth of the seventh month. During this period people visit their ancestral graves.

16. Yamashina Sukeyuki had served GoFukakusa when Lady Nijō was one of his ladies. In Chapter 9 he assisted in making arrangements for GoFukakusa's disappointing affair with the fanmaker's daughter.

17. Because a corpse was considered unclean.

18. This expression of grief draws on lines Genji spoke after the death of his wife, Lady Aoi (Waley, pp. 169 and 172).

19. This refers to Po Chü-i's poem "A Song of Unending Sorrow," which in turn was used in the first chapter of *The Tale of Genji* to describe the relationship between Genji's mother and the emperor, his father (Waley, p. 14).

20. Lady Nijō's son by GoFukakusa died in infancy (Chapter 5), and her illegitimate children had been raised by others. Her daughter by Akebono would have been thirty-one at this time, and her two sons by Ariake, twenty-four and twenty-three.

21. There is a copyist's note here: "Here the manuscript has been cut off with a sword. This is most unfortunate." This is followed by an incomplete sentence: " '. . . and for whom?' The question touched deep emotions."

22. The *Shingosenshū*, the thirteenth imperial anthology, was completed in 1303.

23. The eleventh imperial anthology, compiled in 1265. However, Masatada also has a poem in the earlier *Shokugosenshū*, completed in 1251.

24. In his last talk with her, Masatada warned his daughter against doing anything to tarnish the family's name (Chapter 2).

25. Michimitsu's poem is *Shinkokinshū* Poem 1095; Masatada's is *Shokugosenshū* Poem 63; and Takachika's is *Shokukokinshū* Poem 1521.

26. Kakinomoto Hitomaro, who flourished in the late seventh century, was one of Japan's greatest poets. His poems appear in the *Manyōshū*, the earliest collection of Japanese poetry.

27. Fushimi was GoFukakusa's son, and the custom was to wear mourning for a year after the death of one's father.

28. The *nagi* tree, a tall evergreen, is considered the sacred tree of Kumano Shrine.

29. When she met GoFukakusa at this same shrine in 1291 (Chapter 22).

30. The son of Morochika, a distant relative of Lady Nijō's who had been at the palace when she was.

31. This relative was either Lady Nijō's cousin Michimoto, then age sixty-six, or his son Michio, who was forty-eight.

32. Her dream at Kumano of her father, GoFukakusa, and Empress Yūgi (see Chapter 26).

33. The text ends with another double gloss, even though this paragraph seems quite complete: "The text says 'Here the paper has been cut off with a sword. It is unfortunate. I wonder what happened.' "